# DISNEYLAND AND BEYOND

## SOUTHERN CALIFORNIA FAMILY ATTRACTIONS

### Fourth Edition

*Judy Wade*    *Sharon Gillenwater*    *Stacy Ritz*

RAY RIEGERT
Executive Editor

GLENN KIM
Illustrator

Ulysses Press 🏛 Berkeley

Published by: Ulysses Press
P.O. Box 3440
Berkeley, CA 94703-3440

Library of Congress Catalog Card Number 98-84074
ISBN 1-56975-126-9

Printed in Canada by Best Book Manufacturers

10 9 8 7 6 5 4

Update Author: Lisa Oppenheimer
Managing Editor: Claire Chun
Project Director: Natasha Lay
Editorial Associates: Lily Chou, Nicole O'Hay
Typesetter: David Wells
Maps: Claire Chun, David Wells
Index: Sayre Van Young
Front Cover Design: MIG/DesignWorks
Back Cover Design: Sarah Levin
Cover Photography: Front, Tony Stone Images; Back top, Sea World;
    Back middle and bottom, Robert Holmes

Distributed in the United States by Publishers Group West, in Canada by Raincoast Books, and in Great Britain and Europe by World Leisure Marketing

# DISNEYLAND AND BEYOND

## SOUTHERN CALIFORNIA FAMILY ATTRACTIONS

### Fourth Edition

"A great book to give visitors before packing them off to Anaheim."

*—Los Angeles Times*

"The guide is written with crowds and impatient children in mind; perfect for families planning to hit the sights of Southern California."

*—Orange County Register*

"If you have kids and are headed to Southern California anytime soon, this may be the guidebook to take. . . . Highly recommended."

*—Better Homes & Gardens*

"Sets the pace for (Disneyland) guides, as well as for visiting park goers."

*—Touring America*

# Contents

*Games to Play While Waiting in Line*   x

1.   *Disney Dreaming*   1
     Tourist Seasons   4
     Climate   5
     Calendar   6
     Before You Leave Home   8
     Packing   8
     Getting There   9
     Getting Around Disneyland   11
     Visitor Information   11
     Star System   17
     Lodging   18
     Camping   19
     Dining   19
     Family Necessities   20
     Travelers with Disabilities   21
     Senior Travelers   22
     Foreign Travelers   22
     Planning Your Visit   24
     Sample Itineraries   25

2.   *Magic Kingdom*   31
     Main Street U.S.A.   37
     Adventureland   40
     New Orleans Square   43
     Critter Country   45
     Frontierland   47
     Mickey's Toontown   50
     Fantasyland   53
     Tomorrowland   58
     Disneyland Lodging   63
     Camping   67

|  | Disneyland Dining | 68 |
|  | Dining Outside Disneyland | 71 |
|  | Disneyland Shopping | 74 |
|  | Disneyland Nightlife | 76 |
| 3. | *Knott's Berry Farm* | 77 |
|  | Ghost Town | 84 |
|  | Wild Water Wilderness | 87 |
|  | The Boardwalk | 89 |
|  | Fiesta Village | 93 |
|  | Camp Snoopy | 95 |
|  | Indian Trails | 99 |
|  | Knott's Berry Farm Area Lodging | 100 |
|  | Knott's Berry Farm Area Dining | 102 |
|  | Knott's Berry Farm Area Shopping | 104 |
|  | Knott's Berry Farm Area Nightlife | 105 |
| 4. | *Universal Studios Hollywood* | 107 |
|  | Back Lot Tram Tour | 113 |
|  | Lower Lot | 116 |
|  | Upper Lot | 119 |
|  | Universal Studios Hollywood Lodging | 123 |
|  | Universal Studios Hollywood Dining | 124 |
|  | Dining Outside Universal Studios Hollywood | 125 |
|  | Universal Studios Hollywood Shopping | 126 |
| 5. | *Sea World* | 129 |
|  | The Shows | 133 |
|  | The Exhibits | 137 |
|  | The Rides | 140 |
|  | Sea World Dining | 141 |
|  | Sea World Shopping | 141 |
|  | Sea World Nightlife | 141 |
| 6. | *Orange County Day Trips* | 143 |
|  | Anaheim–Buena Park Area | 144 |
|  | Huntington Beach | 148 |
|  | Newport Beach | 150 |
|  | Laguna Beach Area | 156 |
|  | The Sporting Life | 164 |

7.    *San Diego Day Trips*         167
        The San Diego Zoo       168
        San Diego Wild Animal Park       177
        San Diego       182
        The Sporting Life       199

8.    *Los Angeles Day Trips*       203
        Six Flags California       204
        Long Beach       215
        Santa Monica       217
        Los Angeles       218
        The Sporting Life       232

*Index*       238

*Lodging Index*       247

*Dining Index*       249

*About the Authors and Illustrator*       254

*Maps*
        Disneyland and Beyond       3
        Magic Kingdom       33
        Knott's Berry Farm       81
        Universal Studios Hollywood       111
        Sea World       131
        Orange Coast       147
        Newport Beach       151
        San Diego       171
        Downtown San Diego       185
        La Jolla       191
        Greater Los Angeles       205

## Notes from the Publisher

An alert, adventurous reader is important as a travel writer in keeping a guidebook up-to-date and accurate. So if you happen upon a great restaurant, discover an intriguing locale or (heaven forbid) find an error in the text, we'd appreciate hearing from you. Just contact us at:

Ulysses Press
P.O. Box 3440
Berkeley, CA 94703
E-mail: readermail@ulyssespress.com

It is our desire as publishers to create guidebooks that are responsible as well as informative. We hope that our guidebooks treat the people, country and land we visit with respect. We ask that our readers do the same.

# Games to Play While Waiting in Line

The lines at Southern California's theme parks can try anyone's patience. Fortunately, if you know how to create your own entertainment, the wait can be painless (well, almost).

Kids and adults alike can while away the time, use their creativity and even get a few laughs by playing the games described below. Some of these games relate to specific theme parks, others are appropriate for particular age groups. I have also added trivia questions for extra fun.

If you really want to speed up those waiting lines, create some games of your own!

## Games For All Ages

### ❖ RHYME TIME ❖

Everybody loves to make up rhymes. It's even more fun when you do it together. Begin with a line of poetry. The next player adds a rhyming line, the next player contributes another and so on. The player who rhymes the fourth line gets to start a new rhyme. Example:

> *I read about Disneyland in a book,*
> *And decided I'd go take a look.*
> *I left the dog, but my family I took.*
> *All because of that silly book.*

### ❖ "SENSITIVE" POETRY ❖

Compose a poem that you can see, smell, taste, feel and hear. Give it a try, using the following example as a guideline:

> *I love the smell of old socks.*
> *I love the taste of ham hocks.*
> *I hate feeling blue,*
> *But I love hearing something new.*
> *As you can see I'm a very good poet, too.*

### ❖ A IS FOR... ❖

Look around you and choose objects that begin with particular letters. Start with "A" and proceed alphabetically. For example: animal, bus, carousel, dirt, entrance, etc. Each player must come up with a nearby object that begins with the next letter in the alphabet.

## ❖ *HAVE YOU EVER, EVER, EVER?* ❖

Begin this game by reciting the first three lines of the following ditty and inserting an animal or object in the last word of the third line. The next player then provides a rhyming word for the last word in the fourth line:

> *Have you ever, ever, ever?*
> *Have you ever, ever, ever?*
> *Have you ever seen a MOUSE*
> *Eat a HOUSE?*
> *OH! NO! We never saw a MOUSE eat a HOUSE!*

The last line of the verse is said in unison. The second word doesn't need to be a "real" one; in fact, the sillier it is, the more fun you'll have with the children! Some other examples are:

> *Have you ever seen MICKEY*
> *Be real PICKY?*
> *Have you ever seen a MANGO*
> *Do the TANGO?*

## ❖ *STUPID QUESTIONS* ❖

Making a fool of yourself is easy. Just ask the stupidest question you can think of. Then have everyone decide whose question is the dumbest. The stupid one is the winner!

## ❖ *PINK FLAMINGOS* ❖

Everyone poses a question that has to be answered with the phrase "Pink flamingos." Such as "What did you wear to bed last night?" Pink flamingos. "What did you barbecue for dinner?" Pink flamingos. If you giggle when you ask the question, you're out. The last remaining person is the winner.

## ❖ *SILENCE IS GOLDEN* ❖

Here's a game guaranteed to leave your group speechless. (Parents will love this!) Everyone pledges not to talk for a certain time period, say ten minutes. Only sign language can be used. It's a fun way to be imaginative with body language and visual communication. The last person to speak wins.

### ❖ NUMBER STORIES ❖

Storytelling is even more fun when you use numbers. Begin by using the number "one." The next person adds the word "two," etc. Example: Once upon a time . . . Two bullfrogs went on a date . . . They swam across three lakes . . . Then they saw four speedboats headed straight for them . . . But they escaped with five seconds to spare. . . .

### ❖ PICK A NUMBER ❖

One player picks a number between 1 and 100, but doesn't reveal it to the other players. Each person takes turns trying to guess the number. When someone guesses incorrectly, the player will say "higher" or "lower" depending on whether the guess is above or below the secret number. The person who guesses right gets to pick the next secret number.

### ❖ BODY MOVES ❖

A leader starts the game with a body move, such as winking an eye. The next player performs that move and adds another, like nodding his or her head. For example, they might wink and nod their head. The game continues with each player performing the previous body moves—in the correct order—and adding a new one. Someone who forgets a move, is out of the game.

### ❖ RHYME, RHYME, RHYME ❖

One player begins the game by saying a simple word, such as "mouse." The next player must say another word that rhymes, like "house." Each person takes turns rhyming the original word. When no one can think of a new word that rhymes, the group goes on to a new word.

### ❖ SEE AND TELL ❖

A leader asks each person about what they see in line. Some sample questions: What is the smallest thing you see? What is the prettiest thing you see? What is the brightest thing you see? Other things to look for: tallest, shortest, fattest, skinniest, strangest, funniest, saddest, etc.

### ❖ STORYTELLING ❖

Children are born storytellers. Encourage kids in your group to create tales based on park characters, rides or situations. If you saw Cinderella yesterday, let your child tell you what Cinderella is doing today while you're visiting Sea World—or what a visit to Sea World would be like with Cinderella.

### ❖ COMMON FEATURES ❖

How many people can you find wearing Mickey Mouse ears? How many have braces? Count them. If you're in line at a ride, count the number of people with black hair, children with cameras, people with hats on. . . . You get it? Add to the fun by guessing the number of people you'll find in each category in five minutes.

### ❖ HANG LOOSE ❖

Here's an easy way to loosen up while standing in line. Have every player rub their head and pat their leg at the same time. Then have them touch their nose and their back at the same time. Next, have them lift their right leg and grab it with their left hand. Improvise other variations on this theme. Another familiar version is "Simple Simon Says."

### ❖ QUESTIONS, QUESTIONS ❖

What better way to pass the time than by discussing the highlights of your trip? One player asks the others a variety of questions such as: What is the best beach you've seen? Where is the prettiest place you've been? What is the best ride in all the parks?

### ❖ COLOR ME PURPLE ❖

One player picks a color and other members of the group try to identify it by asking questions. Each player is allowed to ask up to three questions before making their choice. Example: Do you see lots of people wearing this color? Are there fruits this color? Is it the color of a grape?

### ❖ CHALLENGES ❖

Create challenges for your children. Here are four examples: Take ten hops with the left foot then another ten with the right. Count backward from 20. Take as many steps as possible to get from one place to another. Hold your breath for the duration of the song "Zip-A-Dee-Doo-Dah."

### ❖ 20 QUESTIONS ❖

The first player chooses an object. The other players then have (surprise) 20 questions to figure out what the object is. Each question has to be answerable by "yes" or "no." And remember, guesses count toward the 20 questions! A good strategy is to ask general questions in the beginning, such as: Is it alive? Is it very big? Is it soft? As a variation on this classic game, limit the object to things within the theme park.

Another alternative is to allow each person five questions. After five tries, the next player takes a turn. The game continues until one of the players comes up with the correct answer.

### ❖ I SPY ❖

This old favorite is a great guessing game. A player says "I spy something purple," referring to an object clearly visible to the other players. Then the other players ask questions to try to determine what the object is. I Spy can also be played by initially describing the shape, dimensions, smell or sound of an object.

## Games for Kids 6 to 90

### ❖ ODD MAN OUT ❖

The object of this counting game is to avoid saying a particular number. To begin, pick a two-digit, odd number like 25. Go around the circle. The first player can count "1" or "1, 2"; then the next player picks up the count, adding one or two numbers to the progression. For example, the first participant says "1." The next says "2, 3." The third person can say either "4" or "4, 5." Continue until someone (the loser) ends up saying "25."

### ❖ SWITCH HITS ❖

Pick a simple word. The first player must either change a letter in the original word to make another word or create an anagram. For example, start with "BAT." The next player says "BAR" or "TAB." No repeating words! Extra challenge: After completing a round, try reciting the sequence of words from last to first.

### ❖ ALPHABET SOUP ❖

When hunger pangs begin to strike, try moving down the food chain alphabetically. Each player repeats the choices of the previous person. Begin at "A" and continue until you get all the way down to "Z." Here's how: First player: "I'm fond of asparagus." Second player: "I'm dying for asparagus and beets." Third player: "I want asparagus, beets and chicken soup."

### ❖ HINKY PINKY ❖

This word game begins with a player selecting a secret rhyming phrase like "fat cat." The player then defines the phrase—with a clue like "obese feline" or "tubby tabby"—and tells how many syllables are in the rhyming words by saying "Hink Pink" for one syllable, "Hinky Pinky" for two syllables or "Hinkety Pinkety" for three syllables. The other participants try guessing the rhyming couplet.

How about these? What Santa would say during Christmas: "Remember December." An insane flower: "Crazy daisy."

## ❖ PATTERN WORK ❖

Players of this game use clues to discover a pattern. For example, you choose "double letters" as the pattern. Some clues you could give are: "Look at the crook" or "Poodles love noodles." Another example, a little easier for younger children, could be the letter "C": "He likes cats and canaries, cars and cartoons."

## ❖ LINKING UP ❖

Here's a way to bring everyone together. The first player mentions a film, book, celebrity or city. Successive players offer a concept linked to the previous one. Example: First player: Teenage Mutant Ninja Turtles. Second player: Pizza. Third player: Cheesy. Fourth player: Smelly. First player: Socks.

## ❖ BUZZ ❖

Here's a chance to review your multiplication tables. Pick a number between one and nine. That's the buzz-number. Start counting in sequence around the circle of players. When the multiple of the buzz-number comes up in sequence, the number must be replaced by the word "buzz." Players are out if they forget to say "buzz" or if they say it at the wrong time. Example: Pick multiples of 5. When 10, 15, 20, 25, etc. come up they should be replaced by "buzz."

## ❖ THE POWER OF NEGATIVE THINKING ❖

One person thinks of a funny activity like trying to catch a greased pig. Only negative hints can be used to describe the activity: "It really smells." "You slip and slide around a lot." "There's a lot of squealing." The player who comes up with the right answer suggests the next mystery activity.

## ❖ ALPHABET MEMORY ❖

Another fun game involves picking words alphabetically. For example, the first player chooses an "A" word, the second player selects a "B" word and the third player picks a "C" word. Each player must name all the words chosen previously. The game continues through the alphabet, with players being eliminated when they forget the sequence of words.

## ❖ INTERNATIONAL GEOGRAPHIC ❖

See how well you know your way around. The first player names a country. The second player must come up with a city that begins with the last letter of the previously named country. For example, Greenland might be followed by Denver and China could be followed by Athens. Continue in sequence through your group.

## ❖ SPELL CHECKER ❖

Here's an easy game that's a great way to build vocabulary. Pick a word like "Lazy." Then have the players run through the alphabet. When you hit a letter that is in the designated word, say "check." For example: Instead of saying "A" the player will say "check." If you forget to say "Check" for the appropriate word you are out of the game.

## ❖ COCONUTTING AROUND ❖

Coconut is a noun, not a verb. But you can have a lot of fun with this word when you substitute it for a secret verb. Here's how: The contestant goes out of hearing range or covers his or her ears. Other members of the group pick a verb such as "swim." The contestant returns, and can ask up to 12 questions aimed at discovering the verb but must always use "coconut" in the question. For example: "Can you coconut at the beach?" or "Do kids like to coconut in the bath?" After the first contestant finishes, give everyone else a chance to guess other mystery verbs.

## ❖ NAME THOSE RIDES ❖

The first player starts by naming a theme park ride, such as Space Mountain, It's A Small World, etc. The next player must name a different ride, and the game continues with each person naming a new ride. Players have ten seconds to answer. A stumped player is excused from the game. The last person left wins!

You could also try naming Disney characters (Mickey Mouse, etc.), California cities (Anaheim, Los Angeles) or movies (*E.T.*, *Back to the Future*).

## ❖ *DISNEY TRIVIA CONTEST* ❖

1. Who follows the White Rabbit down the hole?
2. What makes Alice shrink and grow?
3. The butterflies Alice meets are shaped like what food?
4. Who was Dumbo's mother?
5. What's the merry tune you hear on the Dumbo ride?
6. Who was Captain Hook's bumbling sidekick?
7. Who are the children Peter Pan takes to Never-Never Land?
8. What did the crocodile swallow in *Peter Pan*?
9. Who was Mr. Toad's horse?
10. What did Mr. Toad trade his family mansion for?
11. What was the name of Mr. Toad's mansion?
12. Why was Mr. Toad arrested?
13. Who sang "When You Wish Upon a Star" in Disney's *Pinocchio*?
14. Princess Aurora is better known by what name?
15. Who led the crew of Jules Vernes' *Nautilus*?
16. What did Tommy Kirk turn into in a 1959 Disney movie?
17. What was the password for the D-Day invasion?
18. Who was the first voice of Mickey Mouse?
19. What kind of television characters were Doreen Tracy, Cheryl Holdridge and Cubby O'Brien?
20. Name Snow White's seven dwarfs.
21. Where did the movie *Pocahontas* have its world premiere?

Answers:
1. Alice.   2. Eating or drinking.   3. Bread. They are called Bread and Butterflies.   4. Mrs. Jumbo.   5. "You Can Fly, You Can Fly, You Can Fly."   6. Mr. Smee.   7. Wendy, Michael and John.   8. A clock.   9. Cyril Proudbottom.   10. A stolen car.   11. Toad Hall.   12. For driving that stolen car!   13. Jiminy Cricket.   14. Sleeping Beauty.   15. Captain Nemo.   16. The Shaggy Dog.   17. Mickey Mouse.   18. Walt Disney.   19. Mouseketeers.   20. Sneezy, Sleepy, Dopey, Doc, Grumpy, Happy and Bashful.   21. New York's Central Park.

# ONE

# Disney Dreaming

Decades old now but still a timeless wonder, Disneyland beckons as **1** a real-life passage to Never-Never Land for the ever-ever young at heart. This purveyor of storybook illusions and cotton candy moods remains one of the most popular travel destinations in the world, drawing millions every year through the Disney door to indulge in its fountain of fantasy, to drink its dreams.

Disneyland truly is the ultimate escape.

That Disney is a world unto itself is undisputed: The 85-acre park has dozens of shops, restaurants, a hotel and even its own fire department. But more than this, Disneyland is a state of mind. The Magic Kingdom has placed its stamp on the American psyche of three generations, sharing the dreams of one man with an entire nation. For here, in 1955, Walt Disney launched the world's first fantasy playground and started a Southern California phenomenon.

Disney sparked a fantasyland fever that spread throughout the Southland. Knott's Berry Farm, which first opened in 1920 as a modest roadside stand hawking berries and rhubarb, has evolved into a 150-acre theme park with 165 rides and attractions. And Six Flags California in Los Angeles made a name for itself with its acclaimed collection of thrill rides, including 11 hair-raising roller coasters.

Universal Studios Hollywood saw the potential in a Hollywood-style theme park where star-struck tourists could get a behind-the-scenes glimpse of television and film production. Today, Universal is a mammoth, 420-acre complex complete with sound stages, theaters, exhibits and live-action shows that give audience members a chance to be sound engineers for a day or even star in a mock television drama.

Of course, Southern California is much more than amusement parks. You can supplement your theme-park tour with visits to many of the region's other attractions. Don't miss seeing the quintessential SoCal burgs of Newport Beach, Laguna Beach and Santa Monica. For healthy doses of history and culture, visit a historic Spanish mission, colorful Olvera Street and the Griffith Park observatory in Los Angeles. And for a bit of the eclectic and downright bizarre, don't forget Hollywood.

Then there is San Diego, which may well be the area's best-kept secret. The city boasts fine museums, award-winning restaurants, superb shopping and a thriving nightlife in downtown's renovated Gaslamp District. Just outside the burgeoning downtown lies more scenic reality. Blessed with an ideal climate and miles and miles of beautiful beaches, bays and parks, sunny San Diego is a year-round playground for both locals and tourists alike.

San Diego is also home to some of the best theme parks in the region. Sea World, the renowned aquatic wonderland, has called San Diego home since 1964. And the city also boasts not one, but two of the best collections of wild animals in the world: the San Diego Wild Animal Park and the famous San Diego Zoo.

This book, *Disneyland and Beyond: Southern California Family Attractions*, takes you through Walt Disney's fantasy world, then shows you the beauty outside it. The focus throughout is on quality and value, the exemplary and the unique, while always keeping families in mind. Why families? Because every day, more and more travelers are choosing the family experience as parents and kids look to share what is offered here.

Throughout this guide you'll discover the best of Southern California's "family friendly" establishments and attractions. You'll also find plenty of tips on saving time and money, as well as on special family needs such as babysitters, breast-feeding and stroller rentals. And the book's short feature articles and one-liner teasers give you insider information, providing local trivia and history and little-known hints at a glance.

Each of Southern California's major theme parks is featured in a separate chapter. There's *Disneyland*, the supreme fantasy factory. The place that children love best, this park of all parks features fanciful rides and scenes and happy vibes. Then there's the more down-home *Knott's Berry Farm* where you can pan for gold or shoot the whitewater rapids.

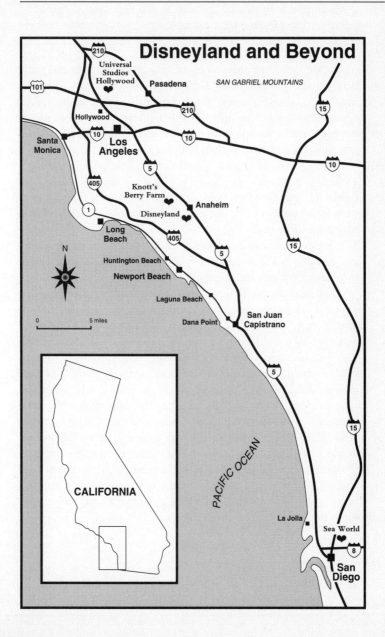

# Disneyland and Beyond

210

Universal Studios Hollywood

Pasadena

*SAN GABRIEL MOUNTAINS*

101

210

Hollywood

10

Los Angeles

Santa Monica

10

5

405

Knott's Berry Farm

Anaheim

15

10

1

Disneyland

Long Beach

405

5

15

N

Huntington Beach

Newport Beach

0        5 miles

Laguna Beach

Dana Point

San Juan Capistrano

5

15

*PACIFIC OCEAN*

**CALIFORNIA**

La Jolla

Sea World

8

San Diego

*Spend a day in a theme park and you've walked three to four miles. If you're not in good walking shape, better get moving!*

But the unfolding chapters of this tourist extravaganza don't stop here. There's *Universal Studios Hollywood*, a dazzling fantasy park fashioned with thrilling movie scenes and rides and fabulous special effects. *Sea World* delves deep into the mysteries of the ocean and its inhabitants. The world's most popular oceanarium, it puts humans in touch with 16,000 creatures both big and small.

When you're waiting to try all those theme-park rides, you'll undoubtedly want to use *Games to Play While Waiting in Line*. This special fun section, which you'll find near the front of the book, features an assortment of games, poems and theme-park trivia to help pass the time in line.

Recommendations on lodging, campgrounds, dining, shopping and nightlife in and around the theme parks are found at the end of each of the theme park chapters.

Away from the parks, the *Orange County Day Trips*, *San Diego Day Trips* and *Los Angeles Day Trips* chapters span the entire Southern California coast, taking in the San Diego Zoo, San Diego Wild Animal Park, Six Flags California, picturesque towns and glorious scenery.

Travel here and you'll find yourself poised on the cusp of reality, a place where, on the same day, you can explore a castle with Cinderella and take a moonlight stroll on a wide, sandy beach. Where you can fly through anytown suburbia with E.T., then stroll a city street lined with postmodern restaurants and surreal shops. Where you can cruise through a concrete lagoon with brightly painted fish and spy dolphins at play in their natural habitat—the waves of the Pacific.

The ultimate paradox, Southern California is the keeper of both manmade empires and natural treasure. The treasure was there long before the empires. With a little luck and a lot of work, it just may stay a permanent part of the landscape.

## Tourist Seasons

Timing is the key to a successful Disneyland visit. If you go during the busy season, you'll spend much of your vacation standing in lines and sitting in traffic. Plus, you'll pay top dollar for everything. One family who went to the Magic Kingdom on Easter Sunday (a peak day) calculated they spent six hours in line and only 35 minutes riding. By contrast, if you go when it's slow, your experience will be the opposite—a *real* vacation.

Unfortunately for families, the summer months—when the children are out of school—are high season. Holidays are also a bad time to visit. Disneyland has its worst crowd crunch from Christmas Day through New Year's Day. Thanksgiving weekend takes a close second, followed by the weeks surrounding Easter. During these frenzied days, Disneyland and Universal Studios are packed by mid-morning. Waits for rides and attractions run a minimum of 45 minutes and a maximum of two hours—not a pretty picture, especially when you have restless children who want to be entertained.

The very best time to visit Disneyland is after Thanksgiving weekend up to the week before Christmas. Other slow times: September and October and the second week of January through May (excluding holidays). As a rule, try to plan your visit in mid-week; Tuesday, Wednesday and Thursday are the slowest days. Fridays through Mondays attract far more visitors.

## Climate

Southern California has an ideal Mediterranean climate with mild temperatures year-round. While the mercury rarely drops below 40 or rises much above 80, some months are more pleasant than others. August and September are the hottest and January and February the coolest. And while rainfall is a rarity in this region, you can expect some showers from December to March. Smog is a big factor in Southern California. If you're sensitive to pollution, you may want to avoid visiting in August and September when it tends to be in greater concentration.

|  | Avg. High Temp. (°F) | Avg. Low Temp. (°F) |
|---|---|---|
| January | 65 | 47 |
| February | 67 | 49 |
| March | 68 | 50 |
| April | 70 | 53 |
| May | 72 | 56 |
| June | 77 | 60 |
| July | 82 | 64 |
| August | 83 | 65 |

| September | 81 | 63 |
| October | 77 | 59 |
| November | 73 | 52 |
| December | 67 | 48 |

# Calendar

## JANUARY

*Los Angeles*   The **Tournament of Roses Parade** kicks off the **Rose Bowl** game in Pasadena on New Year's Day.

## FEBRUARY

*Los Angeles*   The **Chinese New Year** celebration includes a spectacular Golden Dragon parade that snakes its way through Chinatown.

## MARCH

*Orange County*   The **Fiesta de las Golondrinas** commemorates the return of the swallows to Mission San Juan Capistrano. Meanwhile, along the coast crowds gather for seasonal **grunion runs**.
*San Diego*   Kids of all ages flock to a grassy park by the sea for the **Ocean Beach Kite Festival**.
*Los Angeles*   The **American Indian Festival**, held at the Natural History Museum of Los Angeles County, is a colorful celebration.

## APRIL

*Knott's Berry Farm*   Special entertainment, food and arts and crafts highlight the annual **Easter EggMazeMent** festival.
*San Diego*   **Lakeside Western Days** features a parade and a carnival.
*Los Angeles*   **Easter Sunrise Services** are marked at the famed Hollywood Bowl. In Little Tokyo **Buddha's Birthday** is celebrated; along nearby Olvera Street the **Blessing of the Animals**, a Mexican tradition, is re-enacted.

## MAY

*San Diego*   In Old Town, the **Cinco de Mayo** celebration is highlighted by mariachis, traditional Mexican folk dancers, Mexican food and displays. The **Pacific Beach Block Party** features food booths, artisans and live music. Crowds sprout up at the **Julian Wildflower Show** for an artful display of native plants.
*Los Angeles*   Dancers, revelers and mariachi bands around Olvera Street and East Los Angeles mark **Cinco de Mayo**, the festival celebrating the Battle of Puebla in the French-Mexican War. The **UCLA Mardi Gras** offers games, entertainment and food. Little Tokyo

honors kids with **Children's Day**, a two-day festival with arts, crafts and a parade.

## JUNE

*San Diego*    The city kicks off the summer season with several events including the four-month-long **Festival** at the Old Globe Theater, where you can see classic and contemporary plays, and the wacky **Ocean Beach Street Fair and Chili Cookoff**.

*Los Angeles*    The Santa Anita Racetrack in Arcadia comes alive with Irish music, dance and cheer for the **Grand National Irish Fair and Music Festival**.

## JULY

*Orange County*    The **Arts Festival and Pageant of the Masters**, one of Southern California's most notable events, occurs in Laguna Beach.

*Los Angeles*    The **Hollywood Bowl Summer Festival** explodes with a Fourth of July concert.

## AUGUST

*San Diego*    Concerts, festivals and special events mark **America's Finest City Week**.

*Los Angeles*    Little Tokyo's **Nisei Week** honors Japanese-American culture with parades, dances, music and martial-arts demonstrations. The **Children's Art Festival** in Barnsdall Park gives kids hands-on lessons in arts and crafts.

## SEPTEMBER

*San Diego*    Downtown rocks to the sounds of more than 50 bands during **Street Scene**, the city's largest street festival. In Point Loma, the **Cabrillo Festival** commemorates the discovery of the California coast by Europeans.

*Los Angeles*    The **Los Angeles County Fair**, the nation's largest, offers music, food, carnival rides, livestock competitions and just about everything else you can imagine.

## OCTOBER

*Knott's Berry Farm*    The entire park, rides and all, is transformed into one big spookhouse for a **Halloween Haunt** festival.

*San Diego*    In the San Diego area, the **La Mesa Oktoberfest** features Bavarian bands, beer gardens and arts and crafts.

*Los Angeles*    Kids of all ages don masks of many cultures for a colorful parade highlighting the **International Festival of Masks**, held at Hancock Park.

NOVEMBER

*San Diego*    In the San Diego area, families flock to El Cajon for the whimsical **Mother Goose Parade**.

*Los Angeles*    Santa arrives early at the **Hollywood Christmas Parade** and is joined by TV and movie stars. In Pasadena, the rollicking **Doo Dah Parade** parodies the city's more traditional Rose Parade.

DECEMBER

*Disneyland*    The Magic Kingdom hosts a month-long holiday celebration that includes a **Candlelight Procession** and the **Christmas Fantasy Parade** starring 1000 carolers and a celebrity narrator.

*Elsewhere*    Several coastal communities, including San Diego, Huntington Beach, Long Beach and Marina del Rey, mark the season with **Christmas Boat Parades**. Latino communities in San Diego, Los Angeles and throughout the Southland celebrate the Mexican yuletide with **Las Posadas**.

## Before You Leave Home

Nothing makes a trip more enjoyable than a little prep work. This goes for every family member. Parents can learn the layout of the theme parks and what each has to offer, thus avoiding confusion and hurried decision-making after they arrive. Preteens and teens who plan to sightsee on their own should definitely know how to get around. And young children can prepare (and get wildly excited) by reading Disney stories and watching the classic animated films. This helps acquaint them with characters and rides they'll see after they arrive. Some families rent Disney videos before their trip and hold movie nights. A few entertaining movies to rent: *Cinderella*, *Peter Pan*, *Alice in Wonderland*, *Dumbo*, *The Wind in the Willows*, *The Little Mermaid*, *Beauty and the Beast*, *Aladdin*, *The Lion King* and *Pocahontas*.

Children should also be told about height restrictions. Certain rides require minimum heights, including Disneyland's Star Tours, Space Mountain, Splash Mountain and Big Thunder Mountain (all 40 inches) and Indiana Jones Adventure (46 inches). The theme parks strictly adhere to these rules. If your kids are too short to ride, it's best they know *before* you leave.

## Packing

There are two important rules to remember when packing for a "Disneyland and Beyond" vacation: Pack light and pack casual. Unless you

---

*The closer you are to Disneyland, the more expensive the gas will be. Fill up before you get there.*

---

plan to spend your trip dining in ultra-deluxe restaurants, all you'll need in the way of clothing are some shorts, lightweight shirts or tops, jeans or casual slacks, a sweater or sweatshirt for cool afternoons and evenings, a bathing suit and coverup and something relatively casual for any special event that might call for dressing up.

The rest of your luggage space can be devoted to a few essentials. These include a good hat and high-quality sunglasses. You should also take along plenty of strong sunscreen. Even the cloudiest winter days bring out that classic tourist look: scorched skin. A light jacket is a good idea for chilly nights.

Soft, comfortable, lightweight shoes are critical for foot survival. A theme-park visitor walks an average of four miles a day (often on blazing-hot concrete, no less), so you're going to need sole support. Tennis shoes are ideal for sightseeing; save the sandals and flip-flops for poolside.

If you're driving and have extra room, bring plenty of baby formula and disposable diapers. You can buy them inside the various theme parks, but you'll pay dearly. For those afternoon munchies, pack some snacks in ziplocked bags. Crackers, granola bars, the kids' favorite cereal and popcorn are a few that will hold up well. Juice-boxes are also great substitutes for carbonated soft drinks sold in the theme parks.

# Getting There

## BY CAR

**Route 5** will be the main transit corridor during your Disney vacation. Connecting Los Angeles with San Diego, it passes right through Anaheim near the outskirts of Disneyland—you can even spot the famous Matterhorn from the freeway. Farther south, Route 5 passes through Santa Ana, Dana Point and San Clemente, and though it travels inland at times, feeder highways to the beach towns are clearly marked and easy to follow. Several other major highways crisscross Orange County. **Route 1**, known in this area as Pacific Coast Highway, ends its long journey down the California coast in Capistrano Beach. A few miles farther inland, **Route 405** runs from Long Beach to Irvine, with feeder roads leading to the main coastal towns.

## BY AIR

**John Wayne International Airport**, located in Santa Ana, is the main gateway to Disneyland and Orange County. Major carriers presently serving it include Alaska Airlines, American Airlines, America West, Continental Airlines, Delta Airlines, Northwest Airlines, Reno Air, Sky West, Southwest, TWA, United Airlines and USAir.

## BY BUS

**Greyhound Bus Lines** (800-231-2222) serves Southern California, stopping in Anaheim, Santa Ana, San Juan Capistrano, San Clemente, Oceanside, San Diego and Los Angeles. Most stops are flag stops; depots are located in Anaheim (100 West Winston Road; 714-999-1256), Santa Ana (1000 East Santa Ana Boulevard; 714-542-2215), San Clemente (2421 South El Camino Real; 714-366-2646), San Diego (120 West Broadway; 619-239-3266) and Los Angeles (1716 East 7th Street; 213-629-8400).

The **Metropolitan Transit Authority** (213-626-4455), or MTA, serves some areas of Orange County and stops at Disneyland and Knott's Berry Farm.

## BY TRAIN

**Amtrak**'s "San Diegan" (800-872-7245) travels between Los Angeles and San Diego, with Orange County stops at Fullerton, Anaheim Stadium, Santa Ana, Irvine, San Juan Capistrano, San Clemente, Oceanside and Solana Beach.

## CAR RENTALS

Arriving at John Wayne International Airport, you'll find the following car-rental agencies: **Alamo Rent A Car** (800-327-9633), **Avis Rent A Car** (800-331-1212), **Budget Rent A Car** (800-527-0700), **Dollar Rent A Car** (800-800-4000), **Enterprise Car Rent-**

---

*CAR TROUBLE?*

*If your car breaks down at Disneyland, Universal Studios or Sea World, a security officer will come to the rescue. Security vehicles patrol the parking lots, making rounds every five to ten minutes. Simply hail one of the vehicles, which resemble police cruisers. The officers will either start your car or call someone who can.*

*To make traveling time go faster, take along audio tapes of classic Disney stories.*

**als** (800-736-7701), **Hertz Rent A Car** (800-654-3131), **National Interrent** (800-227-7368) and **Thrifty Rent A Car** (800-367-2277).

## Getting Around Disneyland

Disneyland is so built up and spread out that it may seem intimidating at first. Not to worry. The Disney folks are quite practiced at getting visitors where they want to go. Theme-park exits are well marked on all the major roadways. And once you're inside Disneyland, all you have to do is follow the signs.

Arriving in the park, you'll be given a detailed map showing the whereabouts of all rides and attractions. Several modes of transportation carry visitors between the different "lands": the Disneyland Railroad and the Monorail. The Monorail also stops at the Disneyland Hotel and the Disneyland Pacific Hotel, making it easy for families with toddlers to stop off for a mid-afternoon nap before returning to Disneyland for a second round of fun and games.

## Visitor Information

DISNEYLAND
*General Information:* Disneyland Admissions Department, 1313 Harbor Boulevard, Anaheim, CA 92803; 714-781-4565

*Disneyland Hotel Reservations:* Disneyland Hotel, 1150 West Cerritos Avenue, Anaheim, CA 92802; 714-778-6600; Disneyland Pacific Hotel, 1717 South West Street, Anaheim, CA 92802; 714-999-0990

KNOTT'S BERRY FARM
*General Information:* Guest Relations, Knott's Berry Farm, 8039 Beach Boulevard, Buena Park, CA 90620; 714-220-5200

UNIVERSAL STUDIOS HOLLYWOOD
*General Information:* Guest Relations, Universal Studios Hollywood, 100 Universal City Plaza, Universal City, CA 91608; 818-508-9600

SEA WORLD
*General Information:* Ticket Information, Sea World, 1720 South Shores Road, San Diego, CA 92109; 619-226-3901

SAN DIEGO ZOO
*General Information:* San Diego Zoo Guest Relations, P.O. Box 551, San Diego, CA 92112; 619-234-3153

SAN DIEGO WILD ANIMAL PARK
*General Information:* San Diego Wild Animal Park Guest Relations, 15500 San Pasqual Valley Road, Escondido, CA 92027; 619-234-6541

SIX FLAGS CALIFORNIA
*General Information:* Guest Relations, Six Flags California, P.O. Box 5500, Valencia, CA 91385; 805-255-4111

## OPERATING HOURS

Theme-park operating hours seem to change more often than the California tides, but this is to your advantage. Disneyland, Universal Studios and Sea World all base their opening and closing times on the seasons. In general, operating hours are as follows:

❖ During the summer and holidays, the theme parks stay open late, usually closing at 10 p.m., 11 p.m. or midnight.

❖ In the winter, the parks close around 6 or 7 p.m.

❖ Last but most important: At Disneyland and other theme parks, advertised opening times are not always the real opening times. If the Disney folks expect crowds, they may open the park 30 to 60 minutes before the scheduled time. There's no way to anticipate this, but you can take advantage of it by being there early. We recommend arriving at least half an hour early at the theme parks.

---

*BEST SEAT IN THE HOUSE*

*Riding in the front of the Disneyland Monorail is by far the best spot because you get wonderful views out the curved-glass windows as you're cruising through the air. Just as fun, you can sit with the driver and watch him work the control panels. The drivers are extra friendly, offering Disney anecdotes and information on their favorite rides. To ride up front, just ask any attendant. If the crowds aren't too heavy, he or she will escort you to your own special waiting area. Happy monorailing!*

## TICKET OPTIONS AND PRICES

DISNEYLAND   There are several ticket options, called "passports": one-, two- or three-day tickets; two different seasonal passes; or an annual pass. All passports include admission and unlimited use of rides and attractions. Seasonal passports are $99 and $129 for both children and adults and cannot be used on holidays or on varying restricted "blackout days" that occur on weekends during peak season.

|  | Adults | Children 3–11 |
|---|---|---|
| *One-day Passport* | $38.00 | $28.00 |
| *Two-day Passport* | $68.00 | $51.00 |
| *Three-day Passport* | $95.00 | $75.00 |
| *Annual Passport* | $199.00 | $199.00 |
| *Children under 3 are free* | | |

KNOTT'S BERRY FARM   You can opt for a day pass or an annual pass.

|  | Adults | Children 3–11 |
|---|---|---|
| *One-day Ticket* | $35.00 | $25.00 |
| *Annual Pass* | $99.95 | $69.95 |
| *Children under 3 are free* | | |

UNIVERSAL STUDIOS HOLLYWOOD   There are three ticket options: a one-day pass, two-day pass or an annual pass.

|  | Adults | Children 3–11 |
|---|---|---|
| *One-day Pass* | $38.00 | $28.00 |
| *Two-day Pass* | $48.00 | $37.00 |
| *Annual Pass* | $69.00 | $59.00 |
| *Children under 3 are free* | | |

SEA WORLD   Admission options include a one-day ticket, a two-day ticket and an annual pass. If you plan to visit for three or more days, definitely go for the annual pass.

|  | Adults | Children 3–11 |
|---|---|---|
| *One-day Ticket* | $34.95 | $26.95 |
| *Two-day Ticket* | $38.95 | $30.95 |
| *Annual Pass* | $69.95 | $54.95 |
| *Children under 3 are free* | | |

SAN DIEGO ZOO   Visitors can choose from two ticket options: a one-day ticket or an annual membership allowing unlimited visits to both the San Diego Zoo and the San Diego Wild Animal Park. Annual membership for two adults in the same household are $70.

|  | Adults | Children |
|---|---|---|
| *One-day Ticket* | $16.00 | $7.00 (Ages 3–11) |
| *Annual Membership* | $57.00 | $15.00 (Ages 3–15) |
| *Children under 3 are free* | | |

SAN DIEGO WILD ANIMAL PARK    Two ticket options are available: a one-day ticket or an annual zoological society membership allowing unlimited visits to both the San Diego Wild Animal Park and the San Diego Zoo.

|  | Adults | Children |
|---|---|---|
| *One-day Ticket* | $19.95 | $12.95 (Ages 3–11) |
| *Annual Membership* | $57.00 | $15.00 (Ages 3–15) |
| *Children under 3 are free* | | |

SIX FLAGS MAGIC MOUNTAIN    Six Flags Magic Mountain offers visitors one-day and season passes. However, during most of the year they offer a "Twicket," which allows the bearer a second day of admission for a nominal fee.

|  | Adults | Children under 48" |
|---|---|---|
| *One-day Ticket* | $35.00 | $17.00 |
| *Two-park combo Ticket* | $49.00 | n/a |
| *Season Pass* | $65.00 | $65.00 |
| *Children under 3 are free* | | |

SIX FLAGS HURRICANE HARBOR    You can purchase a ticket just for Hurricane Harbor, a combination ticket for Hurricane Harbor and Magic Mountain, or a season pass.

|  | Adults | Children under 48" |
|---|---|---|
| *One-day Ticket* | $18.00 | $11.00 |
| *Two-park combo Ticket* | $49.00 | n/a |
| *Season Pass* | $65.00 | $65.00 |
| *Children under 3 are free* | | |

No matter which theme park you're visiting, the single most important ticket tip is to *buy ahead of time!* If you arrive with ticket in hand, you can avoid standing in long lines. Really, who wants to start their day with a 20-minute wait?

Some area hotels offer theme-park packages and will even help plan your itinerary; ask when you are making room reservations. Or you can order tickets by mail before you leave home or by telephone:

Disneyland (714-781-4043); Sea World (619-222-6363 ext. 2037); Six Flags California (through Ticket Master, 213-480-3232). You can only order Knott's Berry Farm tickets by mail: Department 226, Knott's Berry Farm, 8039 Beach Boulevard, Buena Park, CA 90620; 714-220-5220. Finally, remember that all ticket prices are subject to increase.

## DISCOUNTS

Everyone who goes to Disneyland can get bargains. If you know where to look and whom to ask, you'll find discounts galore for restaurants, hotels, nightclubs and rental cars. Disneyland itself offers only minimal discounts for:

❖ Members of the Magic Kingdom Club. Many employers, including federal, state and local governments, subscribe to the club. If your employer participates in the club, you can request a complimentary membership card from your company's club chapter representative. If your employer doesn't offer the free club membership, you can buy a Magic Kingdom Club Gold Card membership for $65 a year by calling 800-563-4763. As a member, you receive small discounts on Disney admission ($2 off passes, for instance), a 10 percent discount on purchases at Disney stores, and discounts on National Interrent cars, AAA membership and Disneyland restaurants. The Magic Kingdom Club also offers packages that include visits to other Southern California theme parks. Discounts change frequently; call the club headquarters at 714-781-1550.

❖ Southern California residents. During certain months residents receive up to 30 percent off Disneyland admission. A Southern California driver's license is required for proof of residency.

---

### DISNEY DOLLARS

*Leave it to Disney to come up with its own money. As if your own greenbacks aren't good enough, Disneyland offers visitors "Disney dollars." Here's how they work: When visitors enter the theme parks, they can exchange their own U.S. currency for Disney bills, dollar for dollar. Disney dollars are good at restaurants and stores throughout Disneyland.*

*Of course, there's no logical reason to buy Disney dollars. They're not more convenient than real money, and they don't provide any discounts. They can, however, tempt you to spend more. Says one mother: "Disney dollars seemed like play money. I could spend them with wild abandon—something I'd never think of doing with my own money."*

---

*Flash photography is not allowed in most theme-park theaters and in many indoor rides.*

---

❖ Those 60 or older. Seniors are granted a hefty discount all year long. The Senior Fun passport costs just $30 for anyone 60 or over. A driver's license or passport is required for proof of age.

Universal Studios Hollywood and SeaWorld have similar discounts for Southern California residents and/or senior citizens. Check with each park for specifics of the discounts.

The best discounts are outside the theme parks. Remember that rates will always be the lowest during the off-season; during the summer you'll pay top dollar everywhere. Look for motel and hotel bargains advertised in the Sunday travel sections of major newspapers. Many are good deals, but some are not. Beware of cheap accommodations that say "close to Disney" but are really out in the boondocks. If the place is more than five miles away, forget it. You'll waste half your day getting to and from the parks. There are dozens of budget hotels in the blocks surrounding Disneyland. Should you find accommodations here, you'll be able to walk to the park, saving yourself the cost and aggravation of parking. As a general rule, you're better off paying a few extra dollars for convenience and peace of mind.

## VACATION PACKAGES

There are dozens of packages available for the Disneyland traveler. Whether to buy one depends on your individual needs. If you're flying into Orange County and staying at the Disneyland Hotel, a package can probably save you money. Check for packages that combine airfare, accommodations, car rental and theme-park tickets; they often save up to 20 percent. Packages also clue you in on what your vacation is going to cost since you pay for much of it up-front. And they can eliminate a lot of "what are we going to do?" decisions.

On the downside, many packages come with extras you'll never use. Super-deluxe accommodation fees and meals in fancy restaurants represent lost dollars if you don't use them. Some of the Disneyland Hotel's packages, for instance, include everything from unnecessary in-room amenities and meals to access to the concierge lounge. For some families, these are useless, plus they take away the flexibility of being able to enjoy non-Disney restaurants and sights. The Walt Disney Travel Company does, however, offer packages that utilize a variety of Anaheim hotels and motels.

Above all, shop around. Travel agents can help compare package prices and options. Considering the intense competition among area hotels and attractions, you can't help but find a bargain.

## LOCKERS AND KENNELS

A locker can be a lifesaver. Great for stowing extra items such as jackets, packages and diaper bags, they're available for a small fee at all the big theme parks.

Disneyland kennels offer convenient, inexpensive day lodging for pets. Besides Fido and Fluffy, the kennels also accept many unusual boarders such as snakes, birds, hamsters, rabbits and goldfish. If your pet falls into the "unusual" category, bring its cage. Kennels are located just outside the main entrance and cost $10 per pet, per day.

There are also kennel facilities for dogs and cats at Universal Studios and Six Flags California.

## CREDIT CARDS

Don't leave home without your plastic; at Disneyland, you're gonna need it. The major cards—Visa, MasterCard, American Express, Diners Club and Discover—are accepted throughout Disneyland and surrounding attractions. However, some theme-park vendors and fast-food restaurants do not take credit cards. There are ATMs located inside the park and checks up to $100 can be cashed at the Penny Arcade on Main Street or at the Starcade in Tomorrowland.

# Star System

One of the primary goals of this book is to help you sort through the overwhelming number of theme-park attractions, so we have judged them by originality, imagination, design and *overall* family appeal. Obviously, family members aren't always going to agree on the "best" rides, so we've geared our ratings toward the people in charge: the parents. For instance, some rides popular with young children received low ratings because they don't appeal to adults or even older children. In the "Tips" section for each ride, however, we'll point out if it's particularly popular with toddlers or other age groups.

*One Star* signifies "one to be missed," a dullsville attraction that's a waste of time.

*Two Stars* means below average, but with some redeeming entertainment value.

*Three Stars* indicates an average attraction, one that shows at least a little imagination but may not appeal to the majority of visitors.

*Four Stars* signifies above average, offering ingenuity, fantasy and top-notch design.

*Five Stars* is "not to be missed," a very popular, state-of-the-art attraction that makes you want to ride over and over and over.

## Lodging

The Anaheim area, especially the few blocks surrounding Disneyland, offers a smorgasbord of lodging possibilities. In keeping with the Disneyland fantasy, most of the budget-priced motels and inns are built around some kind of theme, much to the delight of children. You'll find cowboy-style lodges, motels named after storybook characters and curious futuristic inns designed for an atomic age. Most sprung up during the Disney boom of the '50s and '60s and could use some renovation. Many offer bland facilities at low prices and are fine if you're economizing and don't plan to spend much time in your room.

No matter where you stay, you should book well in advance, as these budget rooms go fast. During high season, we recommend making your reservation several months ahead of time.

In *Disneyland and Beyond: Southern California Family Attractions*, we have chosen the best family-oriented accommodations that each area

---

*SAY "CHEESE!"*

*There's hardly a bad place to take pictures inside the area's theme parks, but there are some extra-choice spots. Here are ideas for great shots of the kids:*

- ❖ *On the bridge in front of Sleeping Beauty Castle (Disneyland)*
- ❖ *On Dumbo, before takeoff (Disneyland)*
- ❖ *In front of the Mickey Mouse floral portrait located just inside the main entrance (Disneyland)*
- ❖ *With Mickey Mouse inside his Toontown house (Disneyland)*
- ❖ *With the Doo Wop singers in front of Mel's Diner (Universal Studios)*
- ❖ *With Jaws, in the Amity town square (Universal Studios)*
- ❖ *Feeding the dolphins, at the Rocky Point Preserve (Sea World)*

has to offer. You'll find detailed hotel descriptions toward the end of each chapter.

To help suit your budget, we've organized the accommodations according to price. Rates referred to are high-season, so if you are looking for low-season bargains, it's good to inquire.

*Budget* hotels are generally less than $50 per night for two adults and two children; the rooms are clean and comfortable but lack luxury. The *moderate* hotels run $50 to $90 and provide larger rooms, plusher furniture and more attractive surroundings. At a *deluxe* hotel you can expect to spend between $90 and $130 for two adults with children. You'll check into a spacious, well-appointed room with all modern facilities; downstairs, the lobby will be a fashionable affair, and you'll usually see a restaurant, lounge and a cluster of shops. If you want to spend your time in the finest hotels, try an *ultra-deluxe* facility, which will include all the amenities and cost over $130.

## Camping

For families, camping is a great way to stay in the Orange County area. First and foremost, it saves money. Not only is camping much less expensive than staying in a hotel, but it also saves on food bills. By cooking some of your own meals, you avoid falling into the trap of eating overpriced theme-park food three times a day. Camping also provides a physical and mental break from the rigors of theme-park touring. Best of all, most campgrounds are family oriented, providing plenty of outdoor activities for all ages.

Campers will need basic cooking equipment and, except in the winter, can make out fine with only a lightweight sleeping bag and a tent with good screens and a ground cloth. A canteen, first-aid kit, flashlight, mosquito repellent and other routine camping gear should also be brought along.

For campground information see "Camping" in the Disneyland chapter and "Beaches and Parks" in Chapters Six and Seven.

## Dining

It seems as if Southern California has as many restaurants as people. To help you decide on this army of eateries, we've organized them according to family appeal and cost with price ratings of budget, moderate, deluxe or ultra-deluxe.

---

*On a diet? All the major theme parks offer light, low-calorie fare. Check with Guest Relations at each park.*

---

Dinner entrées at *budget* restaurants usually cost $8 or less. The ambience is informal, service usually speedy and the crowd often a local one. *Moderate*-priced restaurants range between $8 and $16 at dinner; surroundings are casual but pleasant, the menu offers more variety, and the pace is usually slower. *Deluxe* establishments tab their entrées from $16 to $24; cuisines may be simple or sophisticated, depending on the location, but the decor is plusher and the service more personable. *Ultra-deluxe* dining rooms, where entrées begin at $24, are often the gourmet places; here, cooking has become a fine art, and the service should be impeccable.

Some restaurants change hands often and are occasionally closed in low seasons. In every instance, we've endeavored to include places with established reputations. Breakfast and lunch menus vary less in price from restaurant to restaurant than evening meals.

## Family Necessities

STROLLERS   A stroller is a must inside a theme park. If you don't bring your own, you can rent one at any theme park. We recommend using a stroller for children younger than three. At Disneyland, it's nice to start the day without one, then pick one up later as little legs start to give out. Keep the paperwork; stolen rental strollers are replaced free of charge with a receipt.

BABYSITTERS   Guests of the Disneyland Hotel who need a babysitter are given a list of recommended licensed sitters upon arrival. The sitters, who will watch your child right in your own room, charge about $8 to $10 per hour, with an additional fee for additional children. Reservations should be made a day in advance. Call the Disneyland Hotel (714-778-6600) for more information.

BABY SERVICES   Available in Disneyland, Baby Services offers quiet, dimly lit rooms with changing tables and comfortable rockers for nursing. High chairs, bibs, pacifiers, formula, cereal and jars of food are also on hand for a fee. Disposable diapers are available here and in restrooms. Most other theme parks offer changing tables in the restrooms, but other services and supplies are limited, so be prepared.

## Travelers with Disabilities

For the most part, Disneyland and the surrounding theme parks are easily accessible to travelers with disabilities. Attractions feature wide, gently sloped ramps, and restrooms and restaurants are designed with persons with disabilities in mind. Wheelchairs and motorized three-wheel vehicles are available for rent at the entrance to every theme park. For hearing-impaired guests, Disneyland offers written descriptions of most attractions. For a small deposit, sight-impaired guests can borrow portable tape recorders and cassette tapes with narrative on each attraction. Check at the Guest Relations desk.

California stands at the forefront of social reform for persons with disabilities. During the past decade, the state has responded to the needs of the blind, wheelchair bound and others with a series of progressive legislative measures. The Department of Motor Vehicles provides special parking permits for the disabled (check the phone book for the nearest location). Many local bus lines and other public-transit facilities are wheelchair accessible.

There are also agencies in Southern California assisting disabled persons. For tips and information about the Orange County and Los Angeles area, contact the **Westside Center for Independent Living** (12901 Venice Boulevard, Los Angeles; 310-390-3611). In the San Diego area, try the **Access Center** (1295 University Avenue, Suite 10, San Diego; 619-293-3500).

The **Society for the Advancement of Travel for the Handicapped** (347 5th Avenue, #610, New York, NY 10016; 212-447-7284), **Mobility International USA** (P.O. Box 10767, Eugene, OR 97440; 541-343-1284) and **Flying Wheels Travel** (P.O. Box 382, Owatonna, MN 55060; 800-535-6790) offer information for disabled travelers. **Travelin' Talk** (P.O. Box 3534, Clarksville, TN

---

### NURSING NOOKS

*Disneyland's relaxed family atmosphere and abundance of cool, dark attractions make it a good place to discreetly nurse an infant. In the Magic Kingdom, try the theaters at the Disneyland Opera House and Fantasyland. For those apprehensive about these locations, there are comfortable rocking chairs at the Baby Services area.*

*Knott's Berry Farm offers three nursing rooms throughout the park. Other theme parks generally provide changing tables.*

---

*Worldwide, 600,000 people ride monorails each day. Disneyland's system was the very first daily operating monorail.*

---

37043; 615-552-6670), a networking organization, also provides assistance.

Be sure to check in advance when making room reservations. Many hotels and motels feature facilities for those in wheelchairs.

## Senior Travelers

As millions have discovered, Southern California is an ideal place for older vacationers, many of whom turn into part-time or full-time residents to take in the mild climate. Many destinations offer significant discounts, and off-season rates make the area exceedingly attractive for travelers on limited incomes. Throughout much of the year, visitors 60 and older enjoy discounts at most theme parks and attractions. The Golden Age Passport, which must be applied for in person, allows free admission to national parks and monuments for anyone 62 and older.

The **American Association of Retired Persons** (AARP) (3200 East Carson Street, Lakewood, CA 90712; 562-496-2277) offers membership to anyone over 50. AARP's benefits include travel discounts with a number of firms.

**Elderhostel** (75 Federal Street, Boston, MA 02110; 617-426-7788) offers reasonably priced, all-inclusive educational programs in a variety of Southern California locations throughout the year.

Be extra careful about health matters. In addition to the medications you ordinarily use, it's a good idea to bring along the prescriptions for obtaining more. Consider carrying a medical record with you—including your medical history and current medical status as well as your doctor's name, phone number and address. Make sure your insurance covers you while away from home.

## Foreign Travelers

PASSPORTS AND VISAS   Most foreign visitors are required to obtain a passport and tourist visa to enter the United States. Contact your nearest United States Embassy or Consulate well in advance to obtain a visa and to check on any other entry requirements.

CUSTOMS REQUIREMENTS   Foreign travelers are allowed to carry in the following: 200 cigarettes (1 carton), 50 cigars, or 2 kilograms (4.4 pounds) of smoking tobacco; one liter of alcohol for personal use only (you must be 21 years of age to bring in the alcohol); and US$100 worth of duty-free gifts that can include an additional quantity of 100 cigars. You may bring in any amount of currency but must fill out a from if you bring in over US$10,000. Carry any prescription drugs in clearly marked containers. (You may have to produce a written prescription or doctor's statement for the customs officer.) Meat or meat products, seeds, plants, fruit and narcotics cannot be brought into the United States. Contact the **U.S. Customs Service** (1301 Constitution Avenue Northwest, Washington, DC 20229; 202-927-6724) for further information.

DRIVING   If you plan to rent a car, an international driver's license should be obtained *before* arriving in California. Some rental companies require both a foreign license and an international driver's license. Many car-rental agencies require a lessee to be 25 years of age; all require a major credit card. Children under the age of five or under 40 pounds should be in the back seat in approved child-safety restraints.

CURRENCY   United States money is based on the dollar. Bills come in denominations of $1, $5, $10, $20, $50 and $100. Every dollar is divided into 100 cents. Coins are the penny (1 cent), nickel (5 cents), dime (10 cents) and quarter (25 cents). Half-dollar and dollar coins are rarely used. You may not use foreign currency to purchase goods and services in the United States. You may, however, exchange your currency at the Passport Processing Center and at the Penny Arcade, both inside Disneyland on Main Street. All other theme parks have limited exchange facilities, so you should arrive at the parks already armed with credit cards and U.S. dollars.

LANGUAGE ASSISTANCE   Disneyland provides translated guides and maps for many attractions. Check with Guest Services inside each park; most have foreign-language maps.

ELECTRICITY AND ELECTRONICS   Electric outlets use currents of 110 volts, 60 cycles. For appliances made for other electrical systems, you need a transformer or other adapter. Travelers who use laptop computers for telecommunication should be aware that modem configurations for U.S. telephone systems may be different from their European counterparts. Similarly, the U.S. format for videotapes is different from that in Europe; U.S. Park Service visitors centers and other stores that sell souvenir videos often have them available in European format.

WEIGHTS AND MEASURES    The United States uses the English system of weights and measures. American units and their metric equivalents are: 1 inch = 2.5 centimeters; 1 foot (12 inches) = 0.3 meter; 1 yard (3 feet) = 0.9 meter; 1 mile (5280 feet) = 1.6 kilometers; 1 ounce = 28 grams; 1 pound (16 ounces) = 0.45 kilogram; 1 quart (liquid) = 0.9 liter.

## Planning Your Visit

You'll be hard-pressed to see all of Disneyland in a single day. To get the most out of your trip, we recommend a two-day visit. Ideally, a Disney vacation should last seven days, with the remaining five days spent sightseeing along the coast or visiting other theme parks in Orange County, San Diego and Los Angeles. Even the most energetic visitors get tired of pounding pavement ten hours a day, and Southern California has much to offer in the way of side trips.

However long you stay, rarely do two visitors agree on how to see Disneyland and its neighboring theme parks. Still, there are good ways and bad ways to spend your days, and following a few touring guidelines can help make your vacation less of a hassle. First and foremost: *Arrive early!*, about a half hour before the official opening time. Second, eat a big breakfast *before* you get to the parks. For the rest of the day, eat during "off" hours, which is before or after the din-

---

### AFTERNOON DELIGHTS

*On those hot summer afternoons, the last place you want to be is rubbing sweaty elbows in a crowded theme park. Instead, head for:*

❖ *Your air-conditioned hotel room (the children can nap while you catch an in-room movie).*

❖ *The Disneyland Hotel swimming pool where you can lay prone in the shade and slurp an icy drink.*

❖ *A Disneyland Hotel restaurant. They're cool and uncrowded in the afternoon.*

❖ *The air-conditioned comfort of the Country Bear Playhouse, Pirates of the Caribbean, Haunted Mansion or a performance at the Golden Horseshoe Stage.*

---

*Take your children to the restroom before getting in a long line, especially at Dumbo!*

---

ing rush hour. Third, have a good idea of the order you'd like to see the various attractions. This guide's five-star rating system can help you decide what goes at the top (and bottom) of your list. You should also remember that kids (as well as adults) like to ride their favorite attractions over and over. Allow extra time for riding again. Last, don't try to cram too much in. Decide what you'd really like to see—then cut that in half. Realize that it's impossible to see everything on your trip.

## Sample Itineraries

To help you along, below are itineraries for a family spending four days at Disneyland and other theme parks, along with suggestions for fifth, sixth and seventh days if you have time for them.

For the first two days, we've given two choices: Disneyland for families with young children three to five years old, and Disneyland for families without young children. We've also provided two choices for the fourth day: Universal Studios Hollywood or Sea World.

These itineraries are guidelines, not marching orders. You may decide, for instance, to visit Disneyland for only one day. All itineraries assume you're staying at either the Disneyland Hotel or at a hotel just a few miles outside. If you're staying more than five miles away, you can take the mid-day breaks at a Disney restaurant. And however you plan your days, remember this is a vacation, not a chore.

### DAY ONE: DISNEYLAND (WITH TODDLERS)

**Early morning**    Be on Main Street early—as soon as the park opens —to pick up maps, strollers and other touring essentials. Then proceed through Sleeping Beauty Castle to the heart of Fantasyland and ride, in this order:

*Dumbo the Flying Elephant*
*King Arthur Carrousel*
*Snow White's Scary Adventures* (may be scary for some youngsters)
*Alice in Wonderland*
*Peter Pan's Flight* (may be scary for some youngsters)
*It's a Small World*

*Lunchtime*   Head back to the hotel for lunch and a nap.

*Afternoon*   Return to Disneyland and take the *Disneyland Railroad* to Toontown station. Enter Mickey's Toontown and visit *Mickey's House*, *Minnie's House*, *Roger Rabbit's Car Toon Spin* and other attractions.

*Late afternoon to early evening*   Board the *Disneyland Railroad* at the Toontown station. Ride to Tomorrowland. Disembark and check out the attractions around the *Rocket Rods* queue area. Proceed to the *Tomorrowland Terrace* for a casual dinner and entertainment by a Top-40 band.

If you have time after dinner (and aren't too exhausted), take the kids for a twinkling night ride on the *King Arthur Carrousel*.

## DAY TWO: DISNEYLAND (WITH TODDLERS)

*Early morning*   Be on Main Street early again. When Disneyland opens, hop aboard the *Jungle Cruise* in Adventureland. Walk across to Tomorrowland and ride *Astro Orbitor* and *Tomorrowland Autopia*. Head over to Fantasyland and ride the *Mad Tea Party* (no spinning the teacups). Then repeat other Fantasyland rides the kids like.

*Lunchtime*   Go to Frontierland and take a raft over to *Tom Sawyer Island*. Relax while the kids burn off some energy. Ride the raft back to the mainland, have a hot dog or a hamburger at the *Hungry Bear Restaurant* and see the *Country Bear Playhouse* in Critter Country.

*Afternoon*   After the bear jamboree, exit Disneyland and take an afternoon break. Arrive back in time to see the live show at Frontierland (check the schedule for show times) in the late afternoon or early evening.

*Evening*   Here are some suggestions for the evening: (1) see a performance at the *Golden Horseshoe Stage* in Frontierland (2) have dinner at the *Blue Bayou* overlooking the *Pirates of the Caribbean*.

## DAY ONE: DISNEYLAND (WITHOUT TODDLERS)

*Early morning*   Be on Main Street early—as soon as it opens—to pick up maps and other touring essentials. Head to Frontierland and make an afternoon reservation for the *Golden Horseshoe Stage*. Then make a mad dash to ride *Space Mountain*. Next head to Adventureland and ride *Indiana Jones Adventure* and *Jungle Cruise*.

*Lunchtime*   In Adventureland, enjoy an early lunch at *Aladdin's Oasis*. After lunch go to New Orleans Square and try to beat the lines at *Pirates of the Caribbean* and *The Haunted Mansion*. Then exit Disneyland, and spend the afternoon relaxing.

---

*Walt Disney's private apartment was built above the fire station on Main Street. It is still used by the Disney family and as a VIP tea room.*

---

**Early evening**   Around 5 p.m., have dinner outside Disneyland, then return to the park.

**Evening**   Walk over to Fantasyland and go on *Mr. Toad's Wild Ride*, *Mad Tea Party*, *Matterhorn Bobsleds* and other rides. After *It's a Small World*, continue into Mickey's Toontown, tackling *Roger Rabbit's Car Toon Spin*, visiting *Mickey's House* and taking in the general atmosphere of this whimsical community. Lastly, go to Frontierland and ride *Big Thunder Mountain Railroad*—a great finale to any evening!

If it's during the summer or the holiday season, stay in the park for the fireworks display.

### DAY TWO: DISNEYLAND (WITHOUT TODDLERS)

**Early morning**   Be on Main Street early. Go directly to Tomorrowland and ride *Space Mountain* again. Then ride *Star Tours* and *Tomorrowland Autopia*.

**Mid-morning**   Walk to New Orleans Square, stopping to repeat *Pirates of the Caribbean* or any other rides you'd like. Then stroll to Critter Country and see *Country Bear Playhouse*. Afterwards, hop aboard the nearby *Mark Twain Steamboat* in Frontierland for a relaxing cruise on the Rivers of America.

**Lunchtime**   While in Frontierland, see a performance at the *Golden Horseshoe Stage*. Then grab a bite to eat at the nearby *Stage Door Café*.

**Afternoon**   After lunch, ride the *Matterhorn Bobsleds* or re-ride favorite Fantasyland attractions. At 2 p.m., head over to Main Street for the character flood from the current parade. Afterwards, exit Disneyland.

**Evening**   Some options are: (1) to dine at the *Blue Bayou* overlooking those outrageous Caribbean pirates (2) visit *Tomorrowland Terrace* for live music (3) have a candlelight dinner at Frontierland's *River Belle Terrace*.

### DAY THREE: KNOTT'S BERRY FARM

**Early morning**   Get to the park before it opens and as soon as the gates open head for *Boomerang*, then *Montezooma's Revenge*.

**Mid-morning**   Stroll Camp Snoopy with small children. Older kids can do the rides in the Boardwalk section of the park, including *Windjammer*, then head to the *Log Peeler* and the rides in Fiesta Village, including *Jaguar*.

---

*Walt Disney once said, "I love Mickey Mouse more than any woman I've ever known."*

---

**Lunchtime**    Just before noon, head back toward the entrance and get in line at *Mrs. Knott's Chicken Dinner Restaurant* located outside the main gate in the *California MarketPlace*. There shouldn't be more than a half-hour wait.

**Early afternoon**    If tots are tuckered out, take them for a whirl on the *Merry-Go-Round* or a relaxing circuit or two on the *Denver & Rio Grande Railroad*. This will constitute a full day for them. Others can walk over to Ghost Town and starting at the *Geode Shop,* move clockwise into the Wild Water Wilderness theme area to the *Bigfoot Rapids,* possibly catching a show at the *Good Time Theatre.* Then, check out nearby *Mystery Lodge.*

**Late afternoon**    On a weekday, crowds will begin to thin, so head to any rides you haven't been on. On a Saturday, crowds will be at their peak so ride *Kingdom of the Dinosaurs* and stroll Camp Snoopy, which will be fairly empty. Then set off for The Boardwalk and ride *HammerHead.*

**Evening**    Grab a tostada at *Herdez Cantina* and watch the *Incredible Waterworks Show* before you leave. If you have energy left, the shops in the *California MarketPlace* will remain open after the park closes.

## DAY FOUR: UNIVERSAL STUDIOS *or* SEA WORLD

### UNIVERSAL STUDIOS HOLLYWOOD

**Early morning**    Plan on arriving at the park 30 minutes before it opens in order to purchase your admission ticket. This way you'll be on the first tram.

**Mid-morning**    Hop off the tram and dash to the *Back to the Future* ride and then move on to a show at *WaterWorld* (schedule permitting).

**Lunchtime**    Order a crêpe from *Crepe de Paris* and stroll with it to *Mel's Diner* to hear the Doo Wop singers.

**Afternoon**    Kids won't want to miss the half-hour *Totally Nickelodeon* show. Those looking for adventure may want to ride *Jurassic Park.* Adults and older children should also work *E.T.* and/or *Backdraft* into their schedules.

**Late afternoon**    Take in any show you've managed to miss and check the *TV Audience Ticket Booth* for shows that might be taping that evening or the next day.

*SEA WORLD*

**Early morning**    Arrive just before the park opens. Once inside, pick up strollers, maps and other touring essentials at the Information Center. Look carefully at the show schedule to plan your day, but first head for either the *Dolphin Show* or the *Shamu Show*, depending on which one offers the earliest starting time. Be at the stadium 20 minutes early to secure seats up close.

**Morning**    If you saw the *Dolphin Show* in the early morning, now see the *Shamu Show* (and vice versa). En route to that show stop by *Rocky Point Preserve* to feed the dolphins and watch the playful sea otters. Also swing by the *Forbidden Reef*, where you can feed bat rays and view moray eels.

**Lunchtime**    Have a leisurely lunch at nearby *Mama Stella's Kitchen* or over at the pleasant bayfront *Harborside Cafe*.

**Afternoon**    After lunch follow the path that circles the outer part of the park. Again, check your show schedule and plan to be at the other shows you want to see, as the *Water Ski Lagoon*, *Wings of the World* and the *Sea Lion and Otter Stadium* are all along this path. Along the way you can beat the afternoon heat by spending time inside the cool buildings that house the aquariums and walk-through exhibits including the *Penguin Encounter* and *Shark Encounter*. Cool off also at the park's only ride, *Wild Artic*. If you're with toddlers who are getting antsy, take them for a romp through *Shamu's Happy Harbor*.

**Evening**    If you visit during the summer season, get your hand stamped and leave the park for dinner. After dinner return to Sea World for *Summer Nights*. Stroll through the park, enjoying the bands and musicians and catch any shows you missed during the day. Stick around for the fireworks spectacular between 10 and 11 p.m. If you're visiting in the off-season, head to *Seaport Village* near downtown San Diego for dinner, then stroll through the shops and beautifully landscaped grounds.

## OPTIONS FOR DAYS FIVE, SIX AND SEVEN

❖ In Orange County, explore the oceanfront towns of *Laguna Beach* and *Newport Beach*.

❖ Spend the day at the *San Diego Zoo* or the *San Diego Wild Animal Park*. In the evening, head to San Diego's *Gaslamp Quarter* for dinner, then stroll through *Horton Plaza*.

❖ Visit *Griffith Park*, *Olvera Street* and other Los Angeles sights. Or go to Six Flags California and try the wild rides at *Six Flags Magic Mountain*. Then cool off and splash around at *Hurricane Harbor*.

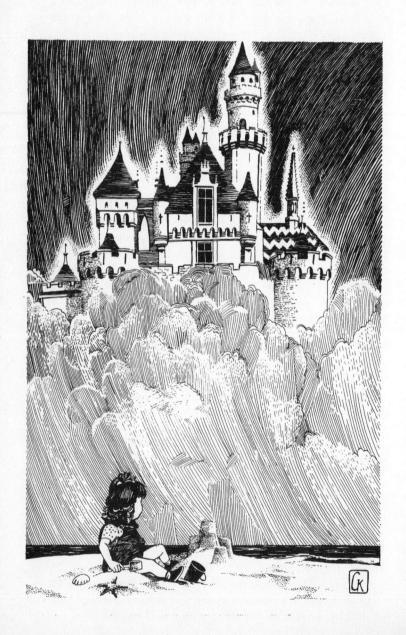

TWO

# Disneyland

It bills itself as "the happiest place on earth," and over 15 million annual visitors will cheerfully agree that Disneyland is without question the most magical 85 acres they know of. On a hot summer day the park often plays host to as many as 60,000 people enchanged by the fairy-tale architecture, whimsical artistry, flourishing gardens and state-of-the-art attractions. Whether you are 6 or 60, Walt Disney's personal stamp of ingenuity will suite you to the letter. The brilliant cartoonist pushed make-believe to its limit, devising a fictional kingdom woven with cartoon characters, simulated towns and jungles, lighthearted music, squeaky clean streets, shimmering lakes and thrilling rides all spun into one colorful, jubilant experience.

Disneyland is fashioned with 63 major attractions, 33 restaurants and 55 shops spread across eight imaginative and vastly different "lands." The most popular is Fantasyland, a dreamy web of storybook architecture, boat rides, carousels and merry music. Adventureland, with its thatch-roofed buildings, jungle journey and stand of huge natural bamboo, offers a tame trek through the wilds of Africa, the South Pacific and the Caribbean and a thrilling expedition through the Temple of the Forbidden Eye.

Frontierland presents a rocky, desert profile in the exciting realm of pioneers and the Old West. Critter Country is as down-home and backwoods as the appealing bears who live there. In contrast, Tomorrowland evokes a completely different era, albeit an imaginary one, with geometric buildings and "Buck Rogers" design and feel. It's home to Star Tours, one of the park's most popular rides. New Orleans Square, filled with ghosts, pirates and quaint shops, is yet another contrast with its intricate wrought-iron trim and turn-of-the-century atmosphere.

---

*During summer months, it takes more than 12,000 park employees to look after the needs of guests.*

---

Then there's Main Street U.S.A., the key to the Magic Kingdom and the first sight that greets visitors. Brick streets, old-fashioned lampposts and intricate building facades create a wonderful facsimile of an idealized American town. There's also the colorful depot for the Disneyland Railroad, an old-fashioned steam train that chugs around the perimeter of the park. Just beyond is a small circular park called Central Plaza with shady benches and beds of colorful flowers. Each evening at dusk the American flag that flies there is taken down in an unabashedly patriotic ceremony. No matter where they're hurrying to, guests inevitably take a moment to join in The Star-Spangled Banner. The magnificent Sleeping Beauty Castle rises ahead, a constant photo spot as guests pose with the castle's fairy-tale spires and turrets in the background.

Each area's remarkable attention to detail from the decorated trash cans to employee costumes and clever restaurant menus continues to inspire admiration in even frequent visitors. There is unbridled pleasure in immersing yourself in the mood of one land, then being transformed by the aura of a thoroughly different realm. Even on the worst days, when the park is crushed with people and heat threatens to suffocate, it is impossible to elude the spirit of Disneyland.

Nighttime brings more illusions to the kingdom, as beads of light trace intricate rooflines and the Matterhorn glows high in the sky. This is the most festive time, when spirited music pulsates from parades, costumed singers pour through the streets and fireworks spray the sky.

There are other theme parks in Southern California. But Disneyland remains the ultimate reality escape for children and provides a spot where adults can think like children. It's a place that tugs at the hearts of dreamers and even impresses those skeptics who chide its corny humor, conservative overtones and idealistic approach.

Anyone who has experienced the fascination of Sleeping Beauty Castle, the adrenaline rush of Star Tours or the happy vibes of It's a Small World knows the Magic Kingdom has no parallel.

## ARRIVAL

Getting to Disneyland is not a problem, except on summer weekends when lines waiting at the entrance can back up at the park's

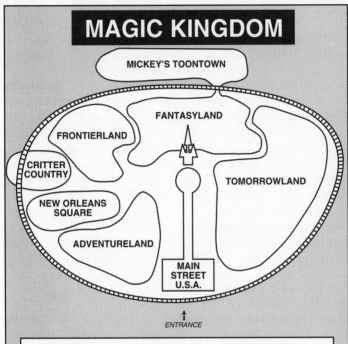

# MAGIC KINGDOM

MICKEY'S TOONTOWN

FANTASYLAND

FRONTIERLAND

CRITTER COUNTRY

NEW ORLEANS SQUARE

TOMORROWLAND

ADVENTURELAND

MAIN STREET U.S.A.

↑
ENTRANCE

### ADVENTURELAND
Enchanted Tiki Room
Indiana Jones Adventure
Jungle Cruise
Swiss Family Treehouse

### MAIN STREET U.S.A.
City Hall
Disneyland Railroad
Main Street Cinema
Penny Arcade
The Walt Disney Story

### TOMORROWLAND
Astro Orbitor
Disneyland Monorail
Honey, I Shrunk the Audience
Rocket Rods
Space Mountain
Star Tours
Submarine Voyage
Tomorrowland Autopia

### FANTASYLAND
Alice in Wonderland
Casey Jr. Circus Train
Dumbo the Flying Elephant
Fantasyland Autopia
It's a Small World
King Arthur Carrousel
Mad Tea Party
Matterhorn Bobsleds
Mr. Toad's Wild Ride
Peter Pan's Flight
Pinocchio's Daring Journey
Sleeping Beauty Castle
Snow White's Scary Adventures
Storybook Land Canal Boats

### MICKEY'S TOONTOWN
Chip 'n Dale Tree Slide & Acorn Crawl
Donald Duck's Boat
Gadget's Go Coaster
Goofy's Bounce House
Jolly Trolley
Mickey's House
Minnie's House
Roger Rabbit's Car Toon Spin

### FRONTIERLAND
Big Thunder Mountain Railroad
Fantasmic!
Frontierland Shootin' Exposition
Golden Horsehoe Stage
Mark Twain Steamboat
Mike Fink Keelboats
Sailing Ship Columbia
Tom Sawyer Island River Rafts

### CRITTER COUNTRY
Country Bear Playhouse
Splash Mountain
Teddi Barra's Swingin' Arcade

### NEW ORLEANS SQUARE
The Disney Gallery
The Haunted Mansion
Pirates of the Caribbean

---

*The Mickey Mouse flower "portrait" at the park's main entrance is planted nine times a year.*

---

entrance. The parking lot opens an hour before the park does. Call 714-781-4565 to verify.

*From Area Hotels:* Most offer complimentary shuttle service.

*From the Disneyland Hotel and the Disneyland Pacific Hotel:* Take the Disneyland Monorail directly to Tomorrowland at no charge. You can purchase your ticket at the Monorail station at the hotel. The parking-lot tram also stops at the hotel and will take you to the park's main gate, or you can make it with a five-minute walk.

*By Car:* The park is approximately 27 miles south of downtown Los Angeles on Route 5. Follow the signs to the Disneyland main entrance.

At the parking lot you'll pay a fee and enter a 15,000-car lot. Be sure to note your parking row because it's easy to lose your car in this giant place. Sections are named after Disney characters such as Bambi, Dumbo, Alice and Mickey. A tram will take you to the main entrance where you'll purchase your ticket.

## TICKET OPTIONS

Disneyland offers several ticket options, called "passports": one-day, two-day or three-day tickets; two different seasonal passes; or an annual pass. All passports include admission and unlimited use of rides and attractions. Seasonal passports are $99 and $129 for both children and adults and cannot be used on holidays or on varying "blackout days" that occur on weekends during peak season.

|  | Adults | Children 3–11 |
| --- | --- | --- |
| *One-day Passport* | $38.00 | $28.00 |
| *Two-day Passport* | $68.00 | $51.00 |
| *Three-day Passport* | $95.00 | $75.00 |
| *Annual Passport* | $199.00 | $199.00 |
| *Children under 3 are free* | | |

## SIGHTSEEING STRATEGIES

If at all possible, avoid Disneyland like the plague on a Saturday. Crowds are huge, and between 10 a.m. and 3 p.m. expect up to a two-hour wait at popular rides such as Indiana Jones Adventure, Star Tours and Space Mountain. Even a Sunday is better, and during the week many rides have little or no wait at all. Oddly enough, though, the most crowded day of the year, according to park officials, seems often to fall midweek sometime during the month of August.

Regardless of the day of the week it is advisable to arrive well before opening and head for Main Street, which opens 30 minutes to an hour before the rest of the park. Here you can rent a stroller or locker, obtain maps and reservations, see "Great Moments With Mr. Lincoln" and get your game plan in order. As soon as the rope is dropped, angle to your right to Tomorrowland and you will be one of the first on either ride.

As soon as you're off one, speed to the other (which will be 30 seconds away). Having polished off those two, you can now dash across the park to the Haunted Mansion and Pirates of the Caribbean, two other attractions that develop lines quickly. This puts you in a perfect position to ride the Indiana Jones Adventure. If you do it right, you will have ridden five major attractions within the first two hours of opening time, and you can see the rest of the park at a more relaxed pace. Don't feel silly doing the "Tomorrowland Dash." You'll find yourself competing with sprinting kids, galloping teens and even grandparents bent on being among the first in line.

Other strategies to consider are the following:

❖ After you've hit the major rides for the day, try to see all of one "land" before moving to another. Otherwise you'll miss something, and it's time-consuming to move backward.

❖ Don't expect to see all of Disneyland in one day. Plan at least two days or you'll become frustrated with lines and the sheer enormity of the park.

---

*LUNCHTIME STRATEGY*

*Between 11:30 a.m. and 2 p.m., and 4:30 p.m. and 8 p.m., park food services are jammed. It's impossible to get near the Blue Bayou, one of the few table-service restaurants. An alternative is to catch the Monorail from Tomorrowland to the Disneyland Hotel. Have your hand stamped and your ticket stubs with you when you disembark, then head for the hotel's* **Stromboli's** *(714-956-6403), a charming indoor/outdoor café along a "waterfront." It's rarely crowded, food is good, and the children's menu (a Pinocchio mask) has familiar fare like grilled cheese sandwiches, spaghetti and hamburgers.*

❖ Unless you're towing toddlers, leave Mickey's Toontown until later in the day, when the youngest children have exhausted themselves and are on their way back to their hotel.

❖ If you want to see one of the four or five daily shows at the Golden Horseshoe Stage in Frontierland, you'll have to make reservations in advance the earlier in the day, the better. Make reservations at the entrance to the Golden Horseshoe Stage. Reservations for dining at Blue Bayou and balcony seating (in the Disney Gallery) for Fantasmic! can be made at the entrance to Blue Bayou.

## NUTS & BOLTS

**General Information:** Disneyland Admissions Department, 1313 Harbor Boulevard, Anaheim, CA 92803; 714-999-4565.

**Stroller and Wheelchair Rentals:** Both are available just inside the main entrance on the right.

**Baby Services:** Located at the end of Main Street closest to Sleeping Beauty Castle. Services include preparing formulas, warming bottles and changing infants. Diapers and other baby needs are available. Some park restrooms also have changing tables.

**Lockers:** Located next to Main Street Cone Shop and Fantasyland Theater on Main Street. Lockers large enough for suitcases are near the Parking Lot Tram Stop, west of the main entrance ticket booths.

**Pets:** The Pet Care Kennel is to the right of the main entrance. Food and water are provided, but you can't leave your pet overnight.

**Lost Children:** Facilities for the care of lost children are at the First Aid Center at the end of Main Street. Messages for lost persons may be left at City Hall in Town Square.

---

*UP CLOSE AND PERSONAL WITH WALT DISNEY*

*Fans of the original Disney won't want to miss the park's latest tour, **A Walk in Walt's Footsteps**. The two-and-a-half-hour guided excursion wends through all the park landmarks where Walt made his mark. There are also lots of neat tidbits of lore, such as the legendary opening-day fiasco wherein a mushy Main Street U.S.A. (the asphalt had been laid just the night before) snatched high-heel shoes right off of women's feet. The tour runs daily at 10:30 a.m. Cost is $14 for adults and $12 for children ages 3 to 11. Theme park admission is required but not included in the tour price.*

**Lost & Found:** Located on Main Street near the lockers between the Market House and Disney Clothiers; 714-999-4565.

**First Aid:** The First Aid Center is at the end of East Plaza Street just off Main Street. Registered nurses are always on duty.

**Banking:** There are ATMs located inside the park and checks up to $100 can be cashed at the Penny Arcade on Main Street or at the Starcade in Tomorrowland.

**Package Pickup:** Serious shoppers should consider this free service, which lets you pick up all your Disneyland purchases at the end of the day at Group Sales, which is outside the main gate on your right as you exit. Expect a wait if you pick up packages within an hour of closing. Guests of the Disneyland and Disneyland Pacific hotels can have their packages sent directly to their rooms.

## GETTING AROUND

To get a feel for the place, think of Disneyland as a giant wheel whose spokes lead to each of the eight themed areas. At the base of the wheel is Main Street U.S.A., which serves as the park's entrance and the place to get oriented. The Disneyland Railroad travels the rim of the wheel.

At the wheel's hub sits Central Plaza, a pleasant park in front of Sleeping Beauty Castle. The plaza is a good meeting place if your party decides to split up during the day or if someone gets lost. There are also grassy areas where parents can rest while children release some energy. From the hub, bridges and walkways lead to each land. Traveling clockwise, you'll encounter Adventureland, New Orleans Square, Critter Country, then Frontierland, Toontown, Fantasyland and Tomorrowland.

On a map the transitions between lands look fairly easy, though in reality there's plenty to foul you up. The entire kingdom is riddled with sinuous waterways and curving lanes that don't always take you along the most direct route. Anyone who's just ridden Space Mountain and attempts a dash to Big Thunder Mountain with kids in tow will find they have embarked on a demanding trek. Translation: Use a map to plot your course, taking it slow until you get your bearings. If you get lost, a Disney employee can always help.

## Main Street U.S.A.

What finer introduction to an enchanted kingdom than a postcard-perfect street? This replica of a beautiful American town affords a

*Main Street stays spotless because it has four employees who do nothing but pick up every scrap dropped by guests.*

visually exciting collage of wrought-iron balconies, ornate balustrades, gingerbread designs, old-fashioned lampposts, painted benches, shade trees, merry music, popcorn and pretzel carts and hanging pots brimming with flowers. Bright-red fire engines clang, horseless carriages putt along and muscled horses haul trolleys packed with visitors.

Much of Main Street is lined with clever shops and businesses whose task seems to be to entertain as well as sell. Disney Clothiers Ltd. sells everything with a Disney logo or character embroidered, painted, sewn or otherwise integrated into its design. Not bad are men's dress socks with tiny Mickeys woven into the pattern. As for The Emporium, if it's not there you probably don't need it. It's the largest store in Disneyland, purveying buttons, books, tapes and CDs, pens and plush toys as well as fashions and gifts featuring your favorite Disney characters.

Interspersed among the shops are nifty sights and eateries that funnel heady aromas out their open doors. The Blue Ribbon Bakery has truly yummy frozen yogurt as well as chocolate chip cookies baked on the premises daily. Chocolate, vanilla and strawberry ice cream plus the special flavor of the day come in sugar cones at Main Street Cone Shop. Each shop has its own ambience, some busy and bright, others formal and Victorian, and still others rustic and woody.

There is so much to keep the eye (and mind) busy here that it takes awhile to absorb everything. Fortunately this area is rarely clogged with people and can be visited anytime. Plan to come between mid-morning and mid-afternoon, when more popular attractions are crowded. Main Street is also a good place for one parent to take the kids while the other goes solo on Space Mountain or Star Tours or any other ride closed to small children.

To explore Main Street, begin by stopping at **City Hall** for maps, entertainment and dining schedules, lost and found and general information. One of Main Street's best spots is the **Penny Arcade**, where a cent will buy you time on an old-fashioned reel machine. There are also mechanical nickel and dime machines and a few modern video games.

Vintage Disney flicks including some great silent cartoons run continuously at the **Main Street Cinema**. Though there are no seats and you have to stand, the octagonal room with six screens is cool, dark and a welcome respite from lines and summer heat. The center circular platform with railing is exclusively for children. Kids are often fascinated by these unfamiliar, black-and-white cartoons, but it's the adults who can while away half an hour or more watching such classics as *Steamboat Willie*. The first cartoon with sound, it has a particularly nostalgic story line: A clever mouse named Mickey falls in love with a rosy-cheeked beauty named Minnie. Main Street is also home to two larger attractions:

***The Walt Disney Story "Great Moments With Mr. Lincoln"*** ★★
In the lobby of this large, comfortable theater is a remarkable scale model of the U.S. Capitol. While you wait for the 15-minute show to begin, video screens display an unabashed "commercial" for Disney. The interesting part, however, shows how the Audio-Animatronic figure of our 16th president was created and explains the research that went into its formulation. The show itself begins with Civil War history and moves to Lincoln addressing the audience from his study. The Lincoln figure is so realistic that he moves his body as naturally as a human and seems to sense the proximity of objects. It is well done but probably would have a better reception as part of a school history lesson.

*Tips:* The theater is hardly ever filled to capacity; it's a good place for a quiet rest.

***Disneyland Railroad*** ★★★ With their striped awnings, brightly painted bench seats and thunderous engines, these old-fashioned steam trains offer loads of fun. You can hop on one of four turn-of-the-century trains at the Main Street station for an 18-minute circuit of the park with stops at New Orleans Square (for Frontierland), Toontown (for Fantasyland) and Tomorrowland. Between the

---

## MAIN STREET STRATEGY

*Main Street generally stays open a half hour later than the rest of the park. While everyone else is funneling out, you can shop and play at leisure. And buying souvenirs just before closing means you won't have to rent a storage locker or lug the bags around all day. If you do shop during the day and you're a guest of either the Disneyland Hotel or the Disneyland Pacific Hotel, you can ask to have your packages sent directly to your room.*

Tomorrowland and Main Street stations the train enters a cave to treat riders to a diorama of the Grand Canyon. To the clopping strains of Ferde Grofe's "Grand Canyon Suite" the train moves slowly through the canyon, close to deer and wolves, as the seasons change from a summer thunderstorm to winter snow. The scene shifts to how the canyon looked centuries before when pterodactyls, apatosarus and other beasts inhabited its depths. Kids love the theatrics, and for adults it's a great way to rest tired bones while getting a splendid introduction to each land.

*Tips:* Trains run every five minutes. Lines can form at all four stations; seats open faster when you're leaving an area that's drawing more people, as New Orleans Square/Frontierland in the evenings, when Fantasmic! is presented.

## *Adventureland*

The crude wooden gate between Central Plaza and Adventureland marks a decided metamorphosis: on one side are brick lanes, cropped lawns and the bright orderliness of the plaza; on the other are dim, watery passages, tangles of vines and croaks of toads. Here in Adventureland, Disney's interpretation of exotica thrives with totem poles, carved spears and bright blossoms that poke across footpaths. The jungly scheme is peppered with the flavors of Africa, the South Pacific and the Caribbean. Even the air is heavy with the musty scent of the tropics (enhanced, no doubt, by the millions of gallons of water that support the Jungle Cruise).

The "faraway place" theme is emphasized by the architecture, a fusion of thatched huts, wrought-iron balconies and Spanish tile roofs. The breezy network of shops across from the Jungle Cruise offers straw Indiana Jones hats, camouflage clothes, whimsical jewelry, treasure chests and other "loot," sold by helpers in tropical-print shirts. A supply raft bringing coconuts "floats" near the ceiling, and a cageful of skulls bears the warning "Past Due Accounts."

Perhaps of all the lands, Adventureland most appeals to all ages. Families, singles, couples, seniors they all savor Adventureland. From the mammoth Swiss Family Robinson treehouse to the adventure-packed Jungle Cruise, each ride features something for every person. No rides here can be classified as "just for kids," and only Indiana Jones Adventure has a height restriction.

---

*Many of the furnishings in the Swiss Family Treehouse, including the pump organ, are genuine antiques.*

---

***Indiana Jones Adventure*** ★★★★★ When this ride opened in 1995, it immediately became one of the park's hottest attractions. And why not? Those of us who'd been thrilled by Indy's big-screen adventures now had the chance to go along for the ride. The "adventure" begins as soon as you enter the lush, tropical grounds of the Temple of the Forbidden Eye, an excavation site somewhere on the "Lost Delta of India." A generator housed in a wooden shed whirs away, while in a tent, presumably Indy's, an old wooden radio is playing 1940s swing music. After climbing several stone steps, you enter the temple and follow a long, cool, twisting passage carved out of rock and earth. Even on a long wait, there's plenty to keep you and the kids entertained. As you descend into the underground excavation, be sure to pull the rope at the well (you can't miss it), and look for a skeleton hidden in a rocky niche. In the "spike room," where skulls are hung atop spiked bamboo poles, *don't* heed the "Don't Touch" warning signs, and see what happens. The real adventure begins when you board a "troop transport" for the final, fast and furiously harrowing leg of the journey. There's nothing terrifying about the ride (unless you cringe at the sight of a wall-full of bugs or rats), and there are plenty of thrills a collapsing rope bridge and the giant rolling boulder from *Raiders of the Lost Ark*, for example. But most of the excitement comes from sharp stomach-churning twists and turns, and the jerking starts and stops the transport makes. Of course, Indy in robotic form shows up a few times (in the dim light, he almost looks real!). Although it would be hard to discern the difference, the transports are programmed by computer so the ride in each car is a bit different.

*Tips:* The usual warnings for this type of fast-action ride apply: it's not recommended for pregnant women or people with back or neck problems. Kids must be 46 inches high to ride. Waits can get up to an hour pretty quickly, especially on weekends, so plan accordingly. The actual ride lasts just over three minutes.

***Swiss Family Treehouse*** ★★★ Some visitors pooh-pooh this attraction as dull and even hard work, but most love the challenge of scaling such a magnificent tree. The multilevel banyan treehouse (made of cement) is fashioned after the island home in the classic tale of

---

*There are at least ten hidden Mickeys on each ride at Disneyland. See if you can find them all.*

---

the shipwrecked *Swiss Family Robinson*. A marvel of design and ingenuity, the tree boasts some 800,000 perfectly applied vinyl leaves and a trunk that's stupendous. Narrow, wooden steps twist around the trunk and through limbs, providing views of rooms furnished so warmly it seems as if the family has stepped out for just a moment. Patchwork quilts are tossed across poster beds, and wood pipes deliver fresh water to each room. Notice the spacious kitchen, located at the tree's base, with its stone floors, brick oven and array of pots and pans. The living room even has a pump organ. There's running water in all rooms, supplied by a waterwheel and a rushing brook with a series of bamboo buckets on pulleys. At the top of the tree there's a small bench, perfectly positioned for pooped climbers to catch their breath.

*Tips:* The tree requires a somewhat arduous climb that may be too strenuous for small children and seniors.

**Jungle Cruise** **★★★★** One of Disney's most famous and best-loved rides is this fun-filled, crazy cruise through a skillfully simulated jungle. Visitors sit elbow-to-elbow on bench seats in canopied riverboats with names such as *Amazon Queen* and *Nile Princess*. A captain, smartly outfitted in safari hat and belted jacket, urges his charges to "Wave goodbye to the people on the dock, you may not see them again," then guides the group on what he warns is a "perilous" subtropical trek. It's one of the few rides narrated by "real" people a refreshing feature and these narrators are amusing, with their corny jokes and wisecracks. ("It's okay to take photos of the elephants. They've worn their trunks today.") During the ten-minute, action-packed voyage, explorers elude elephants, hippopotamuses, zebras, wildebeests, giraffes and pythons (which threaten to "get a crush on you"). They also dodge waterfalls, escape from headhunters and squeak through the ruins of an ancient city. In one shore scene, apes have plundered a camp, leaving a jeep on its back with its wheels still turning and radio blasting. In another scenario that includes a stack of skulls, the "head" salesman is selling arts and crafts. "The one on top is Art," quips the guide. None of the stuff is real, of course, though some scenes are authentic enough to frighten preschool children. Most kids are easily calmed, however, and by the end of the ride don't want to get off despite warnings by the guide to "leave all your jewelry and other valuables but make sure you take your children."

*TIPS:* An excellent steel-drum band often plays on the elevated stage atop the Jungle Cruise boathouse. Besides getting into the irresistible sounds yourself, take the time to watch how children respond to the dynamic rhythms and you'll no doubt see some impromptu choreography.

**Enchanted Tiki Room** ★★ An air-conditioned Polynesian Island Hut is the venue for this tropical serenade by 225 loquacious, robot-like parrots, flowers and tiki gods. You'll either think this is the funniest, silliest thing going, or you'll be bored to distraction. There seems to be no middle ground. You sit on benches while the sound system blasts "In the Tiki, Tiki, Tiki, Tiki Rooooom" which becomes repetitive and eventually borders on the obnoxious. The totem poles that blink and sing are proof that Disney can be overly fatuous.

*TIPS:* If the idea of listening to faux birds and flowers sing for 17 minutes sounds dull, skip this one. Otherwise consider it a chance for a good giggle and to get off your feet.

## New Orleans Square

One of the park's most enchanting areas, New Orleans Square has pirates, a haunted mansion, a restaurant that overlooks a bayou alight with fireflies, and a section of very, very French shops that can distract you for more than an hour if you're in the mood. This representation of New Orleans a hundred years ago, when she was the unchallenged Queen City of the Mississippi, includes iron-trellised balconies, winding streets, sidewalk cafés and wandering Dixieland jazz minstrels. Many consider it the prettiest theme area, and indeed

---

### THE WONDERS OF AUDIO-ANIMATRONICS

*The Audio-Animatronics system used at Disneyland to bring humans, animals, birds and flowers to life is accomplished by recording audible and inaudible sound impulses, music and dialogue on digital laser discs that have up to 32 tracks controlling as many as 438 separate actions. Playback relays music and voice to speakers, while inaudible impulses control lighting and activate the figures.*

with its view of Rivers of the Americas with the majestic *Mark Twain* and *Columbia* making their circuits, it may well be.

Restaurants here offer jambalaya, seafood creole and other creative dishes indigenous to the area.

***Pirates of the Caribbean*** ★★★★★ Arguably one of Disney's greatest feats, this attraction combines the best of the best rides: realistic scenery, spirited music, nonstop action and a couple of short but stomach-lurching drops. Unlike the bright outdoor scenery of Jungle Cruise, this boat trip takes you through the dark and clammy hollows of pirates' dens. In early scenes peg-legged men are chained to stone floors, and buzzards pick at skeletons strewn on a deserted beach while haunts cling to the mast of a ghost ship. For most of the ride, the swashbucklers are plundering, frolicking and raising hell in general. During a chaotic sea battle, the pirate galleon aims across the bows of guests' rafts. Elsewhere pirates carelessly fire pistols, pursue screeching ladies and set the town ablaze. Chickens cluck, dogs bark and drunken pigs twitch their legs in strangely realistic ways. Several sights border on the raucous including the auctioning of women though Disney manages to make it all seem good fun. The attention to detail is masterful, down to the mole on one pirate's chin.

*TIPS:* Small children may be frightened by some of the ride's scenes. The wait here can be up to an hour during the middle of a busy day, but by 7 or 8 p.m. there is rarely more than a 15-minute line. Not to be missed.

***The Haunted Mansion*** ★★★★★ This creepy edifice is home to 999 frighteningly funny ghosts, ghouls and goblins who carry on an incessant search for Occupant No. 1000. "Here lies old Fred. A great big rock fell on his head." So reads one of the wacky graveyard epitaphs outside the Mansion, a vast, ominous house in the far corner of New Orleans Square. It's a fitting introduction to one of Disney's best-ever attractions, an ingenious design with so many special effects and illusions that you find yourself saying, "I know this isn't real, but . . . ."

A gloomy butler greets visitors at the front doors and ushers them into an eight-sided gallery with portraits of "former guests," cobwebbed chandeliers and a ceiling that rises or is the floor sinking? After a sepulchral introduction, he leads everyone to their "doom buggies" for a spirited ride through rooms with phantoms, ghoulies and various netherworld inhabitants. There's a piano player who's nothing more than a shadow, a spooked cemetery and its petrified

*The 11 million gallons of river water in Disneyland are dyed to maintain a clean "muddy" look.*

watchman, a teapot pouring tea and a screeching raven that won't go away. Voices howl, figures skate across ceilings, and ghosts become more vivid as the darkness gets thicker.

All the special effects are great, but the show-stoppers are the "holograms." Using advanced technology and imagination, Disney pushed 3-D projection to its limits. Life-size human images, dressed in everyday attire, float around and mimic the mannerisms of their living counterparts. In one party scene, holograms whirl around the floor in sync with the music while hologram "humans" at a banquet fade in and out. Perhaps the most fascinating (and talked-about) hologram is the woman's head in the crystal ball: Her lifelike image chatters nonstop. The kicker, though, is at the ride's end, when you gaze into a mirror and find you have your own spook (read hologram) nestled beside you.

*TIPS:* Despite the attraction's expert effects, it's not really scary for most people. Small children, however, will likely be frightened by what to them is most certainly "real."

**The Disney Gallery** ★★ Practically above Pirates of the Caribbean, this pleasant gallery is done in the style of a New Orleans mansion with parquet floors and white gingerbread trim. It features a fascinating display of original sketches and artists' renderings done during the park's planning stages. It's interesting to see how concepts for various rides and attractions evolved. Included are limited-edition lithographs, animation cells plus posters and books that are for sale.

*TIPS:* Just off the gallery is a small, cool patio with a fountain plus tables and chairs. Because it's hidden away it's rarely crowded and is a wonderful place to spend a few quiet minutes.

# *Critter Country*

This four-acre backwoods area, Disneyland's rugged Northwest territory, is the setting for Splash Mountain, an enormously popular ride, as well as the Country Bear Playhouse. One of the least-crowded eateries, the Hungry Bear Restaurant, offers "the bear necessities." At Brer Bar food stand you can get a Mickey-shaped soft pretzel.

**Splash Mountain** ★★★★ Considering that the wait here is some-times over an hour, the ride itself is somewhat anticlimactic. You sit in hollowed-out logs that float on a rushing stream for a long uphill pull past old milling gear and machines, then meander outdoors past the homes of Brer Fox, Brer Bear and Brer Rabbit. After a few lit-tle drops the logs float inside the mountain where you're almost Zip-A-Dee-Doo-Daahed to death by what has become the Disney National Anthem. More than a hundred animated *Song of the South* characters are out in force, with Brer Rabbit trying to get honey from a hive swarming with bees and Brer Fox narrowly escaping an alligator.

You're pulled up another hill for a brief drop, then up again, to be plunged over a steep, 47-degree flume drop, screeching five sto-ries into the briar patch of Splash Mountain, spraying spectators as you "watch your life splash before your eyes." From there it's a mel-low float past the Swimmin' Hole and the *Zip-A-Dee Lady* steam-boat where the characters are gathered for the ride's final musical tour de force.

*TIPS:* If you're really averse to getting damp, don't sit in the front seat. And if you don't want to participate at all, the best van-tage point for seeing the ride's steep, speedy final descent is just across from the ride's entrance. There is a height restriction of 40 inches and children must be at least 3 years old to ride.

**Country Bear Playhouse** ★★★ With more puns and cornball jokes than you ever thought you could stand, this silly musical revue fea-tures Disney's unbearably funny bears as they go on vacation. You're encouraged to clap and sing along to such show-stoppers as a female trio belting out "Wish They All Could Be California Bears" with mounted buffalo, moose and deer heads singing backup from the wall. The antics of 18 Audio-Animatronics bears appeal to younger children as well as adults who can appreciate the parody of surfer-dudes singing songs from the '60s.

---

## SPLASH FLASH PHOTO FINISH

*As you exit Splash Mountain you'll see yourself in freeze-frame on a video screen. All your delight, exhilaration or perhaps terror has been captured by the camera on the infamous flume drop and is yours on a souvenir photo for a price, of course. Sit in front for the best shot.*

---

*At 50 feet wide and 30 feet high, the showboat in Splash Mountain is the biggest animated prop ever built.*

---

TIPS: Although there may appear to be a long line for this attraction, the theater is large and cool and doesn't usually fill up.

**Teddi Barra's Swingin' Arcade** ★★ If anyone in your group is drawn to old-fashioned shooting galleries, this is the place. You can challenge animated figures to a quick-draw contest and shoot down mechanical bears as they scamper up trees and through the woods. You need quarters for this frontier-themed fun-and-games emporium.

## Frontierland

Back through New Orleans Square and around the corner from Critter Country, Frontierland places you in the realm of the pioneers. Flags of the original Thirteen Colonies fly proudly over the log-walled stockade entrance. Reminiscent of an 1800s mining town, Frontierland presents a rugged face of cactus, rust-colored rock, adobe buildings and trading posts. River Belle Terrace, which overlooks the route of the *Mark Twain* sternwheeler, serves up yummy pancake and waffle breakfasts. At the Sprit of Pocahontas Shop you'll find American Indian crafts and Pocahontas-themed clothing and toys. The main draw is Big Thunder Mountain Railroad, which simulates the thrills and spills of a runaway mine train. Appealing to all ages, the area recalls early America during the days when the West was still as wild as its reputation.

**Big Thunder Mountain Railroad** ★★★★★ This roller coaster like ride has much more to it than curves and drops. It's a perilous journey aboard a roaring mine train. Boarding open-air ore cars, you embark on a harrowing excursion through the dark caverns of Big Thunder Mountain and some of Disney's most creative scenery. A hint of things to come is evident when the 30-passenger train chugs out of the station with no one at the controls. Within moments, you're engulfed by darkness and become the center of attention for a swarm of bats.

As the train climbs high into the mountain, you pass brilliantly colored phosphorescent pools, and a raging waterfall narrowly misses the tracks. In Coyote Canyon, furry residents howl as the train throttles into the black depths of a chasm. At the top of a natural-arch

*The* Mark Twain *is the first paddle-wheeler built in the United States in half a century.*

bridge you get a momentary view of desert landscape, then re-enter the mountain as the train rumbles like a full-force earthquake. Shoring columns shake and ten-foot rocks tumble toward your teetering train. Miraculously the train finds a way out and returns to the boom town of Big Thunder.

*TIPS:* A very popular ride, even though the wait can be from 30 minutes to one and one-half hours. Children shorter than 40 inches are not allowed to ride.

**Mark Twain Steamboat ★★★** One of the original Disneyland attractions, this sternwheeler with white gingerbread railings is still as beautiful to look at as it is to explore. The ship lazily paddles past plantation docks on the Rivers of America as it circumnavigates Tom Sawyer Island. Keep an eye open for moose, deer and other wild animals in the dense forest of Frontierland.

*TIPS:* Although kids will want to explore the multidecked sternwheeler, adults can find this ride a good opportunity to corral a seat for a 15-minute respite.

**Tom Sawyer Island River Rafts ★★** Guests are transported to a cleverly designed island in the center of the Rivers of America. Steamboats, rafts, keelboats and a giant sailing ship ply these waters, tossing blue-green ripples against the island shore. Visitors crowd onto timber rafts (it's standing only) for fun, motorized transportation to the island. Cool and woodsy, Tom Sawyer Island offers a retreat from lines and plenty of places where children can romp. Guests of all ages can relive childhood escapades, exploring a baffling maze of tunnels inside Injun Joe's Cave, swaying across the precarious suspension bridge and scaling Castle Rock. While children burn off energy, adults can stroll leisurely or rest on one of the island's many benches.

*TIPS:* Unless you want a shady place to sit, adults without kids may want to save this for their second day at Disneyland. There's usually no line, so visit when other attractions are packed. The island closes just before dusk.

**Sailing Ship Columbia ★** Among the ships and boats sharing the Rivers of America is the square-masted sailing schooner *Columbia*. Adults can appreciate the authentic rigging of this 1790-model ship, but kids become a bit bored after they've made their circuit of the deck. It follows basically the same route as the *Mark Twain* with the highlight of the trip occurring when the ship unleashes a cannonade at Fort Wilderness.

*TIPS:* The beauty of the *Columbia* may be better appreciated from a distance than aboard. Skip it if you're pressed for time.

**Mike Fink Keelboats** ★ These two low-slung craft are named for a Mississippi riverboat captain and renowned marksman who lived from 1770 to 1823. The keelboats shoot some rather tame rapids and explore the same scenery as the *Mark Twain*, so there's no need to ride both particularly since the keelboats are much less exciting. Passengers are crowded into a small space, and the narrator's spiel can be dull, although it depends to some extent on which narrator you get. However, there is rarely a long wait.

*TIPS:* This attraction can go to the bottom of your list ride if you have time, but if you miss it you haven't missed much.

**Fantasmic!** ★★★★★ First-time visitors to this nightly show on the River of America can often be heard postulating about what kind of experience they suppose they're in for. But imaginative inventors of this crowd pleaser, the crown jewel of Disneyland entertainment, have come up with a live musical performance that simply defies exact description: a 22-minute spectacle with songs, film clips and special effects that leave the uninitiated and even repeat visitors glued to the action.

The show, performed on Tom Sawyer Island but visible from New Orleans Square, weaves the tale of Mickey Mouse's dream battle between good and evil (read: Disney heroes and villains). In addition to toe-tapping original music and myriad special effects, there's a rope-swinging Captain Hook/Peter Pan battle aboard the sailing ship *Columbia*, as well as live appearances by some classic villains (Maleficent and the Wicked Queen from *Snow White* to name two) and virtually every animated prince and princess ever drawn. Most amazing is the precision interplay between live performers, movie clips and special effects (a feat carried off by nearly two dozen computers). Live characters seem to appear and vanish from nowhere, and film clips, projected off cascading water "screens," create the impression of animated images dancing in midair.

As the show draws to a close, climactic bursts of water and pyrotechnics draw plenty of "oohs" and "ahs" from the crowd, and the grand finale leaves everyone cheering for more. Takes place nightly and is visible from New Orleans Square. Check the map at the Magic Kingdom entrance for show times. An absolute don't-miss!

*The Cider Mill on Tom Sawyer Island houses the special-effects nerve cen-
ter of Fantasmic.*

TIPS: To really appreciate Fantasmic!, you'll have to be able to
see it. Unfortunately, the folks at Disneyland didn't seem to anticipate the magnitude of the event and there are only a few really good
viewing areas to be found. Two of the best: the grassy area at the
River's edge, or the bridge in front of Pirates of the Caribbean. To
secure a spot in either, you'll have to come early we're talking hours
early as crowds for the 8 p.m. shows tend to start gathering as early
as 6 (some devotees get there as early as 4 p.m.). If you're late, you'll
find cast members extremely vigilant about shooing people out of
no-standing lanes. Your best bet: Assign a designated spot-saver while
the rest of your party ventures elsewhere.

**Frontierland Shootin' Exposition** ★ At twenty shots for a quarter, peerless marksmen can sharpen their aim at the infrared-beam
targets. They are interactive and reward you with a stunt whenever
you make a bull's-eye. It's a good place to visit when other parts of
the park are crowded.

TIPS: When there's a line at every other restroom in the park,
the ones in Frontierland will be less crowded.

**Golden Horseshoe Stage** ★★★ Near the *Mark Twain* dock, this
old-fashioned, brass-railed saloon is home to several musical shows,
each with a tongue-in-cheek western theme. Regularly appearing
are the stars Billy Hill and the Hillbillies, who pluck their banjoes,
wail bluegrass tunes and crack corny jokes. If you want to be above
the action, try for a seat in the horseshoe-shaped balcony.

TIPS: Except for the first show of the day (in late morning),
which is first-come, first-served, you must make reservations early
the same day for this show. Or, you can appear at the Golden Horseshoe 15 minutes before show time and stand by for a place vacated
by a no-show. There's a good chance you'll get in. Light meals are
served during the shows.

## Mickey's Toontown

Ever wonder what it would be like to visit the set of an animated
Disney movie? Toontown is as close as you are likely to get. From the

moment you wander under the tracks from Fantasyland or arrive at the Toontown train station, you find yourself in a whimsical land where the pastel-colored buildings slant every which way and cartoons seem to come alive. Round one corner and you'll discover a talking mailbox; round another, you're likely to run head-on into Goofy or Roger Rabbit.

Toontown, you see, is where Disney's animated characters are said to make their homes. You won't find any Do Not Touch signs here. Ring the bell at the camera shop, and a flash goes off. Push the button outside the power house, and the steam spews out. Lift the lid on a crate outside the warehouse, and animal sounds come back at you. Stop by the insurance agency, and you can check on coverage for "Smashing into brick walls disguised as tunnels."

It doesn't take long to walk from the commercial center of Toontown to Mickey's Neighborhood. But for those sore of foot, the *Jolly Trolley* carries up to eight passengers at a time on a wacky, weaving track through town. You can buy cartoon gags at the Toontown Five & Dime or the Gag Factory, or grab a bite to eat at Daisy's Diner, Pluto's Dog House or Clarabelle's Frozen Yogurt.

There's lots to appeal to small youngsters. Donald Duck's Boat, *Miss Daisy*, moored in tiny Toon Lake, features a rope-net ladder, a pipe slide, a rope-pull whistle and bell and a periscope that offers a panoramic view across Toontown. Goofy's Bounce House, set amidst a garden of popcorn stalks and squashed squashes, provides inflated trampoline-like furniture for the over-3, under 4-foot-6 set. The Chip 'n' Dale Tree Slide and Acorn Crawl, built into the branches of a manmade oak, has a spiral staircase to the top of the slide and a bin of plastic roll-in-and-crawl-through "acorns" near its foot. And for the true toddlers, Toon Park has a play area for kids . . . with seats for parents.

***Mickey's House*** ★★★★ This delightful "home" of Disney's first and favorite character should appeal to everyone who visits Toontown, from toddlers to grandparents. Guests enter through the living room and wander through the den, viewing mementoes of the life and career of Mickey Mouse, from photos of Mickey with Walt Disney himself to a replica of Steamboat Willie's boat in a bottle. There's a giant telephone, a smiling radio, a player piano that continually cranks out the Mickey Mouse Club theme, a *Random Mouse Dictionary* on a shelf. Pluto Pup's bed is located inside the house, but his doghouse is through the laundry room in the garden, where a frisky gopher pulls giant carrots back into the ground. The path leads past a small warehouse of cartoon movie props to the screening barn, where you can watch film trailers of *The Sorcerer's Apprentice*, *The Band Concert* and other Mouse classics while waiting to meet Mickey himself shake his hand, get his autograph, pose for a photo.

*TIPS:* There's often a deceptively long line here. It moves fast and is rarely longer than 15 minutes.

**Minnie's House** ★★ This is a much smaller version of Mickey's house next door, with a distinctly feminine touch. Minnie herself often greets guests, who enter through her bedroom and boudoir. There are fruit scents, a computerized makeup mirror on her dressing table, and a phone with answering-machine messages from Mickey nearby. The kitchen tempts with holographic chocolate-chip cookies on the table, a fallen cake (complete with candle) in the oven, a variety of cheeses in the refrigerator, and a working dishwasher with a balancing act of smiling cups. In the garden beyond the back door there is a talking wishing well.

*TIPS:* If time is tight, consider skipping Minnie's House in favor of Mickey's. The spirit of both houses is similar, but Mickey's has more to it.

**Gadget's Go Coaster** ★★ This very short roller coaster often has a very long wait. Once you're on, it's fun, but it's over all too quickly. Credited as the invention of one of the stars of the *Rescue Rangers* cartoon, it looks like a screwed-up junior-high science project built of giant recycled wooden block toys, pencils, straws, toothbrushes, combs, scissors and miscellaneous "stuff." Guests ride in hollowed-out acorns over a red track that weaves over and around a pond from

---

### PARADES

*Disneyland parades usually reflect the animated feature of the moment, with some more entertaining than others. The current daytime procession based on Hercules is a hoot, with lots of lively characters and music, and the big guy Herc himself. This summer, the park expects to add an evening procession based on the upcoming animated movie Mulan. Day or night, if you do plan to hit a parade, arrive early (crowds start filling the Main Street curbs about an hour ahead). One good bet: Use the opportunity to sit down with a gourmet sandwich or baked goody from the Blue Ribbon Bakery.*

which frogs squirt a stream of water. A fish bowl mounted upon a deflated soccer ball provides an unlikely source for a steam engine that ostensibly lifts the acorn train up its first and highest hill.

*TIPS:* Fifty seconds of fun may not be worth waiting 50 minutes or longer in line. Also, it's likely to be frightening to younger children. If time is short, admire the wacky ingenuity of the construction, then move on.

***Roger Rabbit's Car Toon Spin*** ★★★ A taxicab whirls its passengers through the wacky world of Roger Rabbit, his sexy wife Jessica, and the villainous weasels who are plotting to eradicate the residents of Toontown with their toxic "Dip." With black lighting and plywood cutouts, this ride is akin to Fantasyland's popular Snow White and Pinocchio rides, with two major pluses: It's considerably longer and, though your cab follows a track, you have some control over your spin with your steering wheel. In that way, it's rather like putting the Mad Hatter's Tea Party on a track through Mr. Toad's Wild Ride. Adults and older kids may find the waiting line more interesting than the ride itself: It winds through Toontown's back alleys and into the Toontown Cab Co. garage, where you're challenged to decipher such Toon license plates as "ZPD2DA" (Zip-A-Dee-Doo-Dah).

*TIPS:* Lines are shortest in the evening, when many visitors are watching the Fantasmic! show.

## *Fantasyland*

Truly a colorful, whimsical place, Fantasyland is a combination of circus-style canopies, gleaming turrets and gingerbread houses. Dominated by the majestic Sleeping Beauty Castle, it is filled with fanciful lanes that lead you along like the chapters of a fairy tale. Fantasyland has more attractions than any other land (15, more than twice that of most lands). Obviously, children are the biggest fans of these rides, which feature happy lyrics and themes from many of Disney's best-loved films and characters. There are flying Dumbos, whirling Mad Hatter teacups, King Arthur's carousel horses and Snow White's forest. Most adults enjoy the rides, too, and those who don't still delight in the imaginative setting and remarkable attention to detail (in true Disney style, even the garbage cans are splashed with glowing color).

Not surprisingly, Fantasyland is usually the most crowded area of Disneyland. Perhaps that's because this make-believe land epitomizes what Disney does best: bring out the kid in everyone.

***Sleeping Beauty Castle*** ★★★★ This majestic structure gets four stars not for what it contains, but because it is *the* frame of reference for all of Disneyland. Towering above Main Street and encircled by a rock-rimmed moat, the castle is a masterful facsimile of Mad King Ludwig's famous Neuschwanstein castle in Germany. Its royal-blue turrets and gold spires glisten in the sun, providing the ultimate in visual fantasy. You cross the medieval palace's drawbridge into a world of magic and wonder.

The Sleeping Beauty tale is told in colorful, three-dimensional miniature sets, complete with the Prince's tender kiss that brings the fair maiden back to wakefulness. This attraction won't thrill any but the very young, although adults may appreciate the detail in the lilliputian dioramas.

*Tips:* Because this is a walk-through attraction there is rarely a line. During peak periods, however, the movement of the crowd will prevent you from lingering at any tableau that might be a favorite.

***Matterhorn Bobsleds*** ★★★★★ This thriller, down "icy" slopes and through "frozen" caverns, is a unique roller-coaster ride that zooms in and out of Matterhorn Mountain. You'll hold onto your lederhosen while sleek, four-passenger bobsleds climb to an eight-story height inside the mountain, then take a major plunge past waterfalls and a glacier grotto. Sharp, steep turns and gut-wrenching drops elicit the screams of riders that are amplified as they echo through the mountain's hollow interior. Finally, sleds splash into a sparkling alpine lake, usually dampening the riders in the front seat. There's more than ice to chill you while careening down the slopes. The Abominable Snowman may lurch from the shadows to add a frigid

---

## SNOW-CAPPED MATTERHORN MOUNTAIN

*The highest point at Disneyland, Matterhorn Mountain is a 147-foot replica of the famous Swiss peak near Zermatt. It's the first visible sign of Disneyland to those arriving via Harbor Boulevard. It's built to 1/100th scale and was inspired by the Disney feature film The Third Man on the Mountain. Although hollow, it contains enough wood to build more than 300 homes.*

---

*Q: Where in Disneyland can you play basketball?*
*A: At the top of the Matterhorn . . . with the Abominable Snowman.*

---

tingle to the experience. This is one of the park's most visual rides. From almost every angle spectators can watch the sleds whiz in and out of the mountain and decide whether or not to brave the ride.

*TIPS:* Enormously popular, so expect a wait at almost any time. To ride, children must be at least 3 years old.

***Peter Pan's Flight*** ★★★ Small children love this air cruise in colorful pirate galleons. The setting is Never-Never Land, from Sir James Matthew Barrie's 1904 fairy tale about a half-elfin boy who "wouldn't grow up." You glide around brightly lit indoor scenes for rendezvous with Tinkerbell, Captain Hook, Mr. Smee and other favorite Peter Pan characters.

Because of its popularity with families, the short (two-and-a-half-minute) ride typically has long lines. Although adults may not find the wait worth it, children in your party may insist on queuing up for the ride, based on reports from friends who have done it.

*TIPS:* Can be frightening to very small children who don't like the feeling of being off the ground in the dark.

***It's a Small World*** ★★★★ The dazzling, colorful facade of this popular attraction is embellished with stylized versions of European landmarks and adorned with a daffy clock that comes to life with a trumpeting fanfare every 15 minutes. The ride itself is a leisurely cruise in sherbet-colored boats that take you through glittery scenes of hundreds of Audio-Animatronic singing-and-dancing dolls, all attired in their distinctive native costumes. There are Canadian Mounties, hip-swaying hula girls, leprechauns, kings and queens, snake charmers, flying carpets, pyramids, sphinxes, giraffes and hippos, volcanoes, sombreros and even an "underwater" scene representing Hawaii. The theme of world unity shines through in the detailed costumes and settings from countries around the globe. A favorite (if not *the* favorite) Disney ride of small children, it is a feel-good experience with lighthearted lyrics. But be prepared to have the Small World theme jingling in your brain for the rest of the day.

*TIPS:* Though a very popular ride, it has fast-moving lines and rarely more than a half-hour wait.

***Dumbo the Flying Elephant*** ★★ Disney's version of a carnival midway ride is based on the endearing elephant with oversized ears.

---

*In It's a Small World, more than 600 Audio-Animatronic children, attired in native costumes, sing and dance in harmony.*

---

The mouse who befriended Dumbo perches jauntily in the center. Super tame but fun, it features a squadron of Dumbos that glides in a circle and lifts up when riders press a button inside. Kids plead to go on this attraction over and over again.

*TIPS:* Popular mainly with small children and (believe it or not) has one of the slowest lines in the park.

**Alice in Wonderland ★★** This one is as cute to watch as it is to ride. You get into an improbably hued caterpillar that crawls through the queen's castle, taking you down the rabbit hole for Alice's very important date with the White Rabbit. The croquet game, Tweedledum and Tweedledee, the Cheshire Cat, the playing-card guards and the mad tea party are all there. From the outside, the caterpillars present a pastel panorama as they worm their way around oversized flowers and leaves, in and out of the castle.

*TIPS:* Very popular ride with constant lines. Although the ride is slow moving, small children may be apprehensive about the initial downhill trip into darkness.

**Snow White's Scary Adventures ★★★** This Disney-style spookhouse ride features wooden cars that bump and twist their way around boiling cauldrons, screaming witches, ghoulish trees and other creepies. The idea, of course, is that you accompany Snow White on her perilous journey through the forest. Some of the cardboard cutouts and other set work seem hokey, but the rock that nearly lands on your head at the end is a hoot. Though it's not really scary, small children are often uneasy.

*TIPS:* Not popular with seniors and adults without children.

**Mr. Toad's Wild Ride ★★★** Like Snow White's Adventures, this spookhouse jaunt jostles you along a track through various calamities. Following the escapades of Mr. J. Thaddeus Toad from the classic fantasy *The Wind in the Willows*, you joyride down the cobblestone streets of Merry Old England, plowing through cardboard barn doors and haystacks, meeting up with an oncoming locomotive in a dark tunnel.

*TIPS:* Popular with older kids, the ride is often too wild for young children.

*Mad Tea Party* ★★ The faster you turn the center wheel the faster you spin in this 90-second whirl. Sixteen giant pastel teacups turn in one direction while the platform they're on turns in another, practically guaranteeing the dizzys when it stops. But the midway-style ride can be a blast. Indeed, some teenagers head straight here after Space Mountain, waiting in line for consecutive rides, challenging one another to see whose cup spins the fastest. The ride's fanciful theme is taken from an Alice in Wonderland scene where the Mad Hatter throws a tea party for his unbirthday.

*TIPS:* The center wheel can be a chore to turn. If the kids in your group want a real twirl, be sure an adult is with them.

*Pinocchio's Daring Journey* ★★ Pinocchio, that young chip off the old block, finds out that Pleasure Island isn't so pleasurable in this ride. It's the classic tale run through at warp speed. You enter Stromboli's Puppet Theatre through the first of what seem like endless cardboard doors that pop open just in time to let your wood cart through. Along the way Pinocchio's nose grows, he is threatened in the evil amusement park, swallowed by a whale and finally emerges as a real boy back in his own bed, safe with Geppetto. If you don't know the Pinocchio tale, this ride won't tell it, but children enjoy the action and constant movement even if they don't understand it all.

*TIPS:* There's a repetitiveness to this, Snow White's Scary Adventures and Mr. Toad's Wild Ride. If time is short, see just one.

*King Arthur Carrousel* ★★★ A true showpiece of a carousel with 72 graceful, white steeds in a perpetual gallop. One of the original Disneyland attractions, the trusty mounts are decorated with whimsical hearts and flowers on their bridles and martingales. Notice that although most horses are white, no two are identical. Also, instead of traditional merry-go-round music, the carousel organ renders such Disney song classics as "Chim-Chim-Cheree" and "When You Wish Upon a Star." Together with the melodies, the glittering lights, mirrors and almost constant motion make this a singular experience for all ages.

*TIPS:* Lines are rarely longer than 15 minutes.

*Casey Jr. Circus Train* ★★ The little train "who knew he could" (actually there are two of them) winds around Storybook Land for good views of the canal boats and the Dumbo ride. "Let's get this show on the road" says the disembodied conductor's voice that, with a clang of the train's brass bell, sends passengers on their way. Cars are circus wagon cages complete with bars, carrying a cargo of

---

*Each host and hostess at Disneyland has three sets of summer costumes and three for winter.*

---

"wild animals." If crawling into a cage isn't your style, there are two open sleigh-like seats just behind the engine. The mini-choochoo chugs up a hill, goes through a tunnel, and at one point gets moving at a pretty good clip. It stops just above the canal boat waterway for a view of its home station across the lake and a close-up look at a "patchwork quilt" garden with 50 types of wildflowers.

*Tips:* Nice, tame ride outdoors that seldom has long lines.

**Storybook Land Canal Boats** ★★★ Miniature canal boats are piloted through a land where everything is built in detailed miniature. Passing through the mouth of Monstro, the giant whale, you encounter the straw, wood and brick homes of the Three Pigs, then the village where Alice in Wonderland lives. You see London Park, where Peter Pan taught Wendy how to fly, and the home of Ratty, who takes care of the Toad Hole. The Black Forest, home to Snow White and the Seven Dwarfs, Cinderella's cottage and the château where she went to live with her prince, Geppetto's village where he carved Pinocchio, and Mr. Mole's home in the river bank all are represented. The cave at the end? It's the underwater kingdom of *The Little Mermaid*'s King Triton. Nearby is Prince Eric's castle, also from *The Little Mermaid*. Aladdin's palace of Agrabah and Cave of Wonders are also depicted.

*Tips:* The amazing details, right down to miniaturized trees, make this attraction fascinating to anyone who takes the time to appreciate its features.

**Fantasyland Autopia** ★★★ Primary-colored gas-engine cars that look like mini-Corvettes putt into the pastoral back country. What could be fun about driving around the boondocks? Maybe it's the almost total lack of traffic jams and that you'll never, never get a ticket. Drivers can control cars' speed up to about three miles per hour.

*Tips:* A real favorite with kids up to about eight, who then find it boring until they're in their teens, when it becomes camp. Open only during the summer; expect a line.

## Tomorrowland

Walt Disney's original vision for Tomorrowland was as a showcase for the technology of the future. Amid ultramodern buildings with sleek designs, Walt's imagination catapulted visitors into another era; there was the innovative House of the Future (which, as early as the 1950s, predicted gizmos such as electric toothbrushes and large-screen televisions), the Rocket to the Moon and even a "Bathroom of Tomorrow."

Alas, over time, Walt's tomorrow became dated. As the future became the present, the average earth citizen was neither hurdling through space in a flying saucer nor sporting Day-Glo polyester (the 1970s not withstanding) on the job in a plastic office building. Tomorrowland began looking like yesterdayland, more like a 1950s sci-fi flick than a visionary's gaze at the future.

But this update of Tomorrowland, scheduled to open in spring 1998, seems to embrace the fantasy of science fiction rather than the realities of science fact. Much about it is fantastical, from the twirling planets and spaceships of the Astro Orbitor ride, to the area's "Buck Rogers" landscaping and rock designs. Here, in addition to the kitschy classic Submarine Voyage and all-time favorite rides Space Mountain (with updated sound system), Star Tours and Autopia, you'll be able to board the speeding Rocket Rods (still under construction at press time), the park's latest thrill ride, that catapult through Tomorrowland at the speed of a roller coaster.

Still, not everything at today's Tomorrowland comes strictly from the minds of Imagineers. Inspired by the attraction at Epcot in Orlando, Disneyland will offer its own brand of Innoventions. Interestingly, this latest addition seems to take the Land back to Walt's original concept, with corporate sponsors showcasing prototype gizmos and gadgetry of the future in the areas of home, entertainment, workplace/education, recreation/health and transportation. (Who knows, maybe there'll be another Bathroom of the Future.) Housed in the old rotating Carousel of Progress theater, Disneyland offers a unique turn (if you'll pardon the expression) on the Innoventions concept, with the entire building slowly revolving to provide varied points of entry. Fans of Epcot will be happy to find other touches of the Orlando park, from the leaping interactive fountains to the new "Honey, I Shrunk the Audience" attraction.

*Star Tours* ★★★★★ A product of the imagination of George Lucas and the Disney Imagineers, this ride welcomes you to the Tomorrowland Spaceport, complete with R2D2 repairing a battle-scarred StarSpeeder. Mercifully, while you wait in the sometimes-interminable lines, you're entertained with a sales pitch for the latest intergalactic travel packages now being offered.

The action really begins as you approach a set of steel doors where an orange-suited flight attendant ushers you aboard a 40-passenger StarSpeeder. Safety instructions include the usual routine: "Stow your carry-on luggage under your seat and fasten your seat belts." This is no idle advice the visual sensations and motions here are very, very, VERY real. The technology, which is borrowed from the world of *Star Wars*, is similar to the flight simulators the military uses to train pilots.

It's easy to believe you're aboard a StarSpeeder as it takes off for the Moon of Endor. You actually feel what you see on the screen in front of you as you encounter a galaxy full of misadventures. The action is virtually out of control from the word go, as the flight's rookie pilot proves that Murphy's Law applies to the entire universe. You're flung from side to side as the ship takes a wrong turn through a maintenance area, then blasts through the ice crystals in the center of a comet, dodges asteroids and finally plays tag with laser cannons and enemy starships on the *Death Star*. It's an amazing experience, not to be missed.

*Tips:* Very realistic; way too intense for small children. Children must be at least 3 years old and at least 40 inches tall. Do not ride if you get motion sickness or have a bad back. Avoid after a meal.

*Space Mountain* ★★★★★ Next to Star Tours, this roller coaster in the dark is the wildest, most imaginative mind trip in the theme-park lineup. Looming 118 feet above the area, the gleaming, white, concrete-and-steel structure resembles a ribbed, white cone spiked with icicles. After a two-story escalator ride, you begin a two-and-a-half-minute journey through worlds unknown. Meteor showers, whirling galaxies and a gaseous nebula created by three-dimensional aerial projections turn Space Mountain's massive, black interior into a tingling sight-and-sound experience.

Much of the thrill comes from not being able to see where you're going. By roller-coaster standards the ride is quite civilized no upside-down loops, no gut-wrenching drops, and top speed is less than 30 miles per hour. But Disney's packaged the experience along with a new in-vehicle stereo sound system (those are actually speakers on either side of your head) that provides adrenaline-inspiring notes perfectly in time to the heart-pounding climbs and climactic drops. Add the effects of darkness and the ever-moving celestial bodies, and the result is disorientation and an unparalleled rush.

*Tips:* Children shorter than 40 inches are not allowed to ride. Not recommended for pregnant women and those with weak stomachs or bad backs. The dark surroundings and squeals of riders will either scare you off or draw you in. Not to be missed if you like life on the edge.

**Astro Orbitor** ★★★ Kids adore this colorful, carnival-style ride, an updated and faster version of the old Rocket Jets, which puts them airborne for 90 seconds in futuristic aircraft. The open-cockpit vehicles twirl amid a structure flanked by wildly spinning planets. The trip can be tame or mildly exciting, depending on how often you raise and lower your jet. Fans of the old Rocket Jets will find the Astro Orbitor a bit faster, the feeling of speed created by the ride's lower stance, and the effect of the counter-rotating planets. On the down side, you don't get quite the view you did in the jets. The attraction is an exact replica of the Orbitron featured in Disneyland Paris.

*Tips:* Astro Orbitor is a good place for one parent to take young children while the other rides nearby Space Mountain with the older kids. Like the Rocket Jets, the Astro Orbitor can accommodate only about 22 passengers per ride, but the wait may not be as long now that you can board the ride without waiting for an elevator.

**Honey, I Shrunk the Audience** ★★★★★ Welcome to the world of professor Wayne Szalinski, the antihero in Disney's *Honey, I Shrunk the Kids*. After numerous misadventures, Szalinski is tapped to receive the Inventor of the Year Award, and you're invited to the ceremony. In a flash of anticipated mayhem, the entire audience becomes pint sized, menaced by giant snakes, slobbering dogs and stomping, oversized shoes. Like its counterpart in Epcot at Disney World, this 3-D attraction has brilliantly timed its film and live-action effects for action that literally jumps from the screen (and makes most people lit-

---

### MISSION CONTROL

*Space Mountain, like NASA's Houston Control Center, has a sophisticated electronic nerve center that monitors the flight of each "rocket." While in space, the rockets are continuously monitored, and their location is registered on a flight-control console by a series of light-emitting diodes. Any adjustments, such as reduction in speed, are instantaneously initiated by computer.*

erally jump from their seats). The 3-D effects are staggeringly realistic, and there are some startling surprises that I won't ruin by revealing here (suffice it to say that if you don't howl, you're one of the few!). If you're into some scary fun with some good laughs, this attraction is an absolute don't-miss.

*Tips:* As much as it's based on a kids' movie, this is no kids' attraction, and actually sets many little ones (my daughter included) to sobbing. Heed the "Young Children May Become Frightened" warning carefully. I wish I had.

**Submarine Voyage** ★★★ This low-tech ride is admittedly hokey, but the kitschy charm has made it a classic. The underwater cruise through "Liquid Space" takes you beneath the polar ice cap to the North Pole where the view through the portholes is of sunken ships, the lost city of Atlantis, rippling sea grass and mermaids, not to mention some fairly realistic abalone, clams, coral reefs and lobsters. An octopus battles with a shark, and a moray eel peers from its rocky den. The sea serpent at the end is pure fun and nonsense. Kids like the feeling of being underwater (the sensation of descending is created by rising bubbles released as the sub moves past the barnacle-encrusted pier to "deeper" water) and close to the fish, and the unabashedly fake scenery (check out the strings on those mermaids!) is half the fun.

*Tips:* Scuba divers and snorkelers who've seen the real thing may well find this ride unbearably silly, while the claustrophobic will simply find it unbearable (the subs are small and tightly packed). The line here tends to move slowly. Even when crowds don't look terribly big, you can expect a lengthy wait, so it's best to visit early or late in the day.

*Another Tip:* Not recommended for the claustrophobic. It tends to have long lines, so try to do it early or late in the day, or not at all unless the kids insist.

---

## MONORAIL

*The Disneyland Monorail opened in 1959 as a model for urban transit. Its 100-horsepower electric motors operate on 600-volt DC current making it capable of 70 miles per hour at top speed. Rubber-tire wheels on a single-beam trackway make the average 35-mile-per-hour ride smooth and gentle. Riders constantly ask why monorails haven't been built in the "real world." So far no one has an answer.*

*Disneyland's wardrobe department has more than half a million articles of clothing.*

---

**Tomorrowland Autopia** ★★★ As with Fantasyland Autopia, the attraction here is hard to fathom. Internal-combustion autos attached to a track navigate hills and valleys on a mini-freeway system. Drivers can speed up to four miles per hour in sleek, little autos that occasionally bump each other in pseudo fender-benders. Traffic signals, signs like "Prepare to Stop" and gas fumes add to the on-the-road realism of this popular ride.

*TIPS:* Kids seem willing to wait endlessly for this brief ride, seldom longer than five minutes in duration. Find something else to do while young ones stand in line. Kids must be 1 year old to ride or 7 years old and 52 inches tall to drive.

**Disneyland Monorail** ★★★★ The Mark V Monorail System adds immeasurably to Tomorrowland's aura of urban futurism. Though considered an attraction, the Monorail also provides speedy transportation for two-and-one-half miles around the edge of Tomorrowland and off the property to the Disneyland Hotel. Leaving Tomorrowland, its unexciting route runs through the parking lot, but on the return trip you'll get a good overview of the south side of the park and the backside of Tomorrowland. Take the time to disembark at the Disneyland Hotel. This 60-acre extravaganza is the only resort connected to the park by the Monorail.

*TIPS:* The best view is in the first car with the engineer where there's room for four passengers. Most people don't think of this, so even if you're one of the last to board, don't hesitate to approach the engineer with your request.

## Disneyland Lodging

When Disneyland opened on July 17, 1955, Anaheim had five hotels and two motels, with a total of 87 rooms. There were 34 restaurants in the city. Since Mickey Mouse came to town the totals have increased to more than 150 hotels and motels comprising more than 17,000 rooms, and well over 450 restaurants. This, of course, makes for a marvelously varied selection, with accommodations ranging from bare-bones budget motels to super-deluxe mega-resorts.

---

*Each day the Disneyland crew polishes 221 automobiles and 205 ships and boats.*

---

Yet the sheer number of hostelries can be confusing. Along Harbor Boulevard, Anaheim's main strip, dozens of hotels lie within ten minutes of Disneyland's main gate. If you're visiting Knott's Berry Farm as well, see Chapter Three for hotels in that area. Because the two parks are about ten miles apart, one hotel can serve as convenient headquarters for both attractions.

When checking hotels, in addition to price and availability, be sure to ask about packages. Some places have excellent money-saving offers that can include room, breakfast, park admittance plus tax and gratuities. Many are priced per day, some are three-day, two-night affairs. Some even have multi-attraction packages that include Disneyland, Knott's and Universal Studios.

Be sure to inquire about discounts. Especially during winter months hotels and motels are eager to fill their rooms and will gladly extend discounts to AAA members, senior citizens and some airline frequent-flyer members. Don't overlook the corporate discount many hotels extend for the asking. The **Walt Disney Travel Company** (P.O. Box 4180, Anaheim, CA 92803; 714-520-5050) offers help with family travel arrangements and packages. If you'd like to make your own arrangements, the **Anaheim Area Visitor & Convention Bureau** (800 West Katella Avenue; 714-999-8999) will send you an excellent Travel Planner listing hotels and tours.

Unless otherwise noted, the following price categories include two adults and two children under 18 staying in a room. Budget hotels are generally less than $50 per night; moderate-priced hotels run $50 to $90; deluxe hotels are between $90 and $130; and ultra-deluxe facilities cost above $130.

Unless you plan to sightsee or drive to dinner, you can easily settle in at a hotel (many offer shuttle service to both Disneyland and Knott's) and not have to go near a car for several days. Even if you're at a hotel that charges for shuttle service, it's bound to be less than rental-car fees plus parking.

The only hotel connected directly to Disneyland by the Monorail, the **Disneyland Hotel** (1150 West Cerritos Avenue; 714-778-6600) is undoubtedly the most convenient, and also one of the most expensive. For a splurge, and for a total Disney experience, it's worth it. The hotel actually is an extension of the park itself, a kind of mini-Disneyland, with a nightly Fantasy Waters Show and the immensely popular Disney Character Meals.

Within its 60-acre property, the 1136-room resort has beautifully landscaped paths that wind among waterfalls, streams and ponds filled with brightly colored koi. Right in the middle is a mini-marina where guests can ride paddle boats and explore wharfside shops. Kids can pilot remote-control tugboats around a replica of the *Queen Mary*, race scale-model dune buggies by radio control or hit the family arcade for video games. The hotel has three swimming pools, a tropical "beach," a fitness center, a jacuzzi, 11 restaurants and lounges and 20 shops. Rooms, in two-story bungalows or three highrise towers, are spacious and accommodating. Ultra-deluxe.

The **Disneyland Pacific Hotel** (1717 South West Street, Anaheim; 714-999-0990, fax 714-956-6582) is situated on four-and-a-half acres of beautifully landscaped grounds including palm-fringed sidewalks and a koi pond. The Japanese theme continues in the 502 guest rooms, which are elegantly understated with light wood and warm earth tones. The tropical-style lobby is decorated with large oversized chairs and has a glass-enclosed elevator. A swimming pool, spa, recreation area, two boutiques and two restaurants are among the amenities. Located next door to the Disney monorail station, the hotel also provides its guests with special perks such as early admission to Disneyland and other Disney deals. Ultra-deluxe.

The **Anaheim Marriott** (700 West Convention Way; 714-750-8000, 800-228-9290, fax 714-748-2449) offers an outstanding luxury-hotel experience. Two towers, 19 and 17 stories in height, are centered on 15 acres of flower-filled grounds. The lobby reflects a soft, contemporary feel with a sunken sitting area. Framed by a tropical palm court with koi pond, the area has the atmosphere of a sunlit atrium. Just two blocks from Disneyland, it's an easy walk or a short ride on the hotel's streetcar-style tram. The hotel has a connecting indoor/outdoor pool, an outdoor pool, two whirlpools plus saunas and a Nautilus-equipped fitness center. There's also an arcade. Children under 18 stay free and can embark on a treasure hunt anytime during their stay. Its 1033 rooms are medium size with small balconies, some with Disneyland views. The hotel's well-trained, obliging staff seems to feel personally responsible for your good time. Ultra-deluxe.

Two blocks from Disneyland stands the cavernous, 1576-room **Anaheim Hilton and Towers** (777 Convention Way; 714-750-

4321, 800-222-9923, fax 714-740-4737), a glass-enclosed monolith. The airy atrium lobby, set off by brass railings and blue-and-mauve tones, holds four restaurants, three lounges, an arcade and assorted shops, along with a pond and fountain. A 25,000-square-foot fitness center, a pool and a spa are also among the amenities. The modern guest rooms are individually decorated. The Vacation Station, which takes place from Memorial Day until Labor Day, lets kids check in at their own counter and receive a free gift; a lending library allows them to borrow books, toys and games during their stay. The Hilton provides complimentary shuttle service to Disneyland. Ultra-deluxe.

The snow-covered roof at **The Alpine Motel** (715 West Katella Avenue, Anaheim; 714-535-2186, 800-772-4422, fax 714-535-3714) next door to Disneyland will no doubt please the little ones in your family. You won't find five-star luxury here (this is, after all, a budget motel), but the rooms are clean, the service is friendly, the price is right and you won't have far to walk to get to Mickey's front door. Budget.

Families who want some room to spread out might like the **Anaheim Desert Palm Inn and Suites** (631 West Katella Avenue, Anaheim; 714-535-1133, 800-635-5423, fax 714-491-7409). Off season, one-bedroom accommodations rent for less than $70 (they're more expensive during the summer), and the hotel even throws in a continental breakfast (although don't expect it to get too illustrious —we're talking toast, danish and coffee, here). Those who want more elaborate morning munchies can make their own; all rooms come with refrigerators and microwaves. Moderate.

Folks at the family-owned **Candy Cane Inn** (1747 South Harbor Boulevard, Anaheim; 714-774-5284, 800-345-7057, fax 714-772-5462) work hard to make you feel right at home. So named because it was established on Christmas Eve, the Candy Cane is superbly tended, with large (though simply furnished) rooms, lots of gardens and a daily continental breakfast served around a nice pool and jacuzzi. Everyone here is extra helpful; you can either walk to the park or take the shuttle. The rate span here is huge, so be sure to get your room rate when you book. Deluxe rooms have refrigerators and coffee makers. Budget to deluxe.

Little princes and princesses won't be able to resist the ultracute **Castle Inn and Suites** (1734 South Harbor Boulevard, Anaheim; 714-774-8111, 800-521-5653, fax 714-956-4736). The medieval decor features castle towers with faux-stone trim and shield emblems. There's a nice pool to kick back at, and the staff at this family-run property is friendly. Suites here have microwaves. Moderate.

*It takes more than 100,000 lightbulbs of 260 types to keep Disneyland bright and glowing.*

Kids can feel like little cowpokes at the **Ramada Conestoga** (1240 South Walnut Street, Anaheim; 714-535-0300, 800-824-5459, fax 714-491-8953), a place where swinging saloon doors and *Gunsmoke* decor round out the Western theme. Moderate.

The large rooms at the **Anaheim Fairfield Inn by Marriott** (1460 South Harbor Boulevard, Anaheim; 714-772-6777, 800-228-2800, fax 714-999-1727) are brightly decorated and feature refrigerators. Service here is extra friendly, providing one kid-pleasing extra: A nearby McDonald's will deliver Happy Meals via room service! Moderate.

One of the nicest of the hundreds of hotels and motels encircling the perimeter of Disneyland is the 199-room **Best Western Park Place Inn** (1544 South Harbor Boulevard, Anaheim; 714-776-4800, 800-854-8175, fax 714-758-1396), where children under 11 stay free. Crisp, contemporary styling sets it apart from many of its neighbors; accommodations are fresh and colorful. On the premises are a restaurant (kids eat free at certain hours) and gift shop, as well as a pool, a sauna and a jacuzzi. A complimentary continental breakfast in provided. You can walk to Disneyland, right across the street, or hop on the free shuttle. Moderate to deluxe.

**Best Western Raffles Inn** (2040 South Harbor Boulevard, Anaheim; 714-750-6100, 800-654-0196, fax 714-740-0639), situated two blocks from Disneyland, offers a compromise between the huge highrise hotels and roadside motels in central Orange County. Just three stories high and sensibly sized (122 rooms), it actually conveys a bit of the "inn" feeling. It looks like one, too, with its tree-shrouded manor-house facade. Rooms feature Early American furnishings and some contain kitchenettes. Bonuses include in-room movies and Nintendo, an outdoor pool and jacuzzi. Rates include complimentary breakfast and shuttle service to Disneyland. Moderate.

## Camping

In Southern California, camping usually means parking your RV somewhere pleasant. In this highly urbanized area, a spot to pitch a tent is almost impossible to find unless you're willing to wander half an hour or more from Disneyland. Most facilities that bill themselves as campgrounds actually focus on recreational vehicles; some, however, do provide facilities for tent campers. All of the places mentioned here fall in the budget range.

**Anaheim KOA** (1221 South West Street; 406-238-3717) is a ten-minute walk from the Disneyland Hotel where you can hop the Monorail to the park. Besides 221 RV hookups, there's a grassy area where backpackers can set up their tents. This is not exactly camping among the giant redwoods, but the park is clean and quiet. It offers hot showers, clean restrooms, an adult and kiddie pool, spa, gameroom, laundry facilities plus a well-stocked store for groceries and sundries. Pets are permitted.

Five miles from Disneyland and a block and a half from Knott's Berry Farm, **Anaheim Vacation Park** (311 North Beach Boulevard; 714-821-4311, fax 714-761-1743) has 222 spaces with RV hookups in a quiet, friendly, family-oriented park. It has phone and cable hookups, hot showers and laundry facilities, and also permits pets. Children will no doubt gravitate to the rec room, which has a large-screen TV and an assortment of games, and the pool.

Offering 300 sites, including a special area for tents, **Travelers World** (333 West Ball Road, Anaheim; 714-991-0100, fax 714-991-4939) is half a mile from Disneyland. Shaded by palms, this RV park features full hookups, a pool, gameroom, laundry and minimarket. Kids will enjoy the playground, and there's a small car wash on the premises. Pets are permitted.

**CC Camperland** (12262 Harbor Boulevard, Garden Grove; 714-750-6747) is a small, family-type RV park nine blocks from Disneyland with 70 hookups, showers and laundry facilities. It's pleasant and shady with a pool and pool table, and allows small pets. The area for tenters is dirt, not grass, but is close to picnic tables. The public bus stops at the property to take you to Disneyland.

## Disneyland Dining

The park gets high marks for recognizing that modern-day guests may want lighter, healthier fare that is low in the calorie and cholesterol departments. However, most of the eateries are still of the fast-food variety with dishes that suffer from time spent on steam tables or inside plastic wrappings. The small brochure you receive when entering the park lists restaurants by area.

For the convenience of eating on Mickey's turf you may have to contend with long lines, crowded dining areas and a feeling that you'd better hurry because the people standing nearby holding food-laden

*On the park's busiest day, July 4, 1986, the Disneyland kitchens fed 87,000 hungry visitors.*

trays with hungry kids in tow need your table. One solution is to eat anytime other than between 11:30 a.m. and 2 p.m., and between 4:30 and 8 p.m. Two meals a day, a late breakfast and early dinner, might work for your group. Or you can simply eat from vendor carts as you feel the urge. Soft pretzels, popcorn, frozen-juice bars, soft drinks, corn dogs and ice cream are readily available.

On the other hand you'll have a first-class, table-service meal if you're brave enough to handle the inevitable lines at Blue Bayou in New Orleans Square, one of the park's few full-service restaurants.

On the plus side, you have more than 30 restaurants and refreshment centers to choose from in the park. The hosts and hostesses are usually attentive and helpful and are always dressed in costumes reflecting the era and setting of the area where they work.

It's all part of the experience, unless you want to leave the park by taking the Monorail to the Disneyland Hotel where restaurants are rarely crowded at lunchtime.

Disneyland food services are grouped by the "land" in which they are located, and all are budget-priced (under $8 for a dinner entrée) except for Blue Bayou.

MAIN STREET   This has one of the park's most interesting collections of eateries, with its facilities among the most popular in the park. A sit-down breakfast option is **Carnation Ice Cream Parlor and Restaurant**, which specializes in desserts but also has a children's menu that includes hot dogs, hamburgers and sandwiches, served with Mickey chips. The largest restaurant on Main Street is the freshly decorated **Plaza Inn**, which serves buffet-style pot roast, rotisserie chicken and spaghetti. It's cafeteria-style, but the atmosphere is pleasant and upscale.

The bandstand setting at **Carnation Plaza Gardens**, which faces Central Plaza, gives this eating spot a park-like atmosphere. You can order hamburgers here, but the real attractions are the hand-packed ice cream cones and sundaes. Then you can follow your nose to the **Blue Ribbon Bakery**, where over-warmed goodies such as cookies and scones are served alongside gourmet sandwiches made with fresh-baked breads. Budget.

ADVENTURELAND   Located between the Tiki Room and Jungle Cruise, **Aladdin's Oasis** is styled like an Arabian tent and is the place to go for Middle Eastern cuisine like kebabs, rice dishes, tabbouleh and hummus. In keeping with the Adventureland theme, **Bengal Barbecue** purveys portable snacks including spicy barbecue meats and vegetables, Mickey Mouse pretzels and iced cappuccinos.

NEW ORLEANS SQUARE   This area contains the park's premier restaurant, the moderate-to-deluxe-priced **Blue Bayou**. Since the restaurant sits next to Pirates of the Caribbean, you can gaze out on a bayou scene complete with flickering fireflies, chirping crickets and an old-timer who rocks on the front porch of his shanty. The food is quite good, especially the Monte Cristo sandwich (served at lunch only) and the ever-changing fish dishes. Long lines are to be expected, but the restaurant takes reservations.

You can dine to the sounds of jazz at lunch or dinner at the **French Market Restaurant**. This buffeteria features Southern-style entrées including fried chicken, seafood jambalaya and fresh catfish. Close by, **Café Orleans** has prime rib and Cajun-spiced chicken served in a bread bowl. Directly across from the café, **Royal Street Veranda** serves clam chowder in a bowl of French bread. Other gastronomic opportunities include the **Churro Cart**, which purveys sweet Mexican pastries, and the **Mint Julep Bar** where the aroma of espresso and cappuccino (especially in the morning) is irresistible.

CRITTER COUNTRY   For a "honey of a treat," and "the bear necessities," **Hungry Bear Restaurant** will satisfy your appetite with beef burgers, hot dogs, chicken sandwiches and fresh-fruit plates. When all other food facilities are jammed, you may have better luck here because it's tucked away in a corner of the park that doesn't get much through-traffic. The rustic patio is roofed, so it's a good rainy-day destination. Catfish nuggets, Cajun popcorn shrimp and seafood brochette are good takeout choices from **Harbour Galley**, which also has other hot and cold seafood items.

FRONTIERLAND   **River Belle Terrace**, with a view of Rivers of America, serves pancakes, eggs and bacon in generous, brunch-size helpings. The expected salads and sandwiches are there for lunch and dinner, but a standout is the vegetable stew served in a bread basket. For a picnic-style meal on red-and-white-checkered oilcloth, head for **Big Thunder Barbecue**. Down-home favorites such as barbecued chicken and ribs, ranch-style beans, corn on the cob, grilled trout and pie are served cafeteria-style from chuck wagons. The **Casa Mexicana** buffeteria has south-of-the-border specialties including a crisp taco salad.

Chili in a bread bowl, chips and cookies are served at the **Golden Horseshoe** during show times, and you can pick up a burger or hot dog at the **Stage Door Café** next door to enjoy during the performance. You can choose a big, juicy apple, orange or other *au naturel* treat from the **Fresh Fruit Cart**.

FANTASYLAND    The **Village Haus Restaurant**, which re-creates the atmosphere of the film *Pinocchio*, is the primary dining facility in Fantasyland. Intricate turrets, gables and weather vanes adorn the exterior; colorful three-dimensional banners and tapestries decorate the inside. On the menu are salads, burgers, pizza, lasagna and chicken strips for kids. The **Ice Cream Train**, located near Fantasia Gardens, is a possible place to stop for quick snacks and drinks.

TOMORROWLAND    Smoked turkey-breast sandwiches, tuna salad sandwiches and hot dogs are among the offerings at **Tomorrowland Terrace**. There are also special child-size lunches. Because of the popularity of the area, lines form almost constantly. You can eat on a roofed patio in the shadow of a futuristic, Sputnik-like sculpture. Loud, enthusiastic bands often play here during mealtimes. When you're in line for the Astro Orbitor, it's hard to resist the aroma of freshly made popcorn from the **Lunching Pad** snack stand.

## *Dining Outside Disneyland*

Restaurants of every description surround Disneyland, and most offer moderately priced food. At **Goofy's Kitchen** (Disneyland Hotel, 1150 West Cerritos Avenue, Anaheim; 714-778-6600, reserva-

---

### *HAM AND CHEESE AND MICKEY*

*Kids love to eat alongside Mickey Mouse, Donald Duck and the rest of the Disney gang. These galas, called **Character Meals**, feature colorful balloons, favorite Disney tunes and autographs by the animated personalities. Goofy's Kitchen at the Disneyland Hotel offers daily lunch and dinner character buffets, as well as lunch buffets on weekends (ask about special birthday celebrations, too!). The Disneyland Pacific Hotel has daily character breakfasts; weekends in the upstairs parlor, the Pacific hosts the Practically Perfect Tea with Mary Poppins. Call 714-778-6600 and ask for dining reservations. Budget to deluxe.*

tions 714-956-6755), Disney Character Meals are wildly popular. Presented for breakfast and dinner every day and lunch Monday through Friday, the meals are attended by Goofy and other Disney characters who interact with the kids and pose for photos. The all-you-can-eat buffet includes muffins, waffles, cereal and fruit at breakfast, and hot dogs, hamburgers, chicken and roast beef at dinner. Moderate.

A full sushi bar in Disneyland? That's exactly what **Yamabuki** (Disneyland Pacific Hotel, 1717 South West Street, Anaheim; 714-239-5683, reservations 714-956-6755) has to offer, as well as stir-fry dishes, tempura and teriyaki. Laid out in a Japanese-style fashion, the dining area includes a traditional *tatami* room where guests are invited to take off their shoes, sit on cushion-covered straw mats and indulge in the culinary delights of authentic Japanese cuisine. No lunch Saturday and Sunday. Deluxe to ultra-deluxe.

One of the area's best values for atmosphere and satisfying dining is **Mr. Stox** (1105 East Katella Avenue, Anaheim; 714-634-2994), which boasts a versatile menu of rabbit, rack of lamb, veal, pasta and mesquite-broiled fresh seafood. Special touches include savory herbs and spices grown in a garden out back, plus homemade breads and desserts and an award-winning wine cellar. Kids get to select dishes from their own menu. No lunch on Saturday and Sunday. Moderate to ultra-deluxe.

For steak and seafood, try **JW's Steakhouse** (700 West Convention Way, Anaheim; 714-703-3187) at the Anaheim Marriott. Of special interest to those from out of state is the extensive California wine list that includes some of the area's best, but not necessarily most expensive, vintages. Dinner only. Deluxe to ultra-deluxe. Also at the Anaheim Marriott is **Allie's American Grill**, which features a kid's menu that includes staples such as hamburgers, macaroni and cheese, chicken fingers and cheese sticks. The breakfast buffet is a good way to start the day, and for lunch, grown-ups can expect sandwiches, pastas, fajitas and burgers. Glazed teriyaki salmon, New York sirloin steak and Napa Valley chicken are but a few dinner choices. Breakfast, lunch and dinner are served. Budget to deluxe.

In the Hyatt Regency Alicante, **Papa Geppetto's** (Harbor and Chapman avenues, Anaheim; 714-740-6090) is a warm, casual, home-like restaurant with northern Italian cuisine. The bistro-style salad is showily prepared at your table, and the selection of pasta is unusual because of the inventive sauces. All entrées are available in children's

*At the Disneyland Hotel's California Wine Cellar, you can sample vintages from more than 90 California wineries.*

portions. In addition, there's a good children's menu. Dinner only. Moderate to ultra-deluxe.

**Ming Delight Restaurant** (409 West Katella Avenue, Anaheim; 714-758-0978) offers a completely different Oriental dining experience. The Mandarin and Szechuan cuisine is served in a sophisticated setting complete with elegantly carved Chinese chairs and red-and-gold wallhangings. The extensive menu has intriguing fare like Four Delights in a Bird Nest (shrimp, chicken, beef and pork) and Happy Family (shrimp, scallops, chicken and beef). Kids seem to like the grown-up atmosphere and can't keep their hands off the Lazy Susan that adorns the center of each table. Moderate to deluxe.

**Tiffy's Family Restaurant & Ice Cream Parlor** (1060 West Katella Avenue, Anaheim; 714-635-1801) is a winner with kids from the moment they walk in the door and spot the stuffed animals and candy counter. Motherly waitresses make recommendations and help with ordering. The kids' menu includes corn dogs, tacos, hamburgers and hot dogs, but the big hit is the homemade ice cream in flavors like pineapple coconut and chocolate peanut butter. Adults can choose from boneless barbecued chicken, fish and chips, chicken fingers and more. The pseudo stained-glass skylights and etched-glass partitions give the place a vaguely saloon-type atmosphere, but it's a plain old coffee shop that does its job well. Budget to moderate.

**Flaky Jake's** (101 East Katella Avenue, Anaheim; 714-535-1446) is cavernous and informal with ceiling fans and a white gazebo in the center and legions of people lined up to place their orders. Hamburgers and sandwiches come ready to embellish with any of the 20 items from the toppings bar. Other items are ribs, fish and chips, steak and chicken. Pizzas are created to order at the pizza bar, open from 11 a.m. to 2 p.m. Kids love the noisy atmosphere and the mini-arcade in the corner. Budget to moderate.

As buffets go, **Hansa House** (1840 South Harbor Boulevard, Anaheim; 714-750-2411) is unimaginative but reliable. The Swedish-American food is fresh and varied. Captain's chairs are clustered at light hardwood tables, and the walls are papered in a vaguely Scandinavian blue print. Kids are charged according to their age. Breakfast, lunch and dinner are served. Moderate.

---

*Each guest leaves an average of a pound of trash in the park every day. That adds up to about 12 million pounds per year.*

---

The children's menu at **Acapulco Mexican Restaurant** (1410 South Harbor Boulevard, Anaheim; 714-956-7380) provides an impromptu language lesson with sketches of animals that are titled in both English and Spanish; coloring it in will keep them busy. The restaurant loves kids and even has a helium tank to fill balloons for little diners. Kids can have tacos, burritos, taquitos and enchiladas as well as grilled cheese and corn dogs. A favorite with adults is the Fiesta Platter, an assortment of hors d'oeuvres. Budget to moderate.

It's impossible to miss the **Spaghetti Station Restaurant** (999 West Ball Road, Anaheim; 714-956-3250), a funky building surrounded with wagon wheels and antique mining paraphernalia. Inside, the arcade games and Western mini-museum keep you entertained while you wait. Adult fare includes the Bow & Arrow (minestrone and salad) and Bounty Hunter (turkey breast and Swiss cheese). The kids can fuel up with Billy the Kid (spaghetti with meat sauce), Sugarfoot Sal (spaghetti with tomato sauce), Pony Pizza (pepperoni pizza) and Little Bighorn ravioli. Budget to moderate.

Painted bright pink, **Belisle's Restaurant** (12001 Harbor Boulevard, Garden Grove; 714-750-6560) is just a mile south of Disneyland and hard to miss. Once inside this converted house you'll find truck drivers, radically coifed coeds and neat-as-a-pin Orange County families all shoveling away good old-fashioned country-style chow. There's a two-pound steak, "poke" chops, catfish 'n' hushpuppies and baked meat loaf for grown-ups. Spaghetti, fish and chips, hamburgers, chicken fingers and barbecue jumbo ribs are featured on the children's menu. Belisle's is open late (midnight on weekdays; until two on weekends), and most everything on its voluminous menu is moderate to deluxe.

## Disneyland Shopping

Inside Disneyland, Main Street is the prime shopping area. Because it's open earlier and later than the park itself, you have good opportunities to shop when there's nothing else to do. This is also where rental lockers are located, so you can stash your purchases instantly if you don't want to send them to package pickup to collect later.

Guests of either the Disneyland Hotel or the Disneyland Pacific Hotel can have packages send directly to their rooms.

Watches and clocks featuring Mickey Mouse and other Disney characters can be found at **New Century Timepieces**, along with traditional watches. Glass-domed anniversary clocks and wall cuckoos are among the myriad ways to determine the time of day in this interesting shop. Hobbyists can browse for hours through the collection of baseball cards and sports memorabilia at **Great American Pastimes**. The **Market House** is an old-fashioned general store with candies and natural-food snacks, coffee and cider. You're even welcome to sit down to a game of checkers. Expertly crafted glassware and crystal at **Crystal Arts** can be engraved and monogrammed to take home as personalized gifts. Chances are those mouse ears you see on kids all over the park have come from the **Mad Hatter Shop**. It also has Easter bonnets, Tyrolean headgear and Donald Duck hats. Names are embroidered free.

In Adventureland there are shops to remind guests of this area's harrowing adventures, plus camouflage clothing and Indiana Jones hats. At the **Indiana Jones Adventure Outpost**, there's the full range of logo items T-shirts, sweatshirts, mugs and even licorice strips. **South Seas Traders** sells shell jewelry and Polynesian beachwear and swimwear, and you'll find shells, snakes and shrunken skulls at **Tropical Imports.**

One of the favorite shopping areas is in New Orleans Square where unique cooking and serving accessories, gadgets and recipe books tempt the connoisseur at **Le Gourmet**. In the spirit of Mardi Gras, **Mascarades d'Orleans** carries a glittering selection of masks, costumes and accessories. Collectors of Christmas ornaments should not miss **Le Christmas**, where Yuletide decorations and gifts featuring Disney characters are available year-round. You won't want to use it for a rainstorm, but at the **Parasol Cart** you can have your hand-painted parasol personalized. If you decide to have your portrait done at **Portrait Artists**, watch for a few minutes to decide which artist to choose. Although each has an interesting personal style, you may find one artist's technique more appealing than another's.

Shopping's somewhat limited in Critter Country, but if you liked Splash Mountain you might want to stop at **Critter Country Plush**, the ride's official souvenir headquarters. At **Pooh Corner** all the clothing, toys, jewelry and books feature Winnie the Pooh and his friends.

Where else would you expect to find a coonskin cap but in Frontierland? They and other Western-themed items are available at **Western Ho Trading Company**. Browse through the interesting Western and Indian-themed gifts, including well-done turquoise and silver jewelry, at the **Spirit of Pocahontas Shop**. The wonderful, earthy smell of leather at **Bonanza Outfitters** may draw you inside, but once there you'll be fascinated by items like fringed leather vests for one-year olds and tiny moccasins for babies.

Fantasyland is where adults say they most frequently succumb to their tykes' pleas for souvenirs. A quick glance at too-cute-for-words shops like **Tinker Bell Toy Shoppe**, **Small World Gifts** and **Stromboli's Wagon** confirms why. Cuddly plush dolls, toys and Disney characters beg to be picked up and held.

Shopping takes a back seat to the rides in Tomorrowland, although the sports-oriented **Premier Shop** offers some possibilities; it's stocked with apparel, golf balls, collectible pins, cards, plaques and autographed balls. If you missed the mouse ears earlier, there's a second chance here at **The Hatmosphere**.

## Disneyland Nightlife

In the Disneyland Hotel, **Neon Cactus Bar and Grill** (1150 West Cerritos Avenue; 714-778-6600), is a fun nightspot with live rock-and-roll bands Friday through Sunday nights, DJ dancing Monday and Tuesday, and karaoke on Wednesday.

Be sure to check the Disneyland schedule for evening events inside the park. See "Nightlife" in Knott's Berry Farm (Chapter Three) for information on the best nighttime shows for kids Medieval Times and Wild Bill's.

# THREE

# Knott's Berry Farm

Culture isn't something you'd expect to find at a family theme park.
But at Knott's Berry Farm the heritage of the West and genuine learning experiences are combined in 165 rip-roarin' rides, attractions
and live shows. Lest you think that culture and thrills can't happily
coexist, Knott's has some of the acknowledged biggies in the spine-
tingling department. The Boomerang turns your world upside down
not once, but twice, in two 360-degree loops. The Parachute Sky
Jump falls a stomach-grabbing 20 stories. Montezooma's Revenge
accelerates you and your adrenaline to 55 mph in a matter of seconds. HammerHead turns you upside down six times in less than
**one** minute.

When Disneyland opened there were concerns that Knott's Berry
Farm would die on the vine. But it was those fears instead that with-
ered. Even on Disneyland's opening day in 1955, Knott's parking
lots were full of cars. And as it turned out, 1955 was a banner year
for the Berry Farm. Over the years the two have developed a sort
of symbiotic relationship that capitalizes on their differences, and
today Knott's is California's second-largest amusement park.

The Farm, as it is affectionately known in the area, differs from
Disneyland in that it's more of a reality park than a fantasy land.
Things move at a gentler pace, minus the frenetics of scenes like Six
Flags California. There is a real paleontologist at the exit to the Kingdom of the Dinosaurs ride and an actual park ranger/naturalist in
the Wild Water Wilderness Nature Station. You'll find genuine history here, which has a great deal of appeal to grandparents bringing
the newest generation to see how things were in "the olden days."
Fittingly, most attractions are easily accessible to toddlers as well as
senior citizens.

*The 2075-pound Liberty Bell at Independence Hall weighs just five pounds less than the original.*

You may be asking yourself, why in the world is it called Knott's Berry Farm? It all began in 1920 when Walter Knott, his wife Cordelia and their three small children moved to Buena Park. There, Knott soon established himself as a supplier of luscious cherry rhubarb and a superb new strain of berry—the boysenberry—developed by an Anaheim neighbor and grown and marketed for the first time by Knott.

His wife, no slouch herself as an entrepreneur, saw an opportunity to supplement the family income during the Depression by serving chicken dinners on their wedding china. In not too many years, people were flocking to Cordelia's Chicken Dinner Restaurant, often waiting hours in line for her scrumptious meals. By 1940, when the restaurant was serving as many as 4000 Sunday dinners, it was Walter's turn to really crow. As a diversion for the waiting patrons, he began building Ghost Town, and the nation's most popular independently owned family theme park was hatched. Now, doesn't Knott's Berry Farm sound a whole lot better than Knott's Waiting Area for a Delicious Chicken Dinner?

In 1969 Knott opened Fiesta Village, a tribute to California's early Spanish Heritage. The five-acre Boardwalk, the third themed area, opened in 1975 as the Roaring 20's and today pays tribute to Southern California's seaside culture. Camp Snoopy joined the park in 1983, with six acres themed to the California High Sierra. It's the official home of the famous Charles Schulz beagle, Snoopy, plus his pals Linus, Lucy and Charlie Brown.

Dolphin and sea-lion shows were added when Knott's opened its Pacific Pavilion in 1986. In 1988 the fifth themed area was opened —Wild Water Wilderness—a four-acre, river-wilderness area featuring Bigfoot Rapids, a raft ride down a raging, white-water river. The most recent addition here is Mystery Lodge, an exploration of the traditions of the American Indians who lived on the Pacific Northwest coast.

Indian Trails celebrates the arts, cultures and traditions, old and new, of the people who first populated this continent. It's a one-on-one participatory adventure that gives all ages an opportunity to explore the heritage of American Indians.

---

*In 1940 the Old Trails Hotel in Ghost Town was relocated, board by board, from Prescott, Arizona.*

---

The Farm was purchased in 1996 by the Cedar Fair family, who operates four other amusement parks nationwide. Although owned by a corporation, Knott's does an excellent job of maintaining a down-home feel. Knott's Berry Farm is an amusement site that welcomes more than five million guests each year. Attractions appeal to those of all ages and succeed not only because they amuse but also because they provide a sense of nostalgia and history.

## ARRIVAL

At least a dozen hotels are within a ten-minute walk of the park's entrance. If you're visiting Disneyland and are staying in Anaheim, some hotels offer shuttle service to Knott's for a fee.

By car, exit Route 5 at Beach Boulevard and proceed south. Beach Boulevard literally runs into the park. Freeway signs direct you to the farm, and there are signs along the boulevard as well, so it's hard to get lost. Independence Hall is on your left as you approach Knott's. Stay to the right and you'll be directed to one of seven lots where you can park all day for a fee. Trams will take you to the entrance. If you're pointed toward a lot on the east side of Beach Boulevard, a tunnel takes you safely under the busy thoroughfare. You'll also use this tunnel to get from the park proper to Independence Hall, which is outside Knott's.

## TICKET OPTIONS

Two ticket options are available: a day pass and an annual pass.

|  | Adults | Children 3–11 |
| --- | --- | --- |
| *One-day Ticket* | $35.00 | $25.00 |
| *Annual Pass* | $99.95 | $69.95 |
| *Children under 3 are free* | | |

## SIGHTSEEING STRATEGIES

The 150-acre park can easily be visited in a day even when crowds are at their peak. You might want to arrive before it opens, buy tickets and roughly plot your day with the map you're given. Mrs. Knott's Chicken Dinner Restaurant on Grand Avenue serves good, inex-

# KNOTT'S BERRY FARM

THE BOARDWALK

WILD WATER WILDERNESS

GHOST TOWN

INDIAN TRAILS

FIESTA VILLAGE

CALIFORNIA MARKETPLACE

CAMP SNOOPY

↑
ENTRANCE

**GHOST TOWN**
Butterfield Stagecoach
Calico Mine Train
Denver & Rio Grande Railroad
Haunted Shack
Timber Mountain Log Ride
Wild West Stunt Show

**FIESTA VILLAGE**
Dragon Swing
Grand Slammer
Jaguar
Merry-Go-Round
Mexican Hat Dance
Montezooma's Revenge
Sling Shot
Tampico Tumbler

**THE BOARDWALK**
Boomerang
HammerHead
HeadAche
HeadSpin
Kingdom of the Dinosaurs
Nu-Wave Theater
Pacific Pavilion
Parachute Sky Jump
Supreme Scream
Windjammer
XK-1

**WILD WATER WILDERNESS**
Bigfoot Rapids
Mystery Lodge

**CAMP SNOOPY**
Beagle Ballroom
Beary Tales Playhouse
Camp Bus
Camp Snoopy Theatre
Edison's Inventor's Workshop
Ferris Wheel
Flying Ace Balloon Race
Grand Sierra Scenic Railroad
Huff and Puff
Log Pealer
Petting Zoo
Red Baron
Rocky Road Trucking Company
Snoopy's Bounce
Timberline Twister

**INDIAN TRAILS**
Children's Camp

pensive breakfasts. From there you're within three minutes of the gate, poised for opening time.

On a cloudy Tuesday in February, five minutes is the longest you'll wait for a ride, but on a summer weekend day you'll have to plan tactics carefully to avoid mammoth lines. If you're a teenager or un-encumbered adult, the best time-saving idea on entering the park is to make a sharp right through Camp Snoopy and hop aboard Mon-tezooma's Revenge, which is at the edge of Fiesta Village. From there, head through the Village across the train tracks to The Boardwalk and jump on the Boomerang. If you can do both of these rides be-fore 10 a.m. you have a leg up on the day's schedule. Then, proceed to some of the other high-energy rides like Sling Shot and Tampico Tumbler, which will be less crowded.

Toddlers and tykes under six will want to spend most of their time in Camp Snoopy, which was designed especially for them. That, and the merry-go-round in Fiesta Village right next door, can com-prise a full day for little ones. A sit-down indoor show in the after-noon can provide an opportunity for a nap.

The themed sections of the park flow naturally into one another. After hitting the highlights, you should see one area completely be-fore moving to another to avoid backtracking. Parents with kids of different ages will want to split up. A 12-year-old will not be content with time spent in Camp Snoopy, and a four-year-old won't make the height restriction on many thrill rides.

The park is well supplied with shady, comfortable places to sit. Take advantage of them. You'll be able to see everything even with a number of reconnoitering breaks, and you won't feel frazzled at

---

## INDEPENDENCE HALL

*One of the most visible of Knott's attractions is* **Independence Hall**, *located across Beach Boulevard outside the main park. The brick-by-brick replica of Philadelphia's historic hall is so exact you can see fingerprints in the bricks just like in the original. When the real Independence Hall was to be restored for the nation's bicentennial in 1976, the original blueprints were nowhere to be found, so the reconstruction committee contacted Knott's for the blueprints it had drawn. Memorabilia in the hall includes photos and signatures of the signers of the Declaration of Independence, costumed mannequins of the era, even a harpsichord that was the entertainment center of its day.*

---

*The Bottle House is made of 3082 wine and whiskey bottles, all facing inward so they won't whistle when the wind blows.*

---

day's end. The park has 60 food facilities, three full service and the rest buffet, sandwich or fast food. You're welcome, of course, to bring your own lunch. But if you decide to eat in the park on a busy day, try to time it before 11:30 a.m. and after 2 p.m. to avoid long waits. Most weekdays won't be a problem, although you might find yourself checking out several facilities to determine where lines are the shortest.

## NUTS & BOLTS

**General Information:** Guest Relations, Knott's Berry Farm, 8039 Beach Boulevard, Buena Park, CA 90620; 714-220-5200.

**Stroller, Wheelchair and Other Rentals:** These as well as power chairs are available just inside the main entrance on the right.

**Cameras:** Snoopy's Boutique sells disposable cameras.

**Baby Services:** Baby stations with diaper-changing tables and feeding and nursing facilities are next to the schoolhouse in the Wild Water Wilderness area, in Camp Snoopy near the suspension bridge and outside the park next to the first-aid station.

**Lockers:** Lockers are at the main gate on the left, in Wild Water Wilderness next to the baby station and just inside the Ghost Town main gate on the left.

**Pets:** Except seeing-eye dogs, pets are not allowed inside the park.

**Lost Children and Lost & Found:** Both facilities are located outside the main gate at the Information Center.

**First Aid:** A station is located behind the Chicken Dinner Restaurant.

**Banking:** An ATM that honors almost all bank cards is at the left of the main gate.

## GETTING AROUND

Knott's Berry Farm is roughly a square, with the entrance and California MarketPlace at lower left. Ghost Town covers the largest area, but Camp Snoopy has the most attractions packed into its six acres. It's a toss-up as to whether to proceed straight ahead into Ghost Town or to make a sharp right into Camp Snoopy. The kids in your party probably will make the decision for you. The highest-energy areas and the ones that pulse with action at night are Fiesta Village

---

*Knott's narrow-gauge steam train hauls more passengers than any steam train in the United States.*

---

where Montezooma's Revenge lives, and The Boardwalk, home to HammerHead and Boomerang. We've arranged our tour in a roughly clockwise fashion, beginning at Ghost Town and ending at Indian Trails. A good meeting place in case your group gets separated is in front of the church beside the lake in Ghost Town. It's the only church in the park, and the shady area in front is a good place to wait.

## Ghost Town

If Ghost Town looks old, that's because it truly is. But this rickety reincarnation of a piece of the Wild West is still very much alive. Walter Knott was fascinated by tales of the West, having grown up with stories of his mother's trek to California in a covered wagon. It was these tales that inspired him to create Ghost Town.

More than just a designer's imagination of how the West might have appeared, Ghost Town consists of historic structures that were relocated to Knott's Berry Farm. The Haunted Shack originally stood in Esmeralda, Nevada, and was reconstructed nail-for-nail. The Old Trails Hotel, now next to Ghost Town's general store, began its life in 1868 as a hostelry in Arizona. America's last operating narrow-gauge railroad, the Denver & Rio Grande, was bought in 1952 by Walter Knott who moved its engines, passenger cars and even rails to his farm. Adhering to authenticity, he brought in other deserted buildings including a Kansas schoolhouse and a jail. The result is a fascinating, realistic 1880s California mining community.

Ghost Town's population consists of townspeople in period costume who are eager to chat about their lives and professions. At the Geode Shop the lapidist will help you select a promising "coconut"—a round, rough, seemingly uninteresting rock that reveals a swirl of colorful agate or a center of sparkling crystal when cut with his diamond-bladed saw. He'll explain how these 65 million-year-old rocks were formed and sometimes turned up by miners who crowded into California during the Gold Rush. Don't miss the dinosaur egg inside the shop.

You can watch high-kicking can-can girls at the Calico Saloon, pan for gold, or watch Dr. I. Will Skinem set up his Medicine Show and banter with a sheriff trying to run him and his questionable cures out of town. Spinners, weavers and prospectors will spin yarns for anyone who cares to listen. And watch out for the gunfights that break out at any time along village streets.

**Butterfield Stagecoach** ★★★ For a genuinely historic circuit of Camp Snoopy and Fiesta Village, climb aboard this 100-year-old stagecoach. It's so far off the ground (to allow for the rocks and ruts of old-time roads) that you have to climb a set of stairs to reach boarding level. The friendly driver will give you a hand. He'll let you ride shotgun next to him for an up-top view of the park, or you can settle into seats inside as the gentry did in 1890. The stagecoach has been refurbished with 20th-century springs and brakes and is drawn by a team of four spirited horses.

*TIPS:* Those with tired feet will appreciate this gentle ride.

**Timber Mountain Log Ride** ★★★★★ This is the oldest log flume ride in the United States and one of the most popular attractions in the park. This five-minute float in what appears to be a hollowed-out log begins with an uphill climb, then takes you through the inner workings of a sawmill. While transiting the mountain's misty innards, you pass animated scenes of loggers at a crosscut saw and giant timbers being craned and stacked. It ends with a lickety-split plunge down a 70-foot waterfall, guaranteed to douse everyone in the front seat. Exiting the ride you'll see yourself freeze-framed on a television screen in a photo taken as you nosedived over the falls. The photo, of course, is for sale.

*TIPS:* Waits can be up to two hour; plan on doing this one early.

**Calico Mine Train** ★★★★★ You board scaled-down versions of open-ore cars and within seconds are plunged into humid darkness that even smells like you're underground. Blasting noises and the rattle of the train compete with the engineer's running banter as you

---

*PEEK-IN*

*Knott's is crammed with nooks, crannies and unexpected surprises like the "peek-ins" in Ghost Town. You can look through windows of rickety buildings for glimpses of an 1800s assay office where gold is being weighed, and a Chinese laundry where hand washing preceded Maytag by half a century. In the town's telegraph office a dutiful fellow taps out hot bulletins in Morse code.*

tour a working coal mine. The beam of the engine light illuminates narrow tunnel walls that widen to reveal animated miners working a glory hole. Dim lights flicker from their hats, casting eerie shadows of swinging ore buckets on the two-story cavern walls. Farther along, stalactites and stalagmites, underground waterfalls and a damp chill (real or imagined?) add to the realism. As you emerge into daylight across a shaky trestle, there's a good view of Ghost Town. Don't look for physical thrills; the fascination here is the feeling of authenticity and the historical sense of the West.

*Tips:* Because the entire ride is in darkness, it may be a bit unnerving to the very young and claustrophobic.

***Wild West Stunt Show*** ★★★★ Not as slick and polished as the show at Universal Studios, this presentation provides good entertainment nevertheless. The old-fort setting is suitably realistic. The plot is this: The cowboy stuntman's partner doesn't show up, so he recruits a reluctant "replacement" from the audience, a tourist on his honeymoon. But when the macho stuntman sent from central casting finally makes an appearance, the sparks fly. Fistfights, a high fall and lots of shooting keep the action moving as the hesitant volunteer is picked on from all sides.

*Tips:* Arrive at the Wagon Camp early enough and you can garner sheltered seats in the covered wagons that form the 1000-seat theater's periphery. In general, try for seats higher up, as those in the front have limited visibility.

***Denver & Rio Grande Railroad*** ★★★ The train is real, and so are the ear-shattering whistle, clanging bell and billows of steam that hiss from its spiffy engine. At trackside, a fatherly conductor ushers you on old Number 40, then yells out the required "All Aboard!" On this narrow-gauge choo-choo, cars are regulation-size with two-and-two seating. About the time you get settled, your journey is interrupted by a pair of marauding outlaws who seem as intent on cracking corny jokes as on holding up the train. (To a youngster with closely cropped hair: "We'll leave you alone, fellah. Looks like you've already been clipped.") The authentic 1880s steam train, complete with cow-catcher and brass trim, does an eight-minute circuit of Ghost Town and The Boardwalk.

*Tips:* Here is another chance to get off your feet for a while. Once you board you can make the circuit as many times as you like.

***Haunted Shack*** ★★★ As you walk through this house of optical illusions you'll find that water runs uphill and billiard balls end up in the same pocket no matter where you aim them. People appear to change heights, and a faucet produces water from thin air. When a guest is asked to sit in a straight-backed chair, then encouraged to get up, she finds the task almost impossible. Although the chair seems level, in reality it leans backward almost 45 degrees. A sign outside the shack warns visitors not to venture in unless they "can walk on sloping surfaces and are free from vertigo."

*TIPS:* Teens may consider this low-tech attraction hokey, but smaller kids and adults who appreciate the ingenuity of illusion will be fascinated.

## Wild Water Wilderness

At just over three acres, this is the smallest of Knott's themed areas, but it does an excellent job of re-creating a California river wilderness park of the early 1900s. The indigenous trees range from California black oak to coast redwood to Torrey pine and are part of a landscape that includes such enchanting wildflowers as California poppy, bluebell, daffodil, larkspur, lily and horsetail. Point Reyes manzanita and star jasmine also grow along the tidy paths. The deciduous trees that change color add a seasonal feeling to the surroundings, and there is an aviary that is home to native dove, quail and ring-neck pheasant. Once you've experienced Bigfoot Rapids and explored the Wilderness Nature Center, however, there's not much else to see.

**Mystery Lodge** ★★★★ In this age of stomach-churning roller coasters and thrill rides, Knott's has come up with a winner in this

---

### WILDERNESS NATURE CENTER

*Located in Wild Water Wilderness, this is the place to ask the park ranger about Sasquatch, that elusive creature called Bigfoot. He'll show you evidence, in photos and footprints, that such a beast does exist, and you'll hear marvelous tales. The rangers are retired schoolteachers, naturalists and others with a knowledge of the outdoors and an interest in helping kids learn. The **Nature Center** has hands-on displays of indigenous and exotic insects and native plants plus a glassed-in apiary that puts you as close as you'll ever want to get to a working beehive. You can view a honeycomb and watch the industrious insects enter and exit through their own chimney.*

*Bigfoot Rapids features California's longest manmade white-water river.*

captivating Native North American storytelling presentation. Special effects are employed, not to scare you out of your wits but to suggest the power of imagination, magic and wisdom. The experience begins as guests cross a wooden bridge and pass through a hand-carved ceremonial archway alongside Thunder Falls. Entering a "cave," visitors face a full-size replica of a traditional tribal house front. Sounds of birds and other creatures and water lapping at the lakeshore can be heard; then a flash of lightning and a clap of thunder signal an approaching storm. Unfortunately, the mood is broken when the house front opens and you enter the lodge, actually a small modern auditorium, where you'll watch the rest of the presentation. On stage, where the lodge interior has been re-created, a fire glows and the Old Storyteller enters to weave his tale. Images of Raven and other Native totems emerge from the smoke of the fire, dissolving into other forms or dissipating into the air. The effect is gentle and altogether captivating. When it's all over, we are left to believe, as the Old Storyteller has told us, that "if we share the wisdom of elders with the heart of a child, life will be full of wonder and magic."

*TIPS:* A couple of the effects used to create thunder and lightning may startle small children or infants. Out of respect for the Native traditions, photography and videotaping are not permitted in the Mystery Lodge.

**Bigfoot Rapids** ★★★★★ The sign says, "You WILL get wet, you MAY get drenched." Before this white-water rafting ride opened, an Olympic kayaker ran the rapids and rated them very challenging. You, of course, do it a bit differently, strapping yourself into a huge, innertube-like craft with as many as five others for a wild, wet jaunt over a series of churning rapids. A two-story waterfall drops from towering cliffs. If you've ever been white-water rafting, you'll find the boulders and chutes extremely authentic. Just before returning to civilization, you pass through a misty tunnel that echoes with the roar of the ominous creature for which the ride is named. None of this is really scary, though, unless you have a fear of damp trousers and soggy shoes. Great fun for all ages.

*TIPS:* To prevent your shoes from getting soaked, brace your feet high up on the center post when a wave hits. Bigfoot Rapids develops long lines during peak periods. Try to do it early or late in the day. There's a 36-inch height restriction.

# The Boardwalk

The area that was known as Roaring 20's was revitalized in 1996 and reborn as The Boardwalk, a colorfully themed area designed to celebrate the vigor and vitality of Southern California's fabled beach culture. Besides the thrill ride HammerHead, many of the park's old favorites are still here—Boomerang, Parachute Sky Jump, Good Time Theater, Kingdom of the Dinosaurs and Pacific Pavilion. HeadAche and HeadSpin are revamped versions of former rides. The Nu-Wave Theater is home to a multimedia attraction, Cyber Sports in 3-D, in which a three-dimensional sports motion picture is blended with live lasers and 32-channel stereo sound. AirHeadz is an interactive music, food and high-tech arcade center.

**Kingdom of the Dinosaurs** ★★★★★ It's the 1920s and Professor Wells is at work in his lab, developing a time machine. His blackboard is scribbled with equations, and bubbling beakers contain his secret formulas. As you glide along a track in a two-person car, the crackle of electrical charges and the sudden shriek of an emergency signal assault your ears. The professor booms frantically, "Something's gone wrong with the time machine!" As he counts off the epochs and eons, you realize you're being drawn further and further into the prehistoric past. On your left the huge jaws of a *Tyrannosaurus rex* seem ready to snap you in two. To the right a prehistoric wolf battles with the ancestor of an elk. Pterodactyls hover overhead, and a long-necked creature eyes you ominously. Ice Age humans huddle in ragged furs. For four minutes a score of gigantic, fully animated robotic figures from 200 million years ago emerge from their twilight world. Just as you think you'll never escape, the professor announces that he has his machine under control and you're on your way home to the 20th century.

---

## DISCOVERY CENTER

*If you saw something in the Kingdom of the Dinosaurs you didn't recognize, this fascinating, laboratory-like center is the place to ask about it. The resident paleontologist uses a layered chart to explain stages in the earth's development, pointing out when the creatures you've just seen were at their scary best. Displays include petrified wood, touchable fossils and teeth from prehistoric beasts.*

*Tips:* Even though teenagers find it a bit tame, this is one of the most popular attractions in the park. Long lines move quickly, and the wait is usually not more than ten minutes even at peak periods.

**Pacific Pavilion** ★★★ In this marine-mammal show, Atlantic bottle-nose dolphins and sea lions perform in "Dances With Dolphins." The 1200-seat outdoor arena lets you get close enough to feel an occasional splash. At the morning show, handlers demonstrate training techniques that are used to coax the mammals to their performance levels. During the afternoon shows, trainers perform in the water alongside their charges. It's not on a scale with Sea World but is quite entertaining.

**HeadAche** ★ This is a genuine version of the old tilt-a-whirl that those over 40 might remember from 1950s traveling carnivals. While not a thrill a minute, it won't put you to sleep, either.

*Tips:* There is a 42-inch height restriction.

**HeadSpin** ★★ One of the best things about this ride, which is the same thing as a Scrambler, is the beautiful saltwater aquarium at the entrance. It contains tangs in vivid blue and yellow, a clown fish of brilliant orange, even a small eel hiding in the rocks. The darkness surrounding the aquarium is broken by colored strobe lights that illuminate the whirling cars and create a sense of swirling, churning water.

*Tips:* Appeals to teenagers, but adults may find the mashing and slinging more uncomfortable than thrilling. There's a 42-inch height restriction.

**HammerHead** ★★★★ If a head-over-heels 360-degree vertical spin that lifts you 82 feet in the air sounds exciting, then get in line. Just to add to the fun, the 42-passenger gondola rotates independently, so you can find yourself hanging upside down, nearly ten stories above the ground. The ride lasts just over two minutes, but it makes six full 360-degree orbits and gives you a little surprise at the end.

*Tips:* The height requirement is 42 inches. Although shoulder-length restraints keep you from falling out, you will definitely lose glasses, hats or anything else not secured in a pocket.

**Boomerang** ★★★★★ This is the ride you've heard about. As you wait in line, its freight-train sound alone can start the adrenaline rushing. When you step into the four-person car and settle under the padded, horseshoe-shaped restraint, you know you're in for a ride to remember (or one you'll never forget). With a lurch, the chain of cars begins to inch to the top of a tower that seems to go

---

*Sky Tower and the Parachute Sky Jump are patterned after one of Coney Island's most renowned attractions.*

---

nowhere except into space. For a second the car pauses at the top, and then the shrieking begins. You're launched on a terrifying drop from an 11-story height through three loops that not only flip you upside down but twist at the same time. The cars slow as momentum carries you up a second tower. Is the ride over? Not a chance. Boomerang does it to you again, somersaulting you backwards through the same three loops before jolting to a halt at the exit. This unusual, European-designed roller coaster, which lasts just 33 seconds, gives terror a new twist.

*TIPS:* There's a 52-inch height restriction. A park favorite of teens and older kids; ride it early on busy days or expect to wait up to an hour during mid-day.

**Parachute Sky Jump** **★★★★** From the point of view of a spectator on the ground, this could be one of the prettiest rides in the park. Narrow cages drop to earth under multicolor parachutes. Two adults stand side by side inside the chest-high cages as the earth drops away and you begin a slow ascent. For a moment the cage hovers motionless at the top of the tower before plummeting 235 feet to terra firma. There's a momentary feeling of weightlessness, but the ride looks more intimidating than it is because it ends before you've had time for any major stomach flip-flops. If all this seems a bit too exciting, you can get the same view from inside the *Sky Cabin*, an enclosed compartment that rises and rotates slowly around the Sky Tower's colorful center pillar.

*TIPS:* Take your camera along. There are no sudden jerks or wrenches in the Sky Cabin, and you'll be able to get great shots of the park. There is a 36-inch height restriction.

**Nu-Wave Theater** **★★★★★** Don't miss Sea Dream, an underwater-fantasy 3-D movie! It puts a fluttering stingray right in your lap, practically clobbers you with the bowsprit of a three-masted schooner and sends schools of fish scurrying between the heads of the people in front of you. Dramatically beautiful footage shows an octopus capturing its favorite dinner, an unwary crab. Reef sharks, dolphins and whales seem close enough to touch. Watch the entire audience duck the frisbee in the film's opening minutes. The 400-seat theater is all on one level, so you may have to jockey for a clear view of the screen.

*Tips:* The 15-minute film runs hourly. Check your schedule, and be on time: doors close during show time. A perfect place to rest.

**Windjammer** ★★★★ Knott's Berry Farm's latest coaster, the Windjammer, falls between Boomerang and Jaguar in the thrills department; slower than Boomerang, but a good clip faster than the family pace of Jaguar. The minute-and-a-half ride starts off with a quick loop, followed by climbs and plummets and a tight spiral where, if you're lucky (the effect doesn't always work), you may feel the winds of a Pacific storm (created by the folks responsible for the effects in the film *Twister*). An extra-added attraction here is the dual track, which allows two cars to race along side by side; ride creators say you can actually help determine the "winner" of the race by leaning into the turns, and weighting your cars with heavy people (the more you weigh, the faster you'll go).

The entire Windjammer area has a Southern California beach theme. Visitors waiting for riders can drive toy tugboats in the Windjammer Lagoon, or grab an appropriate snack such as a funnel cake at the lifeguard tower's "Surf Side" snack shop. Though the ride makes much of its dual-track format, Windjammer may be disappointing to those who love the extreme thrills of Boomerang, which, with a top speed of 55 miles per hour, goes 15-miles-per-hour faster than Windjammer. As a friend's daughter said, "I'd stand in line much longer to ride the Boomerang than the Windjammer."

*Tips:* One benefit of the dual track format is the capacity; the ride can handle twice as many people in an hour as can Boomerang. So don't be intimidated if the line looks long; it moves quickly.

**XK-1** ★★★★ This futuristic ride creates the sensation of flight as you pilot a craft seven stories above the earth. Two-person cars rotate on arms as they spin from a center post, allowing you to whirl semiplacidly, or climb, dive and perform barrel rolls while being catapulted through space at what seems like warp speed.

---

## INCREDIBLE WATERWORKS SHOW

*Between Fiesta Village and Ghost Town, the park's Reflection Lake is the site of the **Incredible Waterworks Show**. The sound, light and water extravaganza is similar to the "Dancing Waters" show so popular at state fairs and on the Ed Sullivan Show during the 1960s. Hundreds of streams of water, each choreographed to music, soar nearly 100 feet in the air. During the day the show loses much of its impact, but at night it's pleasantly entertaining.*

*Tips:* Unlike most thrill rides on which an out-of-control feeling is part of the excitement, XK-1 lets you control your craft's revolutions. There's a height restriction of 52 inches.

**Supreme Scream**    The ride may be over in just three short seconds, but it'll be worth the wait. At 312 feet, Supreme Scream is the world's tallest ride, and perhaps even the scariest. Facing skyward, feet dangling in mid-air, riders are propelled upward 30 stories. A momentary pause precedes the heart-stopping downward plunge, which reaches speeds of more than 50 miles per hour. The ride is scheduled to open in July 1998.

*Tips:* This ride is NOT for small children or for anyone who is afraid of heights.

## Fiesta Village

Located across the railroad tracks near XK-1, Fiesta Village has high, tiled arches and wisteria-trellised walkways that create a realistic south-of-the-border atmosphere. In this colorful, exuberant section of the park, strolling mariachis and terra cotta fountains pay tribute to California's early Spanish heritage. If you time it right, you can order a giant tostada from Herdez Cantina, then settle in to watch a Mexican band perform at Fiesta Plaza. Good Mexican food is available at a number of restaurants. There's a fast-paced feeling here, created by a collection of thrill rides. Fiesta Village is home to one of the park's premier attractions, Montezooma's Revenge, which has been terrifying riders since 1978.

**Montezooma's Revenge** ★★★★★ If you liked Boomerang, you'll love this gut-wrenching experience. Montezooma does it to you with a vengeance. From a standstill in the launching area, a giant flywheel catapults the cars to 55 miles per hour in just over three seconds. (The flywheel technology used in this ride is the same as that used to launch planes from aircraft carriers.) The gigantic thriller loops you upside-down, comes to a complete halt, then loops you around again, backwards. At mach speed you race to a second tower, hang at its top at a 90-degree angle, then speed back to the launching area.

*Tips:* Do not ride immediately after lunch; in fact, do it early in the day to avoid long lines. There is a 48-inch height restriction.

**Jaguar** ★★★★ "Awesome!" That's the assessment offered by a good many of the riders this attraction was designed for—youngsters and

*Singers, dancers and drummers in traditional costume present American Indian music and dance in Festival Plaza.*

their parents. Rising no more than 60 feet above the ground, this family roller coaster "streaks" out of the Temple of Jaguar Plaza and loops around on 2700 feet of track. The best thing about this ride is that the younger members of your family get to ride on a roller coaster—just like the big kids. Only this one doesn't turn upside down in gravity-defying feats that leave your stomach in the air. Twenty-four passenger cars leave plenty of room for the entire family to ride together.

*Tips:* Children must be 42 inches high to ride Jaguar. The wait to ride can extend up to an hour or more during peak times.

**Merry-Go-Round** ★★★ No one's quite sure what it's doing in Fiesta Village, but this beautifully restored 1896 Dentzel seems appropriately sited here on the banks of Reflection Lake. This carousel is one of the few remaining examples of its type in the country, unique because many of the animals aren't horses. Whimsical ostriches, rabbits, zebras, chickens and lions are typical of Dentzel's designs for his grand carousels.

*Tips:* One of the few rides that is appreciated by all ages.

**Dragon Swing** ★★ This ride is basically a large swing that accelerates sideways to ever-widening arcs until finally you're at right angles to the earth. One adult rider remarked as he disembarked that it made him seasick.

*Tips:* Missable, so visit when you run into long lines elsewhere. There's a 42-inch height restriction.

**Sling Shot** ★★★★ Sling-swings are suspended by a pair of chains from a revolving canopy as centrifugal force flings you out at a 45-degree angle. With your body movement you can control the twists and turns while you dangle tenuously above the watching crowd.

*Tips:* Even though you don't reach enormous heights, this is not for those with acrophobia. There's a 42-inch height restriction.

**Mexican Hat Dance** ★★ Basically the same ride as Disneyland's Mad Tea Party except that this one involves fiesta-colored bowls topped with sombreros. As the bowls revolve on platforms, they also spin. A center wheel lets you control how fast you whirl.

*Tips:* This ride can be as popular with teens as with tots. It seems there's a challenge to seeing just how fast they can get the bowls to spin.

*Tampico Tumbler* ★★★★ The thrill here is feeling like you're on a collision course with the car in front of you. Two-person cars extend from arms that rise from a center stem that revolves as the cars themselves rotate. Halfway through it reverses direction. Fiesta colors of bright red and yellow make the ride interesting to watch. There's a 52-inch height restriction.

*Grand Slammer* ★★★★ From the ground this looks like a simple baby ride, but in fact it simulates a six-story free-fall. You sit in seats at the end of an arm that keeps you parallel to the ground. The arm rotates the seats upwards and out so you go from ground level to a height of 60 feet, then drop back to earth. When your stomach is left at the top and you're at the bottom, you become vividly aware of how deceiving this ride can really be.

*Tips:* Another one to avoid immediately after lunch. There's a 42-inch height restriction.

# Camp Snoopy

If the kids in your group are six and under, you'll probably have no choice but to make this the first stop on your circuit of the park. As you pass through the main gate, you can go straight ahead into Ghost Town or veer right to Camp Snoopy. If Snoopy or one of his pals is near the entrance, it's a cinch your youngster will drag you in that direction. This is home to the most famous beagle in the world, plus friends Linus, Lucy and Charlie Brown, who regularly stroll the streets to shake hands and pose for photos. Kids might need an explanation that these characters don't talk, but that they have no problem communicating with gestures and hugs on a nonverbal level. Everything is created just for kids. Much of the adult delight comes from watching a child's discoveries here. Themed to the California High Sierra, Camp Snoopy features six scenic acres with rushing waterfalls, a meandering stream and swaying pontoon and suspension bridges that challenge a child's sure-footedness. Kids can hop on a mini-steamboat for a 15-minute circuit of Reflection Lake, or for a couple of quarters they can pilot their own remote-controlled tugs, dinghies and ocean liners on a quiet bay. The mule-powered merry-go-round offers an opportunity to experience what the pioneers considered fun.

Camp Snoopy is the one area where you must come *under* a maximum rather than *over* a minimum height requirement to go on many of the rides. Some clearly are labeled "not for parents unless accompanied by a child," and others, like the Huff and Puff, exclude adults altogether. It's a totally happy place, always a family favorite. Senior citizens here for the first time often find some of the rides as exciting as their grandchildren do. Even on crowded days there always seems to be a place to sit to tie a shoe or wipe a face. Many restaurants serve child-sized hamburgers and drinks.

The star rating system here is applied mostly from a small child's point of view and reflects the opinion of a number of two-to-six-year-olds.

**Ferris Wheel** ★★★ Little ones report that they like being up high so they can see everything. This wheel is an old-fashioned, scaled-down version of those found at state fairs, and sometimes kids can get a bit impatient with the loading and unloading, but once it's off and spinning they're thrilled.

**Rocky Road Trucking Company** ★★★ For a taste of the trucking life, kids climb aboard shiny, miniature-sized 18-wheelers, honk the blasting air horns and wind through Camp Snoopy. The path even takes you under Montezooma's Revenge in Fiesta Village.

*Tips:* There are no restrictions, other than that children must be able to sit properly.

**Snoopy's Bounce** ★★★ Reaching 38 feet in height, this larger-than-life, inflated Snoopy contains air-filled cushions. The area is constantly in motion as the movement of children shifts air from one chamber to another.

*Tips:* To enter, a child must demonstrate basic motor skills.

**Beagle Ballroom** ★★★ "Go swim, guys," encourages the attendant at this lively attraction. Little kids leave their shoes at the door to paddle in a "pool" of lightweight, four-inch balls. It's divided by netting into areas for crawlers and walkers, and in both the kids can plow through the two-foot-deep balls in their own inimitable style while parents watch from padded sideline seats.

*Tips:* Children as young as 18 months take to this attraction like ducks to water, while four-year-olds may pooh-pooh it as old hat from child-oriented restaurants. Children must be between 42 and 50 inches.

**Log Peeler** ★★★ This is a scaled-down and tamer version of the classic ride, the Scrambler. You spin around while moving both forward and backward.

*Tips:* Because the ride never leaves the ground, it's a good choice for those afraid of heights.

*When park rides are closed, the explanation posted outside reads "We're fixing the framus and painting the podar."*

**Beary Tales Playhouse** ★★★ A multilevel structure that's home to lovable animated characters whom children can discover while exploring at their own pace. Cave-like corridors, corners and flights of stairs promise a surprise at every turn. At Knott's Berry Farm Canning Company, bears put the famous preserves in jars. Next door, bears in the bakery connive to outwit the wiley fox who's after their fresh-baked pies. A favorite area is Weird Woods with its series of distorting mirrors. The Frog and Toddler Path invites tots to crawl into an "animal cage" for a creature's-eye view of spectators outside.

*TIPS:* A baby center and restrooms are right across from the Beary Tales Playhouse.

**Camp Bus** ★★★ Resembling a traditional yellow school bus, the Camp Bus offers a thrilling way to get a bird's-eye view of Camp Snoopy. This popular ride, designed with the whole family in mind, soars 20 feet in the air.

*TIPS:* Because parents may accompany kids, this is a good ride for those too young to ride others, as they can sit on a parent's lap.

**Timberline Twister** ★★★ Kids who yearn for a ride on Boomerang or Montezooma's Revenge but aren't big enough may find this mini-roller coaster an acceptable substitute. It doesn't have the wild and rowdy curves and speed of the big boys, but there's enough excitement to keep youngsters interested.

*TIPS:* Teens and adults without kids can skip this one.

**Huff and Puff** ★ This very basic ride consists of tiny, one-child mine cars that move along a track solely through the efforts of the small fry. Cars meander the brief route through a piney forest as riders push and pull a hand lever. Some children lose interest within the first 30 seconds as they realize they're not seeing anything interesting and they're doing all the work. Parents sometimes exhort from the sidelines to keep their offspring pumping and prevent them from abandoning the mine cars in mid-track.

**Grand Sierra Scenic Railroad** ★★★ When it's time for a mid-Camp Snoopy break, hop on this little steam train for a circuit of Reflection Lake. While you catch a rest, the route holds kids' interest as they wind past shrimp-colored flamingos in Fiesta Village and wait for the Walter K Steamboat to pass so the drawbridge can close.

*The mural in front of the Dinosaur ride is a photo of Los Angeles in 1927.*

A four-year-old reports he likes the train because "it whistles and makes noise."

*TIPS:* For shutterbugs, one of the best views of Montezooma's Revenge is from the train as it circles the lake's far shore near the entrance to Fiesta Village.

**Edison's Inventor's Workshop** ★★   Call this attraction part science museum, part interactive play station. The turn-of-the-century workshop houses nearly a dozen activities, all with gizmos and gadgets on which pint-size tinkerers can experiment with the powers of electricity and magnetism. In the "Light Tower," you use bicycle power to illuminate a tower of light bulbs; the faster you pedal, the more bulbs light up. In "Magnetic Patterns" and "Magnetic Force" you can manipulate magnets to find truth in the phrase "opposites attract." There is also a bunch of authentic Edison artifacts such as an original gramophone, an early experimental light bulb and some of the inventor's handwritten notes, all on loan from Southern California Edison (cosponsor of the attraction) and the Edison Trust. Mr. Edison himself makes periodic appearances, milling about his workshop to answer questions and to tinker alongside visitors.

*TIPS:* A rarely crowded attraction. Check with employees at the entrance about Mr. Edison's appearances; the experience is more fun when he's around.

**Camp Snoopy Theatre** ★★★   This little 150-seat outdoor gathering place is home to two different performing-animal shows. "Smokey's Animal Friends," in the morning, stars Smokey the Bear and is sponsored by the U.S. Forest Service. The show features tame forest animals including a timber wolf, raccoons and an owl. The boa constrictor, draped around its trainer's body, is touted as the perfect pet. "You feed him once a month, he doesn't bark or wet and he'll give you a big hug when you need it," winks the trainer. The afternoon show, "Man's Best Friend and Then Some," revolves around Roxanne the sheltie, who's challenged for the title of Man's Best Friend by Rover the pig. A French lop-ear rabbit named Bunny Foo Foo, Mable the pygmy goat and a tabby named Junior, who strayed onto the Farm and was put to work, round out the stellar cast.

*Tips:* The 20-minute show is so folksy and casual that kids keep leaving their seats to pet the animals.

**Petting Zoo** ★★  Located next door to the Camp Snoopy Theatre, this barnyard-like enclosure houses a variety of docile animals. Even though it's not particularly well-stocked, it can be a source of fascination to small children. There is an Adalbra tortoise, rabbits, goats, sheep and an Asian pot-bellied pig; a boa constrictor under glass and free-running chickens round out the menagerie.

**Red Baron** ★★★  This ride is very popular with little ones because it's exclusively for them. Kids can choose their own plane and become airborne aces while Snoopy (as the Red Baron) pilots his dog house in the middle of it all. Vintage mini-planes "take off" for a flight filled with gentle dips and swoops.

*Tips:* For tykes, this is one of the area's most popular rides, and lines will form on busy days.

**Flying Ace Balloon Race** ★★★  Another kids-only ride, this is also a favorite because independent-minded youngsters select their own balloon, then hop into the gondola without adult supervision. Huge, colorful pseudo-balloons appear to lift the two-child gondolas six feet in the air, then sink and soar for a three-minute ride.

*Tips:* Kids must be at least 3 years old to ride.

# Indian Trails

This two-acre attraction, located between Ghost Town and Reflection Lake, is a tribute to American Indians and provides an opportunity for authentic historical and cultural experiences. The hands-on adventure appeals to all ages as kids and adults explore the heritage of American Indians.

Unusual architectural styles have been authentically re-created. They include Salish and Kwakiutl longhouses, Tsimshian totem and potlatch poles as well as the tepees of the Blackfoot, Nez Perce, Cheyenne, Crow and Kiowa tribes. Representing the Southwest Indians are the hogans of the Navajo and adobe buildings of the Pueblo Indians; there also are Chumash dwellings and Gabrieleño wickiups from California.

Artisans at work here include canoe makers, ceremonial-mask carvers, leatherwork artists, face painters, basket makers, potters, weavers, sand painters and silversmiths. Indian Trails is filled with representatives whose ancestry predates Columbus. Food facilities offer Navajo fry bread, buffalo stew and corn roasted in the husk.

***Children's Camp*** **★★★★** Created especially for youngsters, Children's Camp lets them assist in handcrafting traditional honor bonnets, beadwork and sand paintings. They can listen as storytellers recount living history and have their faces painted in tribal fashion.

## Knott's Berry Farm Area Lodging

Within a mile in any direction from Knott's, hotels and motels in all price ranges line Beach Boulevard, Buena Park's Hotel Row and nearby side streets. Because Knott's is just five miles from Disneyland, many visitors headquarter at a single hotel for trips to both parks. Hotels listed here are decidedly closer to Knott's. When booking, ask for special park packages that often include admissions and free gifts.

For convenience it's hard to top the **Buena Park Hotel** (7675 Crescent Avenue; 714-995-1111, 800-422-4444, fax 714-828-8590). The 350-room highrise is literally in Knott's parking lot, a three-minute walk from the main gate, with a complimentary shuttle to Disneyland. Rooms are large and appealing. The heated pool, surrounded by a pleasant, grassy area, is a welcome family gathering spot after a day in the park. Moderate.

**Embassy Suites** (7762 Beach Boulevard; 714-739-5600, 800-362-2779, fax 714-521-9650) offers two-room suites with kitchenettes as well as cooked-to-order breakfasts for guests. With a pull-out sofa bed and two double beds, the Spanish-style guest accommodations will comfortably sleep up to six. Well-done natural landscaping surrounds the large pool, which is set in a central courtyard with a barbecue for guests' use. The 201-room hotel is a five-minute walk from the park entrance. Ultra-deluxe.

The 145-room **Buena Park Courtyard by Marriott** (7621 Beach Boulevard; 714-670-6600, 800-321-2211, fax 714-670-0360) is one of the nicer hotels on Beach Boulevard because it's set back from the street, which helps cut traffic noise. Rooms in soft pastels with private balconies and patios surround a charming inner courtyard landscaped with pine trees and lush plantings. Originally designed to appeal to a business clientele, the hotel now caters to parkgoers. The Café is open for breakfast, and there is a lounge open in the evenings that serves appetizers and sandwiches; room service is provided. The park is a five-minute walk away. Moderate.

Set back a bit from the busy boulevard, the green-and-white **Inn-suites Hotel** (7555 Beach Boulevard; 714-522-7360, 800-272-6232, fax 714-523-2883) has 198 guest rooms and an impressive, two-story lobby with fountain and spiral staircase. The quiet courtyard, with heated pool and spa, is surrounded by multilevel landscaping and palm trees. Opposite the lobby is a video-games arcade. Free breakfast buffet is included. The inn is less than a block from Knott's entrance and will shuttle guests to Disneyland. Moderate.

The reliably comfortable **Holiday Inn** (7000 Beach Boulevard; 714-522-7000, 800-522-7006, fax 714-522-3230) is always a good, safe family choice. Large rooms have an agreeable decor. An extra-large adult pool is set beside a children's wading pool, both surrounded with a well-kept, palm-studded lawn. There's a complimentary shuttle to Knott's Berry Farm and Disneyland as well as other area attractions. Moderate to deluxe.

**Travelers Inn** (7121 Beach Boulevard; 714-670-9000, 800-633-8300, fax 714-522-7280), part of a reliable budget chain, offers no-frills accommodations (children under 18 are free with adults) plus a free continental breakfast in a plain but friendly atmosphere, which personnel describe as "1990 motel." The pool and spa are sunny and adequate, and rooms are clean and comfortable. But that's about all. Budget.

Off Beach Boulevard (which means it's quieter), the **Hanford Hotel** (7828 Orangethorpe Avenue; 714-670-7200, 800-727-7205, fax 714-522-3319) has a young, child-oriented staff which obviously enjoys youngsters. The medium-sized, contemporary-decor rooms have a comfortable sitting area with couch or lounge chair. Tidily landscaped pool and patio areas are brightened with white umbrella tables. There's no restaurant, but eateries are just next door. Moderate.

Part of the economy division of Marriott, the **Fairfield Inn** (7032 Orangethorpe Avenue; phone/fax 714-523-1488, 800-228-2800) is not within walking distance of Knott's. The 133 medium-sized rooms are comfortably furnished, and the bare-bones pool is adequate. A young, enthusiastic staff takes the time to get involved with kids. Budget.

Tastefully decorated with desert-style decor, the **Best Western Buena Park Inn** (8580 Stanton Avenue; 714-828-5211, 800-646-1629, fax 714-826-3716) is a two-block walk from Knott's. The pool area is a bit sterile, but the 62 rooms are reliably clean. A few family units with two adjoining rooms are available; some are linked by an archway creating a suite-like arrangement. A modest continental breakfast is served. Moderate.

The **Colony Inn** (7800 Crescent Avenue; 714-527-2201, 800-982-6566, fax 714-826-3826) is a rambling, 128-room, crisp-blue-and-white complex across the street from Knott's. It has a pair of pools and saunas in addition to efficiency units and suites. Budget to moderate.

## Knott's Berry Farm Area Dining

Inside the park you'll find the usual array of fast-food stands, many with menus a notch above what you'd expect in a theme park. Although lines move quickly, expect a wait during peak lunch and dinner hours.

Typically Southern California charbroiled hamburgers, hot dogs and chicken at **Wilderness Broiler** in Wild Water Wilderness satisfy tastes for familiar fare. They'll broil the burgers to order. **AirHeadz** in The Boardwalk area is a good cafeteria-style choice for picky or health-conscious eaters because there's a pleasing array of hot entrées as well as fresh salads. It has indoor seating, or you can eat on the patio. The giant tostadas at Fiesta Village's **Herdez Cantina** have a shell that looks like a sail and are tastily prepared with ground beef and your choice of mild or hot salsa. Enjoy generously sized tacos and burritos while you're serenaded by organ music from the carousel. All are budget. In Camp Snoopy at **Grizzly Creek Lodge**, you will find child-sized hamburgers and hot dogs. Unfortunately this sit-down restaurant doesn't have mini-prices, but it still falls into the budget category.

Just outside the park main gate in the shopping area called California MarketPlace are some very good sit-down restaurants (714-220-5200 for information on all park restaurants). You can park for free without buying a park ticket. If you're in the park, you can exit and return with a hand stamp. Not to be missed is Cordelia Knott's original **Chicken Dinner Restaurant**. Even on a slow day, lines form to taste the world-famous chicken served here since 1934. Grandmotherly waitresses encourage kids to "eat it all so you have more energy for the park!" Wood booths, "antique" buffets and plate rails with grandma's china create a homey atmosphere. While waiting in line, take a look at the framed menus from those bygone days when an entire dinner was 75 cents. Glassed-in pages from old Knott's guests books bear the signatures and comments of notables including John Wayne and Bob Hope. Lunch begins with baking-powder biscuits and can include a small dish of strawberry/rhubarb sauce (delicious!), two pieces of deep-fried chicken and mashed po-tatoes and gravy. Try the boysenberry punch for a zippy, refreshing change. The restaurant also serves broiled and roasted chicken as well as chicken salad for those who eschew fried foods. To avoid the lines but sample the chicken, stop by the chicken-to-go window next door. The restaurant also is open early for breakfast (huge, home-style affairs with biscuits and slabs of ham). It puts you within seconds of the park entrance for opening time. Budget.

Also in the California MarketPlace, just outside the exit gate from Ghost Town, **Knott's Family Steak House** features classic ham-burgers and a good, basic menu. The setting is rustic, early Califor-nia in style, with a Southwest Indian decor, which includes serapes and murals on the walls and oversized pottery pieces. Tasty menu choices include a tangy Chinese chicken salad, Cobb salad and chili that's not too hot for the kids. Moderate.

The choice of restaurants within a mile or so of the park runs heavily to budget-priced chains. Several others are priced in the moderate category and have a special fondness for families.

**PoFolks** (7701 Beach Boulevard, Buena Park; 714-521-8955) epitomizes down-home Southern cookin' and family atmosphere with a hearty, Dixie-style menu. There are turnip greens, black-eyed peas, country-fried steaks, fried chicken and hush puppies. Empha-sizing its homespun style are natural-wood booths and tables with

---

## CALIFORNIA MARKETPLACE

*Knott's California MarketPlace is a separate dining and shopping facility that you pass through before entering the park. This is where Mrs. Knott's Chicken Dinner Restaurant is located, plus two more restaurants. There's a tour de force of Knott's preserves at the Berry Market. Take the time to look twice. Many flavors such as bing cherry, red currant and California plum are available only at the park. Twenty intriguing shops make this area an attraction in itself. If you want to explore California MarketPlace and have a bite to eat without entering the park itself, you can park for free.*

blue-and-white-checked tablecloths and a decor that consists of old kitchen paraphernalia. Framed 1920s newspapers decorate the restrooms, and a period model train chugs around the room to the delight of kids. Budget.

The wait is worth it at **Claim Jumper** (7971 Beach Boulevard, Buena Park; 714-523-3227). The Gold Rush theme includes buffalo, moose, elk and deer heads, which peer over your shoulder while you eat. Kids can hop on a scale when they enter, then pay by the pound (according to their own weight) when they order from the children's menu. There are mini-burgers with fries and apple garnish, barbecued ribs, grilled cheese, chicken, pasta and chicken fingers. Adults can also dine on baby back pork ribs, meat loaf, rotisserie chicken and great Cobb salads. The baked potatoes weigh over a pound. If you have room, try the Motherlode six-layer chocolate cake. Gigantic portions. Moderate.

Located two miles south of Buena Park in Cyprus, **The Olive Garden** (6874 Katella Avenue; 714-894-1330) is so Italian in ambience that it has gondoliers and white-capped mountains painted on the walls. A profusion of plants and natural-wood tables gives the place an outdoor feel. It can accommodate almost 400 guests but is broken into separate sections, avoiding a barn like atmosphere. Entrées include ravioli, spaghetti and lasagne. Regular menu offerings come in children's portions, and kids also like the personal-sized pizzas. Moderate.

## Knott's Berry Farm Area Shopping

The expected T-shirts and souvenir mugs with the Knott's logo are available at the dozen shops in the park. Two unusual shopping opportunities stand out. At the **Geode Shop,** bins of "coconuts"—round rocks that may contain an interesting center—are priced according to weight. The lighter, more expensive ones are more likely to contain a hollow quartz and amethyst-filled center. Make your choice and the lapidist will cut it on his diamond-bladed saw, then polish the surface.

The **General Store** in Ghost Town has a great selection of western wear including classy boots and ten-gallon hats. In Ghost Town's **Crafts Barn** you can watch artisans fashion stained-glass windows, wood carvings and leather bags. **Magic & Sports** offers a selection of tricks and gags that can turn budding magicians into little Houdinis. Your favorite sports team is represented in clothing and souvenirs. If the kids won't leave the park without a Snoopy souvenir, stop at **Rocking Horse Toys** in Camp Snoopy. The famous beagle has his likeness on everything from toys and clothing to illustrated books. Besides plastic totem replicas and other souvenir merchandise, the **Mystery Lodge Store & Museum** offers original (and expensive) ceremonial masks, totems and other native crafts.

Immediately outside the park, California MarketPlace is a mecca for shoppers. You'll have to sort through the chachkas and clutter in its 20 shops, but you'll doubtless uncover some wonderful and unusual finds. It's easy to send gifts home from the **Berry Market**. Gift packs of Knott's products are sold in amazing variety. There's no way to miss **Virginia's Gift Shop**, a large, eclectic shop with plenty of souvenir kitsch as well as high-quality crystal, Lladro porcelains and collector baseball cards. **Knott's International Store** has high-quality Oriental objets d'art in jade and brass. Last thing before you leave, stop by the **Farm Bakery** for a genuine boysenberry pie. It's made with the berry that started it all.

## Knott's Berry Farm Area Nightlife

Any after-hours revelry will often include children, and the area outside the park has two guaranteed-to-please options:

It seems hokey at first: dining with your fingers in an imitation 12th-century castle while knights ride into battle. Actually, **Medieval Times** (7662 Beach Boulevard, Buena Park; 714-521-4740) is a brilliant concept, a re-creation of a medieval tournament, com-

---

### THE SMITHY

*At the Blacksmith Shop, a re-creation of a working smithy, the leather-aproned blacksmith will proudly explain how he's hammered out, link by link, the heavy-duty chain across his doorway. He'll explain how the village smithy once was an entire hardware store, the site for forging tools and utensils as well as shoeing horses. He'll show present-day applications of his work, such as iron pothooks and branding irons for steak, and explain that the word "blacksmith," or "blacksmite," has its roots in "hitter, or smiter, of black iron." For a fee he'll even hammer out a horseshoe bearing your name.*

plete with games of skill and jousting matches. It can get pretty wild when the knights—highly trained horsemen and stuntmen—perform dangerous jousting and sword-fighting routines.

Just up the street at **Wild Bill's Wild West Dinner Extrava-ganza** (7600 Beach Boulevard, Buena Park; 714-522-6414) a two-hour musical variety show takes you back to the days of Wild Bill Hickok. While watching the Wild West show, guests get friendly at long, communal tables in Miss Annie's Saloon, chowing down on fried chicken and barbecued ribs from pewter buckets that the guests pass conveys around the table. The show includes Indian dancers, a comical magician and a lasso artist. Audience members get into the act when they become square dancers.

FOUR

# Universal Studios Hollywood

If Hollywood is one big fantasy, Universal Studios Hollywood is one big set within the fantasy. Here, movieland unfolds like you won't believe as you see the seaside town of Amity featured in *Jaws*, the damp forests roamed by E.T., Norman Bates's *Psycho* house, Baker Street in London and a Parisian courtyard.

There was little more here than fruit trees and coyotes when Carl Laemmle purchased the barren site in 1915 for a movie studio. The entrepreneur invited visitors to his studio, charging them a quarter for the first Universal tour. For that, guests received a box lunch and sat in bleachers watching early silents being made. In those early days the audience could boo the villain and applaud the heroine, but with the advent of sound, visitors were barred from the set.

In 1964 the tour idea surfaced again, this time allowing a tour company to drive its buses through the lower lot to increase lunchtime business at the studio commissary. That first year, 42,000 guests visited the studio, and top brass realized they were on to something. In 1965 the Upper Lot opened, with a better version of the original stunt show, a love animal show and a "screen test" in which guests became "stars." Today, as many as 35,000 visitors a day troop through to get a close-up view of filmland with its sleeves rolled up.

The studio sprawls over a vast lot, flanked by freeways and a small range of hills. The Upper Lot, which also is used for filming, perches atop a hill and down its flanks. From the moment you step out of your car and head for the entrance, you're surrounded with billboards announcing current Universal Studios feature releases.

Technically, the park is split into the Lower Lot and the Upper Lot on the hill. Some areas the Lower Lot are open to visitors only on the tram tour. The Lower Lot is dominated by the sound stages that house Jurassic Park—The Ride, Backdraft, E.T. Adventure, Lucy: A Tribute and World of Cinemagic.

The much more expansive Upper Lot, where you enter, immediately puts you into a movieland mode as you find yourself strolling the Streets of the World. The weathered, rustic buildings of Western Street, New York's enduring brownstones, Baker Street with its reincarnations of typically London shops, Moulin Rouge and the Parisian courtyard and '50s America near Mel's Diner are all so amazingly realistic it's hard to fathom that they're just sets. This is, after all, the world's largest movie studio.

Even restaurants continue the fantasy theme; one is shaped like a steamboat, another is straight out of a Mexican village, and yet another is topped with a revolving windmill. Interspersed with these flights of fantasy are the large, comfortable amphitheaters seating as many as 3000 guests. The shows, one of the park's most appealing features, reveal the secrets of moviemaking magic.

On the studio's well-known tram tour, you're immersed in silver-screen lore as you drive through streets once haunted by Hollywood greats and catch a glimpse of contemporary stars in shows currently in production. Virtually every day (except weekends) it really is possible to witness a motion picture or television show being filmed somewhere on the lot. The authentic-looking sets offer a nostalgic journey from historical films to the screenland homes of the stars of today. It's also possible to be an audience guest at the filming or taping of a television show. For most people, though, simply absorbing all the Hollywood imagery and nuances is intoxicating enough. There is a certain excitement and childlike elation in knowing that the line between illusion and reality runs very thin here.

## ARRIVAL

Universal Studios is located at 100 Universal City Plaza, Universal City (818-622-3801). If you stay at either the Universal City Hilton or Sheraton Universal, both of which are on studio property, you simply take a Universal Trolley or walk up the hill to the Studio attraction.

When arriving by car, you'll exit off the Hollywood Freeway (Route 101) at either Universal Center or Lankershim Boulevard. From the freeway, signs direct you about a half-mile to the park entrance.

You'll drive up the hill past the Sheraton Universal and the Hilton, pay a parking fee and receive a brochure and directions to a large parking lot. A shuttle will take you to the gate. During winter months and on weekdays there's not much of a line at the ticket windows, but if you arrive early you can sit in the courtyard or visit shops for film and souvenir purchasing.

## TICKET OPTIONS

There are three ticket options here: a one-day pass, two-day pass or an annual pass.

|  | Adults | Children 3–11 |
| --- | --- | --- |
| *One-day Pass* | $38.00 | $28.00 |
| *Two-day Pass* | $48.00 | $37.00 |
| *Annual Pass* | $69.00 | $59.00 |
| *Children under 3 are free* | | |

## SIGHTSEEING STRATEGIES

With many major rides and attractions, Universal Studios is best visited over the course of two days. If your itinerary allows for only one day, make sure you know what rides and attractions are your top priorities and do them first. The following sightseeing strategy is for one day only and hits most of the biggies, but it will make for a full day.

The Universal experience has three distinct parts:

1. The Back Lot Tram Tour
2. The Lower Lot
3. The Upper Lot

The 45-minute tram tour covers some of the lower lot, including attractions like King Kong and Earthquake that have been built specifically for the tour. This is where you're most likely to see stars who are working on the lot. Because Universal Studios is a working studio, the route of the tram often changes depending on filming.

The studio back lot occupies a huge, flat acreage with sound stages, offices and equipment-storage buildings. The Lower Lot houses the Jurassic Park ride, the E.T. ride, Lucy: A Tribute and World of Cinemagic are located.

The Upper Lot houses the Back to the Future ride, WaterWorld and the rest of the attractions.

Weekends and summer months are busiest, and you can expect to move at a snail's pace simply because the park areas are small. But

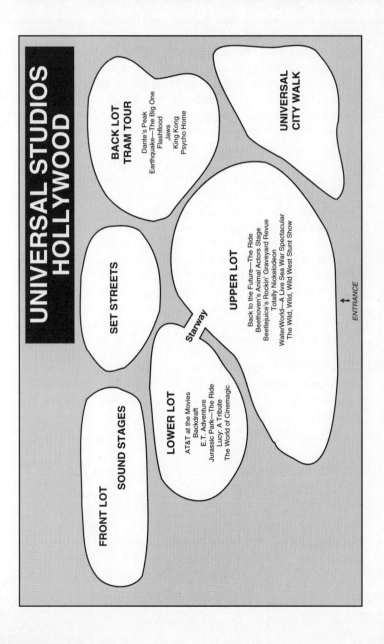

# UNIVERSAL STUDIOS HOLLYWOOD

**FRONT LOT**

**SOUND STAGES**

**SET STREETS**

**LOWER LOT**
AT&T at the Movies
Backdraft
E.T. Adventure
Jurassic Park—The Ride
Lucy: A Tribute
The World of Cinemagic

**Starway**

**BACK LOT TRAM TOUR**
Dante's Peak
Earthquake—The Big One
Flashflood
Jaws
King Kong
Psycho Home

**UPPER LOT**
Back to the Future—The Ride
Beethoven's Animal Actors Stage
Beetlejuice's Rockin' Graveyard Revue
Totally Nickelodeon
WaterWorld—A Live Sea War Spectacular
The Wild, Wild West Stunt Show

**UNIVERSAL CITY WALK**

ENTRANCE

don't be dismayed. Arrive 30 minutes early and get on the first or second tram. This will enable you to get a head start on the lines for the popular rides and attractions.

The Back Lot Tram Tour departs from the Upper Lot. Once you return you have two options, depending on the show schedules. You can either stay in the Upper Lot and dash to the Back to the Future ride and then attend a WaterWorld show (check the schedule), or head immediately down to the Lower Lot via the Starway and ride Jurassic Park and either E.T. or Backdraft, depending on the lines.

After lunch check the afternoon show schedule and coordinate afternoon shows with any rides you missed in the morning. Shows are conveniently staggered and repeated several times a day, so if you plan well you should be able to see all of them. It's important to get to a show at least five minutes before it starts (earlier if you want a good seat). Even though the crowds may look horrendous, the theaters are all large and capable of taking hordes of visitors. The gates close as soon as the theater is full and stay closed during the performance, so get there on time.

You can choose from any of the dozen restaurants in the park. Although food is not of table-service restaurant quality, it does rank high in the world of theme-park dining. It's advisable to eat lunch by 11:30 a.m. and dinner at about 4:30 p.m. to avoid the crowds.

## NUTS & BOLTS

**General Information:** Guest Relations, Universal Studios Hollywood, 100 Universal City Plaza, Universal City, CA 91608; 818-508-9600.

---

*SEE YOUR TELEVISION HEROES IN THE FLESH*

*Many television shows and specials are taped before a live audience, and that live audience can easily include you. At any given time (hardly ever on weekends, though) tickets are available for up to 20 current shows including sitcoms, variety shows, talk shows and specials. Tickets are free, and to assure a full house more are distributed than the studios can hold, so once you have your ticket you must show up early to be certain of a seat. Stop by the* **TV Audience Ticket Booth** *near the Upper Lot exit to see what's available. Tapings are done off the lot, so you should get tickets either for late that same day or for the following day.*

*The entire earthquake stage re-sets in 15 seconds. It shakes 200 times a day.*

**Stroller and Wheelchair Rentals:** Located at Guest Relations, next to the exit.

**Baby Services:** Diaper-changing facilities are located in all restrooms throughout the park.

**Lockers:** Located next to Guest Relations and Jurassic Park–The Ride.

**Pets:** Bring them to the Information Center and they'll be kenneled for the day at no charge.

**Lost Children and Lost & Found:** Located at Guest Relations, Security near the Totally Nickelodeon Theater and near the Back Lot Tram Tour entrance in the Lower Lot.

**First Aid:** There is a station in the Upper Lot next to Animal Actors' Stage and in the Lower Lot near the Back Lot Tram Tour entrance.

**Banking:** ATMs are at the main entrance and in the Lower Lot near the Studio Store.

## GETTING AROUND

Universal Studios' 420 acres make it the largest film and television studio in the world, but just a small portion is open for on-your-own exploring. You'll see a lot of the grounds on the tram, but when hoofing it you're restricted to the lower and upper lots.

Think of the studio as having an upstairs and a downstairs. You arrive in the Upper Lot, where the tram tour departs. The Starway (a series of four plexi-enclosed escalators that must be among the longest in the world) connects the Upper and Lower lots.

The brochure you'll be given contains an overview as well as detailed maps of both areas. Orient yourself with the larger map, then switch to area maps when you're actually within their boundaries.

## *Back Lot Tram Tour*

One of the highlights of any Universal visit is the tram tour, which provides a behind-the-scenes glimpse of the cinema world aboard a four-car, open-air vehicle that accommodates 160 guests. Since seat-

---

*The 30-foot Kong weighs over six tons, has 660 pounds of fur and 10 watts of "growl."*

---

ing is six across, try to sit on the right side if you want a close-up of King Kong's dental work.

As we mentioned earlier, the best strategy is to ride the tram first thing in the morning, before the crowds arrive. As you climb aboard, a guide will begin a corny repartee that actually includes interesting facts about the studio.

As the tram pulls out you'll head to the back lot, which many people find the most fascinating part of the tour. Here you're in another world (or many other worlds) as the tram winds through Rome, the Wild West, Mexico, New York and dozens of other scenes familiar to moviegoers. When the tram rounds a corner, each falsefront building is seen for what it is—a mere facade in which bricks are made of foam rubber and chicken wire and many features are simply painted on.

You'll see Brownstone Street where Abbott and Costello lived; the clock tower and town square of *Back to the Future* fame; and Spartacus Square, where Kirk Douglas once walked in ancient Rome. The buildings of old Mexico were seen in *The Three Amigos*, and the weathered storefronts on Western Street have played in hundreds of horse operas. The settings for hits such as *Coach* somehow seem smaller than they do on television.

As the tram approaches a large building the guide explains that you're about to enter a sound stage where filming is currently in progress. Once inside this re-creation of a modern subway station, you feel a slight lurch. Then the entire earth shakes as telephone poles topple and power cables emit showers of sparks. The roar becomes deafening when the earth collapses and a truck transporting "highly flammable" material falls through from the street above. Smoke and flames engulf the station. If you're not totally involved by this time, you will be when you see a 15-foot wall of water from a ruptured water main rushing furiously toward you ("use your seat cushions for flotation").

The entire experience graphically simulates an earthquake reaching 8.3 on the Richter scale: 32,000 watts of Sensurround audio power blast you with a thunderous gas explosion and the crackling of a raging fire. Lasting about three minutes, the "quake" is most frightening to those who've actually experienced a trembler because it's so realistic.

Amity, the seafaring village seen in the movie *Jaws*, is another stop on the tour. Just as you get your camera poised for a shot of this tranquil scene, old Jaws himself lunges out of the water within inches of your car. The thrills continue in the form of yet another natural disaster (this is California, after all), as the tram descends into a volcano à la *Dante's Peak*. The lava-red tunnel (if you've taken the back-lot tour before, you'll recognize the spinning tunnel as the old "Six Million Dollar Man" avalanche attraction) spouts all the sights, sounds and "flames" of an active volcano. The effect is fun and utterly dizzying, and you'll have to take your tour guide's word for it when he or she explains that it was the tunnel moving, and not your tram.

If that's not enough adventure for one ride, wait until you enter a scaled-down version of Brooklyn that has just been devastated by a rampaging King Kong. It's a tense, frightened city where fires burn out of control and a noisy helicopter blares danger warnings over a loudspeaker. Through tenement windows you see television sets broadcasting accounts of the big beast's destruction. Even as you watch, the screen goes blank when the copter crashes into a power line, unleashing a furious shower of electrical sparks and a tunnel of flames.

As the mighty Kong's towering shadow looms along the buildings, you catch your first glimpse of the big monkey. Then as the tram inches across the Brooklyn Bridge, you come close enough to the gorilla—three feet from those giant jaws—to smell his banana breath. Hang on tight when he grabs the suspension cables of the bridge.

Assuming you survive this part of the tour you'll arrive next in a sleepy Mexican village (a setting in the movie *Butch Cassidy and the Sundance Kid*) where you merely have to withstand a flash flood. In

---

### INTERNATIONAL INCIDENT

*Back in 1985 a group of Soviet diplomats and their guide were on a tram that got stuck in an unpaved area of the lot. Rather than registering dismay, they simply took off their shoes and helped push the vehicle out of the mud. It never occurred to them that it wasn't part of the tour.*

true Hollywood style it drains harmlessly away as you continue along to view the house from *Psycho* (complete with Mother Bates rocking in the window) and many more of Universal's 500 outdoor sets.

## Lower Lot

The Lower Lot is the home of three major attractions—Jurassic Park, Backdraft and E.T. Adventure. It can be seen in under two hours. Unlike the Upper Lot where shows are offered at specific times, attractions in the Lower Lot run continuously. You'll also see some of filmdom's most famous characters—Bride of Frankenstein, Clark Gable, Charlie Chaplin, Woody Woodpecker and others roaming the streets here. They're always willing to pose with you for photos.

***Jurassic Park—The Ride*** ***** You know it's only a ride, but the technological sophistication of this $110-million blockbuster attraction will have you believing that the vicious *Tyrannosaurus rex* that was practically breathing down your neck is real enough indeed. The ride begins with a multimedia introduction by host John Hammond, the creator and owner of Jurassic Park (played by Sir Richard Attenborough). Aboard a river raft, your party of explorers navigates through the misty, exotic world inhabited by huge but gentle prehistoric creatures like the 50-foot-high *Ultrasaurus* and playful *Psittacosauruses*. It's all pretty idyllic, with picturesque waterfalls, pools and geysers. Mother and baby *Stegosauruses* seem glad to see you, and small dinosaurs called "compys" shriek their greetings. But then something goes wrong, and the raft spins off-course into Carnivore Canyon, where the ferocious T-rex and vicious *Velociraptors* are supposed to be behind an electrified fence. But they're nowhere to be seen. . . . Well, even if you didn't see the movie, you can guess what's in store. We don't want to give it away, so suffice it to say, the effects are terrifyingly real. But be warned: Somewhere along that five-and-a-half-minute ride, as your raft travels nearly 50 miles an hour, it will plunge down an 84-foot drop in pitch darkness. It took five years and a creative team that included Steven Spielberg, aerospace scientists, paleontologists and robotic engineers to create this ride, which now comprises a six-acre compound. You won't be disappointed.

TIPS: This is the park's centerpiece attraction, so expect big crowds and long waits during peak times. Portions of this ride are

---

*During her career, Lucille Ball appeared on the cover of* TV Guide *32 times.*

---

not for the faint of heart and may frighten some children (who must be at least 46 inches high to ride).

**Backdraft** ★★★★ This ride is a stunning special-effects display from the motion picture *Backdraft*. It re-creates the film's climactic warehouse conflagration, putting you literally in the line of fire. Surrounded by ruptured fuel lines, melting metal and scalding heat, guests are "trapped" with flames licking at their heels in a completely controlled situation that can be recycled as many as 15 times per hour. The experience begins with a backdraft flame spinning wildly about the building, triggering massive explosions that cause overhead pipes to burst toward onlookers. Red-hot ashes rain down. Ultimately the firestorm encircles the guests, who are protected by an invisible air curtain.

*TIPS:* Average wait in line is 15 minutes; visit when other attractions are busy.

**E. T. Adventure** ★★★★★ Steven Spielberg's celebrated and wildly successful film sets the scene for this airborne bicycle tour to faraway planets. The story line closely follows the movie, with E.T. stranded on earth three million light years from his beloved Green Planet. As you enter the ride, you are asked your first name, then issued a passport that you surrender when you hop onto one of the "bicycles"— cars suspended from above, with handlebars and wheels on the outside. Your first task is to escape government agents and help E.T. save his dying home. As you take flight you feel night winds blow across your face and see the lights of Los Angeles stretch below. You swoop through dizzying star fields en route to E.T.'s eerie home. This spectacular fantasy is created with tens of thousands of fiberoptic stars and 50 cinebotic figures. In what may be the most surprising part of the entire ride, E.T. bids you a fond farewell . . . by your first name.

*TIPS:* This ride has the best waiting area of any in the universe; a cool, dim forest where the air is scented with evergreen. Considering these surroundings, the typical 30-minute wait isn't so bad after all.

**The World of Cinemagic** ★★★ This three-part attraction graphically demonstrates how special visual tricks are staged. On the *Back* *to the Future* set guests (usually an unlikely pair like a teenager and a grandmother) are seated in a replica of the movie's time-travel car and asked to portray Marty McFly and his girlfriend. Rain splatters the windshield, and the car rocks from side to side as another guest playing crazy Dr. Brown is struck by lightning and turned into a smoking skeleton with singed hair and electricity dancing around his body.

On another set, dominated by an enormous Statue of Liberty, the "matte" process is demonstrated as volunteer actors take a heart-stopping fall from atop the statue's torch (you could be one of them!) hundreds of feet above the ground. Portraying the climactic scene in the movie *Saboteur*, this stunt re-creates one of Alfred Hitchcock's milestone special effects. Finally, the creation of mood and image through sounds is explored at the "Harry and the Hendersons Sound Effects Show." If you want to be part of the action, sit in the front row and volunteer. You may be assigned to a thunder sheet, wind machine, squeak device or other audio equipment that re-creates a storm complete with swirling wind and crashing windows. You can also help bring film to life by stomping through loose audio tape to create the sound of walking on leaves, or drawing a metal rake across a chalkboard to simulate tree branches scratching a window pane. Meanwhile you'll be treated to a fascinating demonstration of how sounds become real once they're integrated with the images on screen.

*TIPS:* Since this attraction is entirely in a dark, cool sound stage, it's a good one to see when you need a break from summer's heat.

**Lucy: A Tribute ★★★** This heart-shaped art deco facility traces the Hollywood career of Lucille Ball from 1933 until her death in 1991. Filled with Lucy memorabilia, the displays portray her years at Columbia Pictures and RKO Studios, with costumes and props from her famous films. There is home video footage of Lucy and her husband Desi Arnaz, plus letters from the comedienne's fans and a collection of her Emmys. True Lucy fans have been known to stand for hours admiring the re-created set from *I Love Lucy* and watching re-runs of the television show. If movie history fascinates you, the interactive "California Here We Come" game lets you test your knowledge of the series while "traveling" with the Ricardos and Mertzes to California.

*TIPS:* This is a good attraction to visit when waiting for the next tram ride or World of Cinemagic Show.

*The Starway escalator connecting the Lower Lot and the Upper Lot is a quarter-mile long.*

*AT&T at the Movies* ★★★ The interactive video devices that fill this room should prove fascinating if you can get through the kids who line up six deep to play them. One machine allows you to freeze-frame your face, then replace parts of it with such Hollywood makeup effects as Dracula teeth and Wolfman hair. In another, your face is scrambled and you are left the task of reassembling it. You can test your color perception by trying to match a computer-selected hue to its surrounding border, or call your hair stylist from a phone booth that's equipped with a four-foot speaker phone.

*Tips:* You'll inevitably stand in line to play one of these games. While you're killing time waiting, watch the interesting reactions of kids as they play with these interactive machines.

## *Upper Lot*

This is Universal Studios' major area, where most of the shows and attractions are located, and the place you'll spend the most time. It's a good idea to make a decision about which shows you'd like to see and note the schedule so you can be there on time. Between shows, stroll the **Streets of the World**. There are Baker Street from old London, Western Street, Moulin Rouge, '50s America where you'll find Mel's Diner and a Parisian courtyard with quiet tables for lunch or a rest.

Among the Upper Lot's numerous attractions you'll encounter is a series of tents housing carnival games. Outside Mel's Diner you can catch the Doo Wop Singers, who croon '50s songs from the seat of a '57 Chevy Bel Air. Clad in hero jackets and sunglasses and sporting outrageous pompadours, they perform "Goodnight Sweetheart," "The Lion Sleeps Tonight" and other familiar favorites from a simpler era. Check the show schedule for performance times.

By comparison, the 15-minute "Blues Brothers Show" simply doesn't measure up. The characters that Dan Ackroyd and John Belushi made famous just never seem to develop the punch of the original. Not even an appearance by Frankenstein, who jives with the black-suited white-soxed duo, can raise this show out of the ordinary.

***Back to the Future—The Ride*** ★★★★★ This flight-simulator ride is a super symphony of speed, fantasy, terror and mind-blowing special effects. When it's over, your throat aches because you've unwittingly screamed so long and hard. It's the kind of ride where 12-year-olds do high-fives at the end, then turn to Mom and announce: "We're going again!"

Based on the *Back to the Future* smash-hit trilogy, the five-minute journey hurls you through centuries at supersonic speed. The action begins in a briefing room where the mad scientist Doc Brown tells guests that Biff (the movie's bully) is threatening to end the universe. The pursuit to find him is on. Eight riders climb into a fancy De-Lorean Time Machine, which spews liquid-nitrogen fog that looks like ice on fire. Your car eerily floats out of its garage, and suddenly you're enveloped by a room-sized video screen that takes you on a brain-blasting visual trip: you tumble down volcanic tunnels, collide with a glacier and get chomped and spit out by a growling *Tyranno-saurus rex*.

TIPS: This is a *very* rough ride! Children shorter than 40 inches are not allowed to ride. Not recommended for expectant mothers, people prone to nausea or claustrophobia, or those with bad backs. Just about everyone who visits Universal wants to ride *Back to the Future* (even those masochists with queasy stomachs and bad backs). Given this fact, know that unless you ride as soon as the park opens, you'll face up to an hour's wait.

***Totally Nickelodeon*** ★★★★ It's got a face-smearing pie shooter, a bath-sized chocolate sundae and a green-goo-dispensing "Slime-nator." Need I say more? Fans of the popular Nickelodeon network (or any kid who just longs to see mom or dad get slimed!) won't want to miss this outrageous (and messy) audience participation game show based on Nickelodeon favorites such as *Family Double Dare*, *Hey Arnold* and *Rugrats*. The competition features whipped cream, pies in the face, and plenty of slime, all the ingredients for an instant kid hit. Audience volunteers take the stage and compete in games chosen by the crowd; contests range from rubber-band obstacle courses to sweaty-sock-piling contests to target practices (moms and dads: guess who's the target?!).

Adults, beware; this is grown-up annihilation, Totally Nickelodeon style! In one game, moms and pops get made into human hamburgers: salad, special sauce and all. In another, they're strapped into baby walkers and made to wear baby bonnets. A third might be called

TV Dinner à la Dad. Of course it's all in good fun, and the winner (yes, the winner) gets the ultimate honor of being "slimed" with Nickelodeon's famous green goo (if the Slimenator fails to deliver, there are other creative options in store).

Volunteers for the Nickelodeon show can expect to get extremely messy. As one friend put it: "The slimenator was pretty effective and pretty gross. It was perfect!" Fortunately, you don't have to worry about your clothes. Universal provides jumpsuits and a post-show cleanup backstage. Totally Nickelodeon shows are approximately 30 minutes long; show times change daily. Check the map for show times as you enter the park.

*TIPS:* Although the theater holds 1200, this is a popular show, and long waits during peak summer months are not uncommon. Your best bet is to head for the earliest show when most people are focusing on Jurassic Park. Try to show up at least 30 minutes ahead in order to get one of the best seats up front.

*ANOTHER TIP:* Volunteers for the show are selected at random from throughout the theater. If you want to improve your chances of getting slimed, try to sit near the aisle, as employees like to select participants who don't have to climb over people to reach the stage. Your chances are even better if you can coerce your entire family into joining up.

***WaterWorld—A Live Sea War Spectacular*** ★★★★★ If this live-action extravaganza doesn't impress you, nothing will. It's based on the Kevin Costner movie and has enough action to keep you rapt for the 15 minutes it takes for the show to unfold. All that and a plot, too: The polar ice caps have melted and the survivors live on floating islands—eerie, mist-shrouded structures made of sheet metal, driftwood and debris. Helen, one of the good guys, returns to the floating atoll with the news that she's found dry land. Deacon, leader of the bad guys, attacks, hoping to kidnap her and get to dry land. The battle that ensues involves explosions that send water cascading

---

### ALL QUIET ON THE SET!

*Because Universal is a working studio, the tram route may change from day to day to avoid areas where shooting is in progress. Some directors love an audience and encourage visitors on their set; you could be lucky and get a close-up look at a popular show.*

over the audience, fireballs radiating heat you can feel, a seaplane that practically crashes in spectators' laps, a bullet-spraying gunboat, water cannons and stunts galore. Thundering music and the realistic set add to the excitement.

*TIPS:* This show draws big crowds; some people line up an hour before to get into the 3000-seat outdoor theater. The best seats are in the center section, about halfway up, where you can take in all the action. The first four rows of seats are designated as "wet seat" sections. If you sit there, make sure you cover up cameras and video equipment.

**The Wild, Wild, Wild West Stunt Show** ★★★★★ This 15-minute, live-action Wild West show features over 100 stunts amid disintegrating buildings, noisy gun battles and flailing fistfights. It's every little kid's cowboy fantasy come to life. The show features Ma Hopper and her boys Cole and Clod, who set out to prove that their stunt skills are better than those of the Universal stunt team. Actors are hurled through wood doors, off balconies and down a well. After a knock-down melee atop the set's roof, a stuntman flings himself off a three-story building onto sheets of knotty pine that have been specially laid across saw horses to break his fall. Called a "plank high fall," it was a stunt used in the early days of cowboy shenanigans before foam fall pads were invented. Watch closely to see how the stuntmen employ their skills to avoid injury as they dodge shotgun blasts and endure chairs broken over their heads. Kids love the gory finale, during which a stuntman is hit by a bullet that splatters the wall behind him with "blood." Young children may be frightened by the gunshots, but older kids generally enjoy the loud, frantic action.

*TIPS:* Arrive here as early as possible so you can watch "Charlie Chaplin" before the show begins. He directs guests toward their seats, then follows behind, imitating their walk or posture. He'll spot a parent with child in tow, then quietly substitute his hand for the parent's. When the child finally looks up and discovers Charlie, the crowd howls.

**Beethoven's Animal Actors Stage** ★★★★ An entertaining show with great family appeal, this live-animal extravaganza is presented in a pleasant, breezy amphitheater before a crowd of 2000 people. The star of the show is the St. Bernard, Beethoven. Other animals who perform are two Borneo orangutans named Sunshine and Jethro. The show also includes trained dogs, cats, cockatoos and even a rat. The trainer explains that the animals have a list of credits that includes *Beethoven*, *Steel Magnolias*, *Coach* and *Batman Returns*.

*TIPS:* If you're seated in one of the front rows you can watch the animals watching you. They seem to be as curious about people as we are about them.

**Beetlejuice's Rockin' Graveyard Revue** ★★★ The dead man is back, this time for a song and dance fest featuring some of his best ghoul friends around including Dracula, the Phantom of the Opera, the Wolfman, Frankenstein and Frankie's bride. The musical performance is mostly rock-and-roll silliness, with featured creatures altering the lyrics to fit their grave humor. Like all Universal gigs, this one's a lot of fun, with performers hamming it up big time, and tossing around lots of special effects and pyrotechnics (when they sing "Great Balls of Fire" here, they mean business) that really get the crowd going. The 20-minute show is performed several times daily. Check the map at the entrance for times.

*TIPS:* The Beetlejuice theater is big and rarely full, but you'll want to arrive about 15 minutes early to get a good seat.

## Universal Studios Hollywood Lodging

There's no motel row in this area, but two excellent hotels are adjacent to Universal property. Both offer free shuttles to the studio, and their central location puts them within 45 minutes of Six Flags California and ten minutes from Hollywood.

The **Sheraton Universal** (333 Universal Terrace Parkway, Universal City; 818-980-1212, 800-325-3535, fax 818-985-4980) rises 21 luxurious stories and overlooks a glistening pool, lush gardens and the San Fernando Valley. It's generally considered the premier place to stay when visiting Universal Studios. The hotel's 442 guest rooms are large and well furnished. Prices at the Sheraton are in the ultra-deluxe range, but packages and weekend rates are available.

A bit taller and farther up the hill, the **Universal City Hilton** (555 Universal Terrace Parkway, Universal City; 818-506-2500, 800-444-8667, fax 818-509-2058) is a gleaming, 24-story tower with guest rooms overlooking Universal Studios, Warner Brothers, Paramount and Disney Studios. Rooms here are spacious and well appointed, and most enjoy spectacular views. Kids love the large pool and jacuzzi. Children under 12 stay free in their parents' room.

Although rates are tabbed in the ultra-deluxe range, there are packages available combining Universal Studios tickets with reduced room rates.

The **Beverly Garland's Holiday Inn** (4222 Vineland Avenue, North Hollywood; 818-980-8000, 800-238-3759, fax 818-766-5230) is a smaller, comfortable place within one-and-one-half miles of Universal Studios that genuinely welcomes families. The seven acres of park-like grounds create a country club–like atmosphere with tennis courts and a pool. Here, too, rates are ultra-deluxe, but special packages are available.

## Universal Studios Hollywood Dining

Universal Studios Hollywood, with some of the best food of any theme park in Southern California, features two full-service restaurants as well as many smaller outlets. They are priced budget to moderate.

Superhero-loving kids and adults will find comic-book heaven at **Marvel Mania Hollywood** (1000 Universal Center Drive; 818-762-7835). The eatery is awash with larger-than-life comic book artifacts, as well as continuous light, sound and video shows. The total effect is like a living comic book: enter through the whooshing decompression chamber, feel the vibration in your dining seat and listen for comic book sounds throughout. Spiderman, the Incredible Hulk and other comic book big guys mill around outside, and you can choose from themed menu selections such as Ghost Rider's Ribs (barbecued ribs), Dastardly Dip (spinach appetizer dip) and Fin Fang Foom (fruit dessert). The restaurant does not typically accept reservations, but inquire ahead if you're going with an unusually large party. Budget to moderate.

Also part of the Universal complex is **Fung Lum Restaurant** (222 Universal Terrace Parkway; 818-763-7888), a Chinese restaurant with yet another panoramic view of the San Fernando Valley. A lovely, quiet place for lunch or dinner, it specializes in lemon chicken, spare ribs and an ever-changing selection of fresh fish. Moderate.

Within the park's Lower Lot, take a break at the **Studio Commissary** for cafeteria-style Philly steak sandwiches, chicken tostadas and croissant sandwiches; dining is on an umbrella-shaded patio.

In the Upper Lot, restaurants are either cafeteria style or via window service, but there are always eating areas with clean tables and chairs nearby. Some of the most creative crêpes around are dished out at **Crepe de Paris** near Moulin Rouge. Family meals that serve four people, with fried chicken, mashed potatoes, gravy and biscuits, are available at **Doc Brown's Fancy Fried Chicken**. Right next door, the **Hollywood Cantina** has traditional Mexican tortillas, tacos and burritos. **Ristorante Italia** makes their own pizza dough. A white steamboat called the **River Princess** dispenses submarine sandwiches, turkey hot dogs and a boxed kids' meal with a prize. As might be expected, the *Moulin Rouge* has French dip sandwiches, rotisserie chicken, croissant sandwiches and other vaguely French fare.

The most entertaining park restaurant is **Mel's Diner**, an extravaganza complete with neon and chrome trim, quilted metal walls and a black-and-white-checkered floor. There's no curbside service, but helpers in roller skates bus trays and wipe tables. Hot dogs and hamburgers (with a tiny American flag on top) are served in red plastic baskets with a side of fries.

## Dining Outside Universal Studios Hollywood

Places outside the park tend to cluster on Cahuenga and Ventura boulevards in Universal City/Studio City within a mile of the studio. The neighborhood is filled with both starving actors and wealthy hill-dwellers, and restaurants reflect their mixed tastes.

---

### UNIVERSAL CITY CINEPLEX

*If you're looking for evening entertainment, this 18-theater complex offers a wide choice of films. There are always several family-style movies being shown, or parents and kids can split up and see different films. A small café serves cakes and cappuccino. The complex is a ten-minute walk from the Hilton and Sheraton hotels.*

***Universal City Walk*** *(1000 Universal Center Drive, Universal City; 818-622-4455) is a three-block-long pedestrian mall that connects Universal Studios Hollywood to the Cineplex Odeon movie theaters. Although the emphasis is on shops and restaurants (Hard Rock Cafe, Wolfgang Puck Cafe, Jody Maroni Sausage, Tony Roma's, etc.), you can stroll down the middle of this "city street" and enjoy a collection of vintage neon signs and wacky, eclectic architecture. Occasionally street performers entertain, and in the central court (located by Tony Roma's), kids enjoy darting in and out of jets of water shooting up from the sidewalk fountain.*

For a glimpse of a rising star or celebrity, the funky **Good Neighbor Restaurant** (3701 Cahuenga Boulevard West, Studio City; 818-761-4627) is as likely a place as any. This low-key, no-frills coffee shop has standard American fare. Breakfast and lunch only. Budget.

The decor at **Teru Sushi** (11940 Ventura Boulevard, Studio City; 818-763-6201) is as inviting as the cuisine. Handpainted walls and carved figures combine with slat booths and a long dark wood sushi bar. The sushi menu includes several dozen varieties; they also serve a selection of traditional dishes. There is a beautiful garden dining area with a koi pond. No lunch on Saturday and Sunday. Deluxe.

Look no farther for gospel brunch than **B. B. King's Blues Club** (1000 Universal Center Drive, Suite 222, Universal City; 818-622-5464). Every Sunday at noon, folks flock here for an unusual (an uplifting) dining experience. In the evenings people choose from an eclectic menu of soul food with a twist and hear top-notch blues musicians spilling their hearts out. Moderate.

**Hard Rock Cafe Hollywood** (1000 Universal Center Drive, Suite 99, Universal City; 818-622-7625) forms a new link in the famous restaurant chain devoted to music memorabilia. One of the prized possessions here is Bill Clinton's autographed gold saxophone. As far as the eats go, choose between a variety of salads, sandwiches, burgers and entrées, which include barbecue chicken, ribs and fresh fish of the day. Moderate.

**Miceli's Restaurant** (3655 Cahuenga Boulevard West, Universal City; 213-851-3344) is noisy and a bit Italian-kitschy with its stained-glass windows and opera-singing waiters, but the food is excellent. Try the pizza and spaghetti and don't miss the hot dinner rolls. Moderate to deluxe.

**Thai BBQ Restaurant** (3737 Cahuenga Boulevard West, Universal City; 818-760-9691) prepares broccoli chicken, chicken satay, beef dishes and a host of other Southeast Asian entrées. While some meals are very spicy, many are mild enough for children. Budget to moderate.

## Universal Studios Hollywood Shopping

Inside the park, shops have more Universal Studios Hollywood T-shirts, mugs and other logo-emblazoned merchandise than you ever imagined. A few stores, however, are noteworthy. Information about all the stores may be obtained by calling 818-622-3716. If you

*Alfred Hitchcock used more than 30 cameras to shoot the famous* Psycho *shower scene.*

get home and wish you'd bought something, don't despair. Just call the studio mail order department at 800-447-0373.

In the Lower Lot, the **Backlot Store** is a multimedia shopping experience. You can watch clips from your all-time favorite television shows while browsing through the shop. At the **E.T. Toy Closet** there are giant tinker toys that hold such intriguing items as articulated robot hands. **Jurassic Outfitters** features the widest array of dinosaur merchandise imaginable.

The largest store in the park, **Universal Studios Store** offers souvenirs from every attraction in the park. **Silver Screen Collectibles** shop, also located in the Upper Lot, features a "Wardrobe Dept." where little girls can buy "dress-up" clothes (glittery, chiffony fairy princess–like dresses, sequined tiaras, gold and silver slippers, hats with feathers and fancy hair clips). There's also movie memorabilia; collectors can pick up framed, signed photos of stars (Brando, Hepburn, Crawford), plus lobby cards, publicity stills and limited-edition animation cels. There's a Wizard of Oz scarf depicting all the movie's characters, which was a promotional item when the film opened in 1939. It's framed, and the asking price is $5000 (it's been there two years so far). **Animal Stars**, a menagerie of stuffed creatures, has mounted lion and tiger "trophy" heads for children's rooms, plus leopard, lion and zebra print T-shirts.

Kids of all ages should head over to the **Emporium** for clothing and souvenirs sporting their favorite cartoon characters.

# FIVE

# Sea World

San Diego attracts thousands upon thousands of tourists with its win- **129** ning combination of surf, sand and sea. For many of these visitors, Sea World, a manmade aquatic wonderland, is number one on the itinerary. The 150-acre marine park, chock full of shows and attractions that probe the puzzles of the deep, is the jewel of San Diego's Mission Bay.

The 16,000 creatures that call Sea World home hail from as close as San Diego Bay and as far as Antarctica. Here at the best-known oceanarium on earth are whales the size of your house and clown fish the size of your toe. Add to them slick black seals and pink-fringed invertebrate, clever dolphins and endearing penguins, whiskered sea lions and mischievous otters. There are less-familiar characters, too, such as puffins and buffleheads, unicorn fish and slithering sea snakes.

Many of the critters hang out in big, blue swimming pools that dot Sea World's lush landscape. Every day thousands of people file into stadiums around these pools to watch the fascinating animals play while they work: whales that whistle and do somersaults, seals that slap one another on the back and dolphins that swim the backstroke.

Amphibious actors (plus a few human performers) steal the shows that have made Sea World world-famous. But this place is much more than shows. The multimillion-dollar aquatic theme park and research center boasts over 20 attractions that delve into underwater mysteries. From the mammoth World of the Sea aquarium and chilly Penguin Encounter to the den of scary sharks, they paint a poignant portrait of the sea.

Outside the exhibits, the park looks like a seaside painting in motion. Seagulls shriek overhead, and salty breezes shift across lawns of soft grass. Rock ponds weave through palmy gardens, and pink flamingos make clawprints on patches of sand. Speedboats and skiers roar across a rambling lagoon. Sea World's definitive landmark, the 320-foot Skytower, affords visitors a panoramic view of the city's skyline, foothills, bays and beaches.

Within this briny setting you can stroke a slippery, slimy bat ray. You can hand feed a hungry dolphin or a greedy walrus. Or you can lunch on the shady patio of the Harborside Café and maybe get a glimpse of the wild sea lion that hangs out on an adjacent ledge, hoping for a handout.

If this sounds like quintessential Southern California touristing, it is. Since Sea World opened in 1964, it has offered marine-life education with a kick-back-and-take-your-shoes-off attitude. Today, Sea World endures as an old-style California theme park. Unlike Disneyland, that big mouse house nearby, Sea World offers little in the way of high-tech attractions.

But those are really the best things about Sea World. Life here is more relaxed, more tuned to the out-of-doors. This is a place where you can downshift into slow gear and think about what happens below sea level. A place that, for many people, is the only real thread to that strange, liquid cosmos.

## ARRIVAL

Hurray! Sea World is easy to find: It's right off Sea World Drive on Mission Bay, about five miles north of downtown San Diego. From Route 5, exit west onto Sea World Drive. From Route 8 heading west, exit onto West Mission Bay Drive and then go east on Sea World Drive. Remember to *make a note of where you park* (rows are numbered) so you'll be able to find your car at the end of the day. There is a fee for parking.

## TICKET OPTIONS

You can buy a one-day ticket, two-day ticket or an annual pass. If you plan to visit for three or more days, go for the annual pass.

|  | Adults | Children 3–11 |
|---|---|---|
| *One-day Ticket* | $34.95 | $26.95 |
| *Two-day Ticket* | $38.95 | $30.95 |
| *Annual Pass* | $69.95 | $54.95 |
| *Children under 3 are free* | | |

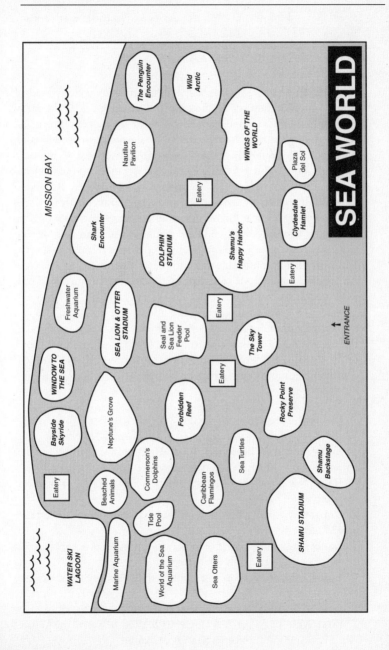

---

*Baby Shamu, born July 9, 1991, was the sixth killer whale to be born at the Sea World family of marine parks.*

---

## SIGHTSEEING STRATEGIES

As a first-time visitor, you may expect the same crowd craze faced at Disneyland and Universal Studios. Don't. Laid-back Sea World rarely has gridlock and is so well planned it hardly ever has lines. The main thing to know is that the big attractions are shows, so you should plan your day around their starting times. Allow at least 45 minutes between shows. This gives ample time for restroom stops and enjoying the "walk-through" exhibits such as the Forbidden Reef and Penguin Encounter. It also lets you arrive ten minutes early for each show so you get a seat. Some shows fill up fast, particularly during midday. If you have small children, take a seat near an aisle so you can easily make restroom or other emergency trips during the shows. Sea World helps you decide what to see and when to see it with a computer-generated Map and Show Schedule, which are passed out as you enter the park.

Parents also will want to schedule a midday stop at Shamu's Happy Harbor playground. Children love all the nifty activities, and you'll be happy to take a break in the shade. Above all, don't rush from show to show. Half the fun of Sea World is taking the leisurely way around and enjoying the "walk-through" exhibits.

## NUTS & BOLTS

**General Information:** Ticket Information, Sea World, 1720 South Shores Road, San Diego, CA 92109; 619-226-3901.

**Stroller and Wheelchair Rentals:** Both are available in the entrance plaza just inside the main entrance.

**Baby Services:** There are changing tables next to or in most restrooms.

**Cameras:** Forgot your camera? Disposable cameras can be purchased inside the park.

**Lockers:** Located near the Information Center. Lockers cost 50 cents to $1 each time you open them.

**Lost Children:** Report lost children to Guest Services inside the main entrance.

**Lost & Found:** Contact Guest Services.

**First Aid:** The First Aid Center is located between the Whale Gift Shop and the California Sea Otter exhibit.

**Banking:** ATMs are located at the main entrance and in between the Rocky Point Preserve and the Skytower.

**Package Pickup:** This free service lets you shop without having to tote the bags around all day. Just inform any Sea World store clerk you want package pickup, and they will send your purchases to the California Surf Shop or the Dolly Dolphin Emporium where you can pick them up on your way out of the park.

GETTING AROUND

Sea World is a breeze. Just think of it as a lopsided doughnut. The doughnut's center is marked by the Skytower; the hole is made up of a circle of eateries, marine-life pools, Rocky Point Preserve, Forbidden Reef and the Sea Lion and Otter Stadium. Along the doughnut's outer edge are eight other major exhibits and shows. Traveling clockwise they are Shamu Backstage, Shamu Stadium, Water Ski Lagoon, Window to the Sea, Shark Encounter, Dolphin Stadium, Penguin Encounter, Mission: Bermuda Triangle, Wings of the World and Shamu's Happy Harbor.

If you're in a wheelchair, Sea World is easy to navigate. Paths are broad, and ramps are abundant and gently sloped. Stadiums and theaters offer plenty of wheelchair seating (often front-row).

## *The Shows*

*Shamu Stadium* ★★★★★ Outside the Disney domain, no theme-park character has gotten more hype than Shamu the killer whale. Not to worry: Everything you've heard is true. Sea World's best-

---

*IT'S CHOW TIME*

*Want to get close to Sea World's animals? Just feed them. Buy a tray of herring, squid or smelt and head over to the Forbidden Reef, Rocky Point Preserve or the Seal, Sea Lion and Walrus attractions. The California bat rays and dolphins will eat right out of your hand, and you can even pet them. The sea lions and seals put on a real show, barking for food and rolling on their backs. Get there late in the day and you'll see the whiskered fellows all fat and happy and snoozing in a big heap. The blubbery, ton-plus walruses rarely do much more than sleep and eat. (But be careful. They will spit at you!)*

loved mammal—all 8000 pounds of him—lives up to his reputation in this splendid attraction called "The Shamu Adventure." Black and white and glossy all over, the big guy does a graceful underwater ballet and waves to the crowd with his tail, then sends a mini-tidal wave over the first few rows. He also parks himself on the platform so audience members can see. During the show, Shamu is joined by Baby Shamu and their friends. The action is captured on state-of-the-art cameras that broadcast Shamu's feats (and the crowd's reactions) on a 300-square-foot video screen above his pool.

*TIPS:* This is the only attraction that regularly fills up well before show time. Consider arriving at the stadium 20 or even 30 minutes ahead of time. The folks at Sea World tell us that the afternoon shows are the least crowded. Be advised that spectators sitting in the first 15 rows will undoubtedly be drenched. (P.S. If you'd like to be an audience participant, see "Tips" for Dolphin Stadium, below). Not to be missed.

***Water Ski Lagoon*** ★★★ Each summer humans are at center stage of a waterskiing extravaganza. The skiers—all professionals—perform an astounding series of stunts, including headstands on jet skis, ramp jumping on wet bikes, acrobatic pairs skiing and barefoot waterskiing. Jet skis and power boats burst across the lagoon at hair-raising speeds. One of the highlights is a graceful, precision-skiing quartet of skiers looking straight out of *Baywatch*. Don't miss this production; the aquatic antics are spectacular.

*TIPS:* For hilarious entertainment before the show, settle in a few minutes early. Some of the players warm up the crowd by clowning around in the lagoon in small motor boats, capsizing, colliding and even falling overboard.

---

## A SEA LION OR A SEAL?

*How can you tell a sea lion from a seal? If you don't know, sign up for Sea World's **Behind-the-Scenes** tour. The 90-minute, guided excursion features oodles of sea life trivia and a backstage look at Sea World attractions. You'll see animals that were injured and rescued by the park, and the place where penguins incubate. The tour costs $5 (plus park admission) and is offered several times a day. To sign up, visit the Information Center near the main entrance. (P.S.: A sea lion is a seal with earflaps.)*

*Sea World's penguin population gobbles about 750 pounds of fish every day.*

**Window to the Sea** ★★  This simulated voyage under the sea takes place in an indoor theater with a 40-foot-wide series of video screens that show underwater footage from various oceans throughout the world. Most of the film focuses on Sea World's research programs and attractions. This is all done with the best of intentions, but we'd rather be outside seeing the animals in the flesh. Of all the shows at Sea World, this would be the one to skip—unless you're hot and tired and need a dark, cool place to catch a quick nap.

*TIPS:* Energetic children with short attention spans become terribly restless during this show. If you've got a little dynamo on your hands, you'd best skip this one.

**Dolphin Stadium** ★★★★★  Remember that Sea World television commercial where the dolphin rockets into the air and does a really great triple flip? It was a teaser for this "One World" Show that reveals just how clever dolphins can be. For 25 minutes the jovial creatures perform gracefully on command, doing backstrokes, acrobatics and even the hula. The crowd oohs and aahs at just the right times, like when a child from the audience does a flipper shake with a dolphin. Pilot whales do some pretty neat things, too, such as taking their trainer on a high-speed spin around the pool. The show climaxes with a multispecies finale. If you've ever doubted the intelligence of whales or dolphins, this show will change your mind.

*TIPS:* Ready to take the plunge? If you'd like to be an audience participant, be there 30 minutes early. Go to the front of the stadium and ask for an operations employee. There is, of course, no guarantee you'll be chosen, but then again, you just might be.

**Dolphin Interaction Program** ★★★  Dolphin lovers have been lining up in droves since Sea World inaugurated its Dolphin Interaction Program (DIP), the event that invites guests 13 and older to stand nose to bottlenose with these popular aquarian mammals.

The two-hour program begins at 8 a.m. with an hour-long class on dolphin anatomy, followed by a wetsuit fitting and a few minutes of calisthenics. Then it's everybody into the pool. After everyone has acclimated to the 55-degree salt water (even with a wetsuit, it's c-c-cold!), trainers take you through a series of behavior signals where dolphins respond with such behaviors as shaking flippers, doing flips,

*Sea-otter fur has approximately 600,000 hairs per square inch.*

jumping and stopping on a dime. The program wraps up with a dolphin volleyball game.

Program creators are careful to refer to DIP as an "interaction" rather than a "swim" with the dolphins (the rule here is "two feet on the floor at all times"), which is an important distinction for those who have visions of frolicking around with Flipper. Though the whole program lasts two hours, only 20 to 25 minutes is actually spent in the water, wading at that (Sea World is currently pondering a second deep-water interaction program, but nothing has been decided). Still, such encounters with dolphins are rare and many visitors are genuinely enamored of the whole experience. For my money, the $135 price tag (per person including same-day park admission and souvenir towel; observers can brought along for just the price of park admission) is a little steep for the reward.

The Sea World franchise's original dolphin interaction program (there are now replicas at other Sea World parks), DIP was closed in 1997 and reopened in April 1998 after some retooling.

*TIPS:* Sea World's DIP has been a popular sell since it first opened in 1995. The program is strictly limited to nine people so if you are interested, a year ahead is not too early to make your reservation.

**Sea Lion and Otter Stadium** ★★★★ Whimsical scenery, a wacky script and great animal shenanigans make this the liveliest, zaniest show at Sea World. It stars Clyde and Seamore, a sea-lion duo that sets out to solve the riddle of the island's mysterious Mighty Surlaw (Walrus spelled backwards). During the show Clyde and Seamore are joined by a North American river otter and a Pacific walrus. Everyone seems to enjoy this fast-paced show, but it's the preschoolers who can't get enough of the adorable animals.

*TIPS:* Avoid the seats on the far sides of the stadium; the view is lousy.

**Wings of the World** ★★★★ More than 30 birds from as far away as South America, Africa and Australia take to the stage and to the air for this fine feathered revue. The 25-minute show includes dramatic displays of the habits of wild birds. A fish eagle pounces on simulated prey in a demonstration of its hunting ability. Colorful, precocious parrots shamelessly mimic their human co-stars. An ominous-looking vulture circles over the audience showing off its ten-foot wingspan.

The highlight comes when a trio of aerodynamic hawks takes a 300-foot dive, reaching speeds of 100 miles per hour.

*TIPS:* Seating is divided into three sections. Get here early to get a seat in the middle section as the view is far superior to those from the side.

## The Exhibits

**Forbidden Reef** ★★★★★ This fascinating exhibit affords a safe, wonderful way to experience some creatures you would probably not want to encounter in the wild. Outside the entrance, slippery bat rays glide through a shallow pool; their stingers have been surgically removed so they're safe to touch. The slimy creatures even seem to enjoy being stroked as they swim around the pool's perimeter. Inside, the mood is darker and eerier as giant aquariums hold enormous, dark-rock formations. A closer look reveals hundreds of snake-like figures emerging from holes in the rock. These moray eels stay almost motionless, suspended in the water, half-emerged from their hiding places. Their beady eyes and needle-like teeth are frightening but mesmerizing. It's difficult to drag the kids—and sometimes even the adults—out of this one.

*TIPS:* The bat rays can take a while to swim over to the edge of the pool. Be patient and they'll come around. Don't miss out on touching one of these intriguing creatures; they feel like slimy velvet.

---

### SEA WORLD'S WORLD OF THE SEA

*In addition to all the shows and exhibits, Sea World's landscape is dotted with smaller ponds, pools and aquariums filled with thousands of intriguing sea critters. Turn a corner and you may encounter a thriving colony of flamingos, a frisky bunch of otters or ancient sea turtles basking in the sun. Sea World is also home to three aquariums that simulate the natural habitats of aquatic creatures from all over the globe. The **Marine Aquarium** features hundreds of ocean fish, a chambered nautilus and a giant Pacific octopus. The **Freshwater Aquarium** houses creatures from Africa, Asia and the Amazon River basin, including a large tank of archerfish, capable of shooting airborne prey with liquid "arrows." At the **World of the Sea Aquarium**, four 55,000-gallon tanks feature kelp-bed fish, a coral reef and the world's first Pacific blacktip born in captivity.*

***Rocky Point Preserve*** ★★★★★ Resembling the rocky California coastline, this 700,000-gallon pool houses the world's largest display of Atlantic and Pacific bottlenose dolphins. Visitors are invited to participate in their feedings and observe them surfing waves created by a machine. Residing in an adjacent pool are Alaskan sea otters rescued from the oil spill in Prince William Sound. Visitors are kept abreast of their rehabilitation through videos and displays.

***The Penguin Encounter*** ★★★★ Sea World's most charming creatures live here in an icy den of snow-capped rocks, freezing waters and blustery breezes. As visitors drift by on a moving beltway, the little guys waddle across the floor, dive into their seapool and zoom around underwater. Occasionally they cock their heads at you through the viewing window as if to say, "What's the big deal?" To many people, the Penguin Encounter is a big deal. The simulated polar world is the largest penguin home away from home. Hundreds of the flightless birds live where the light is arctic dim and the air is a penguin-comfy 28°F. Next door in a similar room are dozens of alcids, arctic birds that look like a cross between a parrot and a duck. Actually a relative of penguins, alcids have wonderfully bizarre names like buffleheads, puffins, smews and murres. If you have small kids, take them to the alcids: They'll love seeing the strange creatures and learning to pronounce their names.

*TIPS:* After stepping off the beltway, guests can take longer looks at the birds from a separate viewing area. There's also a Learning Hall where exhibits and videos detail penguin research and exploration.

***Shamu's Happy Harbor*** ★★★★ "I wish you hadn't shown them this. I'll never get them out," lamented one mom after dad brought the kids here. Getting small fry to leave is a common problem, and little wonder: It's filled with stuff kids love best. There are tunnels to roam and water muskets to fire, bells to clang and wheels to turn.

---

## GLASS WITH CLASS

*Tucked away in a small shop between the Skytower and the Forbidden Reef, a true artisan practices his craft. Ruben Ducheny fashions delicate whales, dolphins, seals and other marine creatures out of shimmering handblown glass. A third-generation glassblower, he has been creating these works of art at Sea World since the park opened in 1964. Stop by and see this very talented man do his thing.*

There are shallow pools and rigging-net ladders, and rooms where children can wade thigh-high in plastic balls. All day, jubilant kids pour across the two-and-a-half-acre playground, testing one gadget after another. The crowd favorite is a 55-foot pirate galleon with zillions of places to run, climb and hide. For parents, there's a sheltered area with good views of the kids and (yes!) plenty of seats for resting those aching feet.

*TIPS:* To play, kids must be between 37 and 61 inches tall.

*Plaza del Sol* ★★   The name seems to imply an outdoor marketplace with food vendors and souvenirs, but Plaza del Sol is actually an indoor exhibit, Sea World's tribute to Latino culture, a large and important part of the Southern California population. The colorful displays feature exploration of various parts of Latino life including music, sports and education. Attractions include videos, touch screens and interactive features such as bongo drums you can really bang on.

*TIPS:* The future of Plaza del Sol may some day include musicians and other live Latino entertainment. For right now, it's just an exhibit, but a nice, air-conditioned place with things to tinker on.

*Clydesdale Hamlet* ★★   What has four legs, is six feet tall and weighs more than a ton? Answer: A Clydesdale, and Sea World is home for six of these huge animals. Horses at a marine park? Go figure. The world-famous animals are owned by Sea World's parent company, Anheuser-Busch, which is how they ended up sharing their turf with Shamu.

*TIPS:* Small children delight in these creatures as their sheer size and bulk are really something to see.

*Shark Encounter* ★★★★   The spectacular, three-part exhibit allows visitors to view sharks from above, below and within their environment. No, you're not expected to dive in, but you'll actually walk along a transparent tunnel through the center of the shark tank. There's nothing like being face to face with nine-foot tiger sharks, moray eels and hundreds of tropical fish. You enter the exhibit along a sandy path surrounded by palms. In the distance you'll see ominous-looking shark fins circling about a lagoon. The path takes you down into a 400,000-gallon tank filled with lemon, nurse, bull, brown and leopard sharks. Don't miss the chance to see these sea scaries up close.

*TIPS:* Kids of all ages give this attraction high marks because, as one eight-year-old said, "It's like being inside a big aquarium." They also like being able to walk through again—and again—and again.

---

*Sharks smell a single ounce of blood in a million ounces of water.*

---

**Wild Arctic ★★★★** Sea World has creatively packaged this exhibit of Arctic animals into a theme attraction featuring the only ride in the park. Visitors first board the jet helicopter (à la flight simulator) for a flight over the frozen north, soaring over rocky glaciers and tumbling through an avalanche. The helicopter lands, and guests exit into Base Station Arctic where resident scientists are ostensibly there to explore two capsized sailing ships from a century-old wreck. The base station has lots of neat areas to explore, as well as windows and decks for above- and below-water viewing of native Arctic mammals such as polar bears, walruses and beluga whales.

Creators have taken great pains to carry out the research station theme here, from the long johns hanging on the clothesline, to the snowshoes and jackets piled hastily in a corner. The vast pools of chilled (and chilly!) salt water are nattily disguised, with plenty of "ice" and "glaciers" to simulate the Arctic. If you're lucky, you may catch a glimpse of "researchers" venturing out into the terrain via kayak, and there are plenty of "resident scientists" on hand to answer questions. There are also interactive touch screens and cameras for getting a closer look. Interestingly, the attraction is based on a real event; the disappearance of the sailing ships *Erebus* and *Terror* in the Arctic in 1845. One little extra: Being that it's in the Arctic, this is one of the coolest places in the park.

*TIPS:* As the park's only ride, this attraction has the longest lines and is most crowded between 11 a.m. and 2 p.m.

*ANOTHER TIP:* The attraction has two theaters for the helicopter portion: one with motion and one without (ask which line is for which). If you'd like to skip the helicopter ride entirely, you can ask to be let into the Base Station through the gift shop.

## The Rides

**The Skytower ★★★** Often called "the needle in the sky," this ink-blue tower rises a skinny 320 feet from the center of the park. A round, windowed elevator ferries people back and forth to the summit and looks like a top in slow motion spiraling up and down a string. A ride on the Skytower will cost you $2 extra. The 15-minute vertical voyage is quiet, leisurely and scenic, and the view from the top is enough to make your day. Whether it's worth the extra bucks is, of course, a matter of opinion.

*TIPS:* Some preschoolers are frightened when they see the ground start to shrink below. Older kids, however, love it.

**Bayside Skyride** ★★★ Almost every theme park in America has one of these skyrides where you board a hanging gondola for a bird's-eye view of the activity below. Sea World's gondola ride reaches a height of 100 feet for a half-mile roundtrip journey over the park and Mission Bay. Like the Skytower, this attraction costs an extra $2.

*TIPS:* Small children and even adults who are afraid of heights may find this ride a bit unnerving.

## Sea World Dining

The **Harborside Cafe** is the only full-service restaurant at Sea World and a good choice for a quiet, leisurely meal. The food is a cut above what you'll find in the rest of the park. The menu is limited to a few fresh, crisp salads, grilled chicken and fish, and hamburgers and sandwiches. If the weather is fine, ask for an umbrella table on the bayside deck. Budget to moderate.

For a quick budget meal, Sea World visitors have the choice of several casual cafeteria and takeout eateries. **The Ranch House Grill** serves up decent salads and smoked, mesquite-grilled chicken and ribs. The park's largest eatery, **Mama Stella's Kitchen**, is a large, efficient cafeteria serving pizza, pasta and other Italian specialties. Freshly carved turkey and roast beef sandwiches are featured at the **Hospitality Center Deli**.

## Sea World Shopping

Sea World's few shops are of the souvenir variety and offer little in the way of interesting browsing. For those who insist on a campy memento, there are stuffed Shamus, dolphins and sea lions, shark hand puppets and an assortment of ocean-themed T-shirts.

## Sea World Nightlife

San Diegans usually wait until the summer season to visit Sea World, when the park comes alive after dark with Summer Nights. Special night shows are offered at both Shamu Stadium and Sea Lion and Otter Stadium. Bands perform throughout the park, and every evening concludes with a brilliant fireworks spectacular that reflects in the pools, ponds and adjacent bay. Summer Nights takes place Memorial Day through Labor Day; the park is open until 10 p.m. weeknights and 11 p.m. on weekends; Summer Nights is included with regular admission.

# SIX

## Orange County Day Trips

If you need an escape—or just a breather—from the ultimate escape itself, you don't have to travel far to find it. Active cities, picturesque towns, beaches, parks, the ocean, museums, theater—you name it, they're all practically on your doorstep. Disneyland and Knott's Berry Farm are by no means the only thing going in Orange County.

Within only a few miles of the theme parks, Anaheim and Buena Park offer numerous attractions. Away from the urban crush, Orange County has soft beaches galore, curving hills, ocean bluffs and towns along its fabled "Gold Coast" that are separate and unique. Do not fail to take a leisurely drive along Route 1, the coast road that parallels the ocean through most of the state and is lovingly known as the Pacific Coast Highway. It may just lead you to the perfect California beach town.

Seal Beach, Orange County's answer to small-town America, is a pretty community with a sense of serenity. To the south lies Huntington Beach, a place that claims the nickname "Surfing Capital of the World." The social capital of this beachside society is Newport Beach.

There's more. Corona del Mar is a model community with quiet streets and a placid waterfront. Laguna Beach shelters an artist colony, along with spectacular beach coves. Dana Point represents an ultramodern marina development. San Juan Capistrano, a small town surrounding an old mission, is closer to its roots than any place in this futuristic area.

Among them these coastal towns offer an amusement park, marine preserves, fishing piers, shopping malls, historic sights and miles of white-sand beach. All are splendid diversions when you tire of the hot, crowded theme-park scene. Since Newport Beach and Laguna

Beach are located so conveniently close to the Disneyland area, you might even consider alternating days at the theme park with days at the beach. Or spend some time touring Orange County's inland realms, where you'll discover parks, children's museums and roads that lead east into the distant mountains.

## Anaheim-Buena Park Area

Located in a 1923 restored railroad station, **The Children's Museum** (301 South Euclid Street, La Habra; 562-905-9793; admission) is a hands-on learning center. With exhibits and programs devoted to science, history, the arts and humanities, children here can excavate fossil replicas or step on stage and make their theater debut, among other challenging adventures.

Far from being the only visitor attractions in the inland reaches of Orange County, the theme parks themselves have spawned the growth of other travel destinations. **Hobby City** (1238 South Beach Boulevard, Anaheim; 714-527-2323; admission) looks like a miniature Knott's Berry Farm, anchored by a "perfect half-scale replica" of the White House and featuring a doll and toy museum. There are thousands of dolls from around the world including special exhibits dating back to the time of the Egyptian pharaohs. Arranged in chronological order, the doll exhibits sweep through the Middle Ages all the way up to the height of the Cabbage Patch dynasty and the late Barbie period. A special display features dolls of the first ladies from Martha Washington through Jackie Kennedy. The entire complex is encircled by the wee tracks of the "Hobby City Choo Choo," a mini-train for kids. Also featured is an intriguing array of 24 specialized shops, each devoted entirely to the hobbyist and collector. Among them are baseball card, stamp, coin, gem, antique, stitchery and doll stores. Perhaps the most unique is a shop devoted to miniatures all built on the scale of one inch to the foot.

In the shadow of Knott's Berry Farm, **Movieland Wax Museum** (7711 Beach Boulevard, Buena Park; 714-522-1155; admission) spans the history of the film industry with more than 250 wax figures of stars ranging from Charlie Chaplin to Arnold Schwarzenegger. Realistic scenes of the stars in their best-known roles prompt many visitors to wax enthusiastic about the museum. Roseanne, Ed Asner, Gene Kelly, Michael Jackson and Mr. Spock are just a few of the

---

*One Wild Rivers water ride, The Abyss, plunges ten stories through a pitch-black tunnel.*

---

celebrities immortalized here. A special Chamber of Horrors brings alive the macabre from *Frankenstein* to *Friday the 13th*. Large scenes provide a detailed look at the Poseidon Adventure, and you'll also have a chance to see the spaceship *Enterprise*. A complete tour takes about two hours.

Located on a prehistoric fossil field that may be as extensive as the famed La Brea Tar Pits, **Ralph B. Clark Regional Park** (8800 Rosecrans Avenue, Buena Park; 714-670-8045; parking fee) offers tours of centuries-old fossil beds. Admission charge for tours (by reservation). This unique facility also features an interpretive center with fossil displays and a working paleontology lab. Providing marvelous educational opportunities, the digs and lab activities are structured as part of an organized tour program.

The **Discovery Museum of Orange County** (3101 West Harvard Street, Santa Ana; 714-540-0404; admission) is a blast from the past. This turn-of-the-century, living-history museum re-creates the region's early days in four turn-of-the-century buildings spread across an 11-acre site. Children can dress up in period clothing, listen to a victrola, pump water from a well, do laundry with a scrub board and enjoy a guided tour of the orchard. Closed Monday, Tuesday and Saturday.

The largest store of its kind in America, **Doll City USA** (2080 South Harbor Boulevard, Anaheim; 714-750-3585) is a 6000-square-foot extravaganza. Thousands of dolls are featured, ranging in price from $3.99 to $14,000. The modern collectibles include the best work of the world's leading doll makers. Closed Sunday.

Serpentine descents, tube rides, swimming pools and jacuzzis make **Wild Rivers** (8770 Irvine Center Drive, Irvine; 714-768-9453; admission) Orange County's ultimate waterfront attraction. Flume rides, swirling rapids, waterslides, wading pools, river safaris and bodysurfing are all part of the fun. Some popular rides, like the white-water trip down Wild Rivers Mountain, are off-limits for small children. But miniature versions of the most popular thrill rides do give the little ones a taste of big-time fun. The major pools all have lifeguards, and a wave pool creates an ideal boogie-boarding envi-

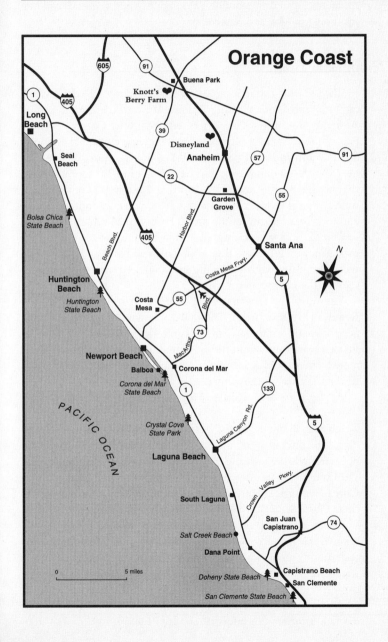

Orange Coast

ronment. Open daily from June through August; weekends and holidays only in May and September.

## Huntington Beach

It's hard to beat a stretch of coastline that's up there in the mythology of surfing with Hawaii's Waimea Bay and the great breaks of Australia. Since the 1920s, surfers with boards have been as much a part of the seascape as blue skies and billowing clouds. They paddle around **Huntington Pier** (end of Main Street), poised to catch the next wave that pounds the pilings. First built in 1904 for oil drilling, the pier has been damaged by storms and extensively repaired four times. The last monster storm hit in 1988, when 20-foot waves tore 250 feet from the end of the pier. The new pier, which opened in July 1992, is 1856 feet long, 38 feet above the water and has a life expectancy of 100 years. But, as anyone who has lived by the ocean will agree, that century-long life span could be shortened dramatically by the next winter storm.

Stop in at the **International Surfing Museum Huntington Beach** (411 Olive Street; 714-960-3483; admission) for a historic perspective on Southern California's favorite pastime. The showplace sits two blocks away from the beach and features boards, boards, and more boards as well as an array of surfing paraphernalia. Closed Monday and Tuesday in the winter.

At the **Newland House Museum** (19820 Beach Boulevard; 714-962-5777) visitors can see what life in 19th-century Huntington Beach was all about. Listed on the National Register of Historic Places and built in 1898, the house is filled with furnishings and antiques from the town's early days. Closed Monday, Tuesday and Friday.

In addition to its many beaches, Huntington Beach features **Bolsa Chica Ecological Reserve** (accessways across from the entrance to Bolsa Chica State Beach and at Warner Avenue). An important wetlands area dotted with islands and overgrown in cord grass and pickleweed, this 300-acre preserve features a mile-and-a-half long loop trail. Among the hundreds of animals inhabiting or visiting the marsh are egrets, herons and five endangered species. There is an interpretive center with scientific displays, educational materials and trail guides. Reserve is always open; interpretive center is open Tuesday through Saturday. For information, call 714-897-7003 or 714-960-9939.

## HUNTINGTON BEACH DINING

At **Louise's Trattoria** (300 Pacific Coast Highway; 714-960-0996), you can dine on fine Italian cuisine for reasonable prices. Try one of their fresh pasta dishes, such as rigatoni with grilled vegetables tossed in olive oil, or a California-style pizza with one of their inventive salads. The restaurant is open and airy with modern decor, plenty of windows, and a patio overlooking the ocean for open-air dining. A separate kids' menu features chicken fingers, small pizzas and cheese raviolis. Moderate.

The **Harbor House Café** (16341 Pacific Coast Highway; 562-592-5404) is one of those hole-in-the-wall places packed with local folks. In this case it's "open 24 hours, 365 days a year" and has been around since 1939. Add knotty-pine walls covered with black-and-whites of your favorite movies stars and you've got a coastal classic. The menu, as you may have surmised, includes hamburgers and sandwiches. Actually, it's pretty varied—in addition to croissant and pita-bread sandwiches there are Mexican dishes, seafood platters, chicken entrées and omelettes, with the option of kid-sized portions. Budget to moderate.

Close to Huntington Beach and dating back to 1930, the **Glide 'er Inn** (1400 Pacific Coast Highway, Seal Beach; 562-431-3022) is an unusual landmark indeed. The motif is aviation, as in model airplanes dangling from the ceiling and aeronautical pictures covering every inch of available wall space. The menu is covered with depictions of biplanes and, almost as an afterthought, includes an extensive list of seafood selections as well as European dishes like wiener-schnitzel and veal smetana (sautéed in light cream with mushrooms). There's also a separate children's menu. Moderate.

## HUNTINGTON BEACH BEACHES AND PARKS

A local favorite tucked in between Huntington Beach and Long Beach, **Seal Beach** features a swath of fine-grain sand and a fishing pier. The swimming is good, and surfers can be seen riding the good breaks at the pier around 13th Street.

With three miles of fluffy sand, **Bolsa Chica State Beach** (714-846-3460) is another in a series of broad, beautiful beaches. There are regular grunion runs (in season) and rich clam beds. Since the summer surf is gentler here than at Huntington Beach, Bolsa Chica is ideal for swimmers and families. Big breakers for surfing spice up the winter months. Complete facilities, including beach rentals, restrooms, lifeguards, outdoor showers, picnic areas and a snack bar make Bolsa Chica a convenient place to spend the day.

One of Southern California's broadest strands, **Huntington State Beach** (714-536-1454) extends three miles along the Pacific Coast Highway. In addition to a desert of soft sand, it has those curling waves that surfers' dreams (and movies) are made from. Pismo clams lie buried in the sand, a bike path parallels the water and there is a five-acre preserve for endangered least terns. Before you decide to move here permanently, take heed: these natural wonders are sandwiched between industrial plants and offshore oil derricks.

Located immediately to the north, **Huntington City Beach** (714-536-5280) runs several miles more and features a five-acre preserve for endangered least terns.

## Newport Beach

The main resort town on the Orange County coast, Newport Beach is a mélange of manmade islands and peninsulas surrounding a small bay. For help finding your bearings around this labyrinth of waterways, contact the **Newport Harbor Area Chamber of Commerce** (1470 Jamboree Road; 714-729-4400) or the **Newport Beach Conference & Visitors Bureau** (3300 West Coast Highway; 714-722-1611, 800-942-6278).

Although it cannot compete with Laguna Beach as an art center, the town does offer the **Orange County Museum of Art** (850 San Clemente Drive; 714-759-1122; admission). Specializing in contemporary art, this facility possesses perhaps the finest collection of post–World War II California art in existence. Closed Monday.

One of Newport Beach's prettiest neighborhoods is **Balboa Island**, comprising two manmade islets in the middle of Newport Bay. It can be reached by bridge along Marine Avenue or via a short ferry ride from Balboa Peninsula. Walk the pathways that circumnavigate both islands and you will pass clapboard cottages, Cape Cod homes and modern block-design houses that seem made entirely of glass. While sailboats sit moored along the waterfront, streets that are little more than alleys lead into the center of the island.

The central piece in this jigsaw puzzle of manmade plots is **Balboa Peninsula**, a long, narrow finger of land bounded by Newport Bay and the open ocean. High point of the peninsula is **Balboa**

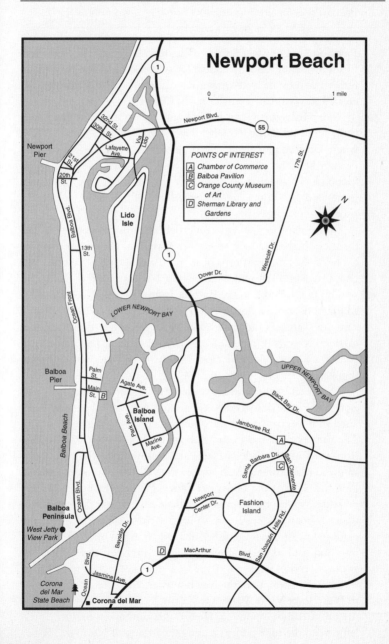

# Newport Beach

0 _____ 1 mile

POINTS OF INTEREST
- A  Chamber of Commerce
- B  Balboa Pavilion
- C  Orange County Museum of Art
- D  Sherman Library and Gardens

Newport Blvd.

55

17th St.

Westcliff Dr.

32nd St.
30th St.
Lafayette Ave.
Via Lido
21st St.
20th St.

Newport Pier

Balboa Blvd.

Lido Isle

13th St.

Ocean Front

Dover Dr.

LOWER NEWPORT BAY

UPPER NEWPORT BAY

Balboa Pier

Palm St.
Main St.  B

Agate Ave.

Back Bay Dr.

Park Ave.

Balboa Island

Marine Ave.

Jamboree Rd.

A

Santa Barbara Dr.

San Clemente

C

Balboa Beach

Fashion Island

Newport Center Dr.

Balboa Peninsula

West Jetty View Park

Ocean Blvd.

Bayside Dr.

D

MacArthur  Blvd.

San Joaquin Hills Rd.

Corona del Mar State Beach

Ocean Blvd.

Jasmine Ave.

1

■ Corona del Mar

*Balboa Pavilion hosted the nation's first surfing tournament in 1932.*

**Pavilion** (end of Main Street), a Victorian landmark that dates back to 1905 when it was a bathhouse for swimmers in ankle-length outfits. Marked by its well-known cupola, the bayfront building once created its own dance sensation, the "Balboa."

Today Balboa Pavilion is the home of a waterfront amusement park, **The Fun Zone** (600 East Bay Avenue, Balboa; 714-673-0408), where kids can practice defensive driving in a bumper car, ride the Ferris wheel and merry-go-round or take a dark ride through the funhouse. In addition, they can try their hand at skee ball, video games and pinball machines. To see more of the harbor area, rent a pedal or pontoon boat.

Cruise ships to Catalina Island debark from the dock here, and there are harbor cruises offered by **Catalina Passenger Service** (714-673-5245; admission) aboard the *Pavilion Queen*, a mock riverboat that motors around the Newport Bay mazeway.

This is also home to the **Balboa Island Ferry** (714-673-1070), a kind of floating landmark that has shuttled between Balboa Peninsula and Balboa Island since 1919. A simple, single-deck ferry that carries three cars (for about $1.50 each) and sports a pilot house the size of a phone booth, it crosses the narrow waterway every few minutes.

The beach scene in this seaside city extends for over five miles along the Pacific side of Balboa Peninsula. A broad, white-sand beach lined with lifeguard stands and houses reaches along the entire length. The centers of attention and amenities are **Newport Pier** (Balboa Boulevard and McFadden Place) and **Balboa Pier** (Balboa Boulevard and Main Street). At Newport Pier, also known as McFadden's Pier, the skiffs of the **Newport Dory Fishing Fleet** are beached every day while local fishermen sell their catches. This flotilla of small, wooden boats has been here so long it has achieved historic landmark status. At dawn the fishermen sail ten miles offshore, set trawl lines and haul in the mackerel, flounder, rock fish and halibut sold at the afternoon market.

To capture a sense of the true beauty around you, take a walk out to **West Jetty View Park** (Ocean Boulevard at Channel Road) at the tip of Balboa Peninsula. Here civilization meets the sea. To the left extend the rock jetties forming the mouth of Newport Harbor.

Behind you are the plate-glass houses of the city. A wide beach, tufted with ice plants and occasional palm trees, forms another border. This is also the place where the truly courageous (or the truly crazy) challenge the waves at "The Wedge." Known to bodysurfers around the world, the area between the jetty and beach is one of the finest and most dangerous shore breaks anywhere, the "Mount Everest of bodysurfing."

The richness of the natural environment is evident as well when you venture through **Upper Newport Bay Ecological Reserve** (Back Bay Drive; 714-640-6746). The road passes limestone bluffs and sandstone hills. Reeds and cattails line the shore. Southern California's largest estuary, the bay is a vital stopping place for migrating birds on the Pacific Flyway. Over 200 species can be seen here, and two endangered species, Belding's savannah sparrow and the light-footed clapper rail, live along the bay.

NEWPORT BEACH LODGING

You'd have a heckuva time docking your boat at the **Sail Inn Motel** (2627 Newport Boulevard; 714-675-1841, fax 714-673-1057 [let it ring seven times]). Actually it's on an island, but the "island" is a median strip dividing the two busiest streets on the Balboa Peninsula. Offering 17 standard motel rooms, the Sail Inn is a block from the beach and walking distance from many restaurants. It's also just one mile from the rides and arcade games of the Fun Zone at Balboa Pavilion. Moderate to deluxe.

The **Balboa Inn** (105 Main Street; 714-675-3412, fax 714-673-4587), next to the beach at Balboa Pier, is a Spanish-style hotel built in 1929. With its cream-colored walls and tile-roofed tower, this 34-room hostelry is vintage Southern California. Adding to the ambience is a swimming pool that looks out on the water. Kids will have a ball building sandcastles and paddling around in the Pacific. At night they can head over to join the crowd at the Fun Zone. The rooms, some of which have ocean views, are furnished in knotty pine, decorated with colorful prints and supplied with jacuzzis, brass fixtures and fireplaces. Suites are ideal for families. Deluxe to ultra-deluxe.

By way of full-facility destinations, Southern California–style, few places match the **Hyatt Newporter Resort** (1107 Jamboree Road; 714-729-1234, 800-233-1234, fax 714-644-1552). Situated on a hillside above Upper Newport Bay, it sprawls across 26 acres and sports three swimming pools, a wading pool, three jacuzzis, a nine-hole pitch-and-putt course, a tennis club and ping-pong. Within walking distance is the Back Bay area featuring playgrounds, excellent beaches and swimming. Kids' meals are available at the restaurants, and Camp Hyatt, a supervised children's program, operates from 6 p.m. to 10 p.m. on Friday and Saturday, and 9 a.m. to 3 p.m. on Sunday, April through September. Beautifully landscaped with a series of terraced patios, the resort features a lavishly decorated lobby. Guest rooms are modern in design, comfortably furnished and tastefully appointed. An inviting combination of elegance and amenities. Ultra-deluxe.

## NEWPORT BEACH DINING

Everything in Newport Beach was built last week. Everything, that is, except **The Cannery Restaurant and Cruises** (3010 Lafayette Avenue; 714-675-5777). This 1921 fish cannery is today much as it was way back when. The conveyor belts and pulleys are still here, their gears exposed; and there are fire wagons, a fierce-looking boiler and more tin cans than you can imagine. All are part of a waterfront seafood restaurant that serves lunch, dinner and weekend brunch at deluxe prices. Special children's meals feature hamburgers, chicken and fried fish. Ultra-deluxe weekend brunch cruises aboard a 58-foot boat are also offered.

You won't miss **The Crab Cooker** (2200 Newport Boulevard; 714-673-0100). First, it's painted bright red; second, it's located at a busy intersection near Newport Pier; last, the place has been a local institution since the 1950s. Actually, you don't *want* to miss this crabby place. The informal eatery, where lunch and dinner are served on paper plates, has crab (surprise!) as well as fish, scallops, shrimp and oysters. A skewer of cod comes on the children's plate. A fish market is attached to the restaurant, so freshness and quality are assured. Moderate to deluxe.

Around **Balboa Pavilion** you'll find snack bars and amusement-park food stands that are particularly convenient for families.

A place nearby that's worth recommending is **Newport Landing** (503 East Edgewater Avenue; 714-675-2373), a double-decker affair where you can lounge downstairs in a wood-paneled dining room or upstairs on a deck overlooking the harbor. Serving lunch, dinner and weekend brunch, it specializes in fresh fish and also features hickory-smoked prime rib and chicken with artichokes. Special kids' choices include hamburgers, grilled-cheese sandwiches and spaghetti. Lunch is moderate, dinner is deluxe.

Who could imagine that at the end of Balboa Pier there would be a vintage 1940s-era diner complete with art deco curves and red plastic booths? **Ruby's Diner** (1 Balboa Pier; 714-675-7829) is a classic. Besides that it provides 270 views of the ocean. Of course the menu, whether breakfast, lunch or dinner, contains little more than omelettes, hamburgers, sandwiches, chili and salads. Kids' meals include cheeseburgers and grilled-cheese sandwiches with fries. Budget.

Because there are very few restaurants on Balboa Island, one place stands out: **Amelia's** (311 Marine Avenue; 714-673-6580), a family-run restaurant serving Italian dishes and seafood, is a local institution. At lunch you'll find them serving a handful of pasta dishes, fresh fish, sandwiches and salads. Then in the evening the chef prepares calamari stuffed with crab, scallops, Icelandic cod, bouillabaisse, veal piccata and another round of pasta platters. No breakfast, but they serve Sunday brunch. Kids' portions are available. Moderate to deluxe.

If you were hoping to spend a little less money, **Wilma's Patio** (225 Marine Avenue; 714-675-5542) is just down the street. It's a family-style restaurant—open morning, noon and night—that serves multicourse American and Mexican meals. Kids can order from a special menu that has space on the back for crayon artwork. Smaller portions of many items, ranging from dollar pancakes to hot dogs, are available year-round. Budget to moderate.

Ironically enough, one of Newport Beach's top dining bargains lies at the heart of the region's priciest shopping malls. Encircling the lower level of **Fashion Island** (Newport Center, 401 Newport Center Drive; 714-721-2000) is a collection of stands dispensing sushi, soup and sandwiches, Mexican food, pasta salads, burgers and other light fare. Budget to moderate.

---

*SURF'S UP*

*In the 1960s, brassy sounds of Newport Beach's Big Bands surrendered to the twanging strains of electric guitars as the Orange Coast earned the nickname "Surfer Heaven." Dick Dale, the "King of the Surf Guitar," hit the top of the charts with "Pipeline," setting off a wave that the Beach Boys and Jan and Dean rode to the crest. Down in Dana Point, local boy Bruce Brown contributed to the coast culture in 1966 with a surf flick called* The Endless Summer, *which achieved cult status and earned for its director a reputation as "the Fellini of foam."*

---

*Sea stars, urchins, crabs and octopuses serve as the entertainment at Little Corona del Mar Tidepool Reserve.*

---

## NEWPORT BEACH BEACHES AND PARKS

In addition to the beach that extends the entire length of Balboa Peninsula, you'll want to consider several other spots.

**Newport Dunes RV Resort** (1131 Back Bay Drive; 714-729-3863; admission) is a private facility with a broad, horseshoe-shaped beach about one-half mile in length. It curves around the lake-like waters of Upper Newport Bay, one mile inland from the ocean. Very popular with families and campers, it offers a wide range of activities, including volleyball, playground activities and boat rentals. There are also restrooms, a snack bar, groceries, picnic areas, laundry, pool, jacuzzi and beach rentals. Swimming is fine, with lifeguards on duty in the summer.

Located at the mouth of Newport Harbor, **Corona del Mar State Beach** (714-644-3047) offers an opportunity to watch sailboats tacking in and out of the bay. Throngs congregate because of its easy access, landscaped lawn and excellent facilities. It's well protected for swimming, and also popular for surfing, sailing and fishing. Located at Jasmine Avenue and Ocean Boulevard in Corona del Mar.

**Little Corona del Mar State Beach** (Poppy Avenue and Ocean Boulevard, Corona del Mar; 714-644-3047) is another in the proud line of pocket beaches along the Orange Coast. This preserve includes the **Corona del Mar Tidepool Reserve**, where classes and tours of the tidepools are held. The bluff to the north consists of sandstone that has been contorted into a myriad of magnificent lines. There's a marsh behind the beach thick with reeds and cattails. Fishing is good from the rocks. The beach is also popular with swimmers, surfers, snorkelers and skindivers.

## Laguna Beach Area

Another stop on Orange County's cavalcade of coastal cities is Laguna Beach. Framed by the San Joaquin hills, the place is an intaglio of coves and bluffs, sand beaches and rock outcroppings. It conjures images of the Mediterranean with deep bays and greenery running to the sea's edge. Little wonder that Laguna, with its wealthy residents and leisurely beachfront, has become synonymous with the chic but informal style of Southern California. Its long tradition as an artist colony adds to this sense of beauty and bounty.

Part of Laguna's artistic tradition is the **Festival of the Arts and Pageant of the Masters** (Irvine Bowl, 650 Laguna Canyon Road; 714-494-1145; admission), staged every year during July and August. While the festival displays the work of 160 local artists and crafts-people, the Pageant of the Masters is the high point, an event you *absolutely must not miss*. It presents a series of *tableaux vivants* in which local residents, dressed to resemble figures from famous paintings, remain motionless against a frieze that re-creates the painting. Elaborate make-up and lighting techniques flatten the figures and create a sense of two-dimensionality.

During the 1960s, freelance artists, excluded from the more formal Festival of the Arts, founded the **Sawdust Festival** (935 Laguna Canyon Road; 714-494-3030; admission) across the street. Over the years this fair, too, has pretty much joined the establishment, but it still provides an opportunity to wander along sawdust-covered paths past hundreds of arts-and-crafts displays accompanied by musicians and jugglers. It also runs from late June to late August and has hands-on craftsmaking booths for children.

Laguna Beach's artistic heritage is evident in the many galleries and studios around town. The **Laguna Beach Visitors Bureau and Chamber of Commerce** (252 Broadway; 714-494-1018), with its maps and brochures, can help direct you. They can also assist with hotel and restaurant reservations.

Beauty in Laguna is not only found on canvases. The coastline is particularly pretty and well worth exploring. One of the most enchanting areas is along **Heisler Park** (Cliff Drive), a winding promenade set on the cliffs above the ocean. Here you can relax on the lawn, sit beneath a palm tree and gaze out on the horizon. There are broad vistas out along the coast and down to the wave-whitened shoreline. Paths from the park descend to a series of coves with tidepools and sandy beaches. The surrounding rocks, twisted by geologic pressure into curving designs, rise in a series of protective bluffs.

DANA POINT   South on Route 1, you will pass through Dana Point. This ultramodern enclave, with its manmade port and 2500-boat marina, has a history dating back to the 1830s when Richard Henry Dana immortalized the place. Writing in *Two Years Before the Mast*, the Boston gentleman-turned-sailor described the surrounding countryside: "There was a grandeur in everything around."

---

*The swallows returning to Capistrano come all the way from Argentina!*

---

Today much of the grandeur has been replaced with condominiums, leaving little for the sightseer. There is the **Orange County Marine Institute** (24200 Dana Point Harbor Drive; 714-496-2274) with a small sea-life aquarium (open Saturday and Sunday only) and a 130-foot replica of Dana's brig, *The Pilgrim* (open Sunday only). They also lead evening cruises (admission) on weekends and selected weekdays.

Then, for a lighthouse keeper's view of the harbor and outlying coastline, take in either of the **lookout points** at the ends of Old Golden Lantern and Blue Lantern streets.

SAN JUAN CAPISTRANO    Seventh in the state's chain of 21 missions, **Mission San Juan Capistrano** (Camino Capistrano and Ortega Highway; 714-248-2048; admission) was founded in 1776 by Father Junípero Serra. Considered "the jewel of the missions" it is a hauntingly beautiful site, placid and magical.

There are ponds and gardens here, ten acres of standing adobe buildings and the ruins of the original 1797 stone church, destroyed by an earthquake in 1812. The museum displays American Indian crafts, early ecclesiastical artifacts and Spanish weaponry, while an Indian cemetery memorializes the enslaved people who built this magnificent structure.

The highlight of the mission is not the swallows, which are vastly outnumbered by pigeons, but the chapel, a 1777 structure decorated with Indian designs and a baroque altar. The oldest continually used building in California, it is the only remaining church previously used by Father Serra.

Of course the mission's claim to fame is the 1939 ditty, "When the Swallows Return to Capistrano." The tune, like many schmaltzy songs about California, seems to remain eternally lodged in the memory whether you want it there or not. The melody describes the return of flocks of swallows every March 19. And return they do, though in ever-decreasing numbers and not always on March 19. There is also a living-history program (admission) on the last Saturday of every month, with costumed "characters" playing the role of Father Serra and others, and craftspeople showing how old-time crafts were made.

At the **O'Neill Museum** (31831 Los Rios Street; 714-493-8444; admission), housed in a tiny, 1870s Victorian, there are walking-tour maps of the town's old adobes. Within a few blocks you'll discover about a dozen 19th-century structures. The museum is furnished with Victorian decor. Closed Monday and Saturday.

The **Capistrano Depot** (26701 Verdugo Street; 714-488-7600) appeared a little later in the century but is an equally vital part of the town's history. Still operating as a train station, the 1895 depot has been beautifully preserved. Built of brick in a series of Spanish-style arches, the old structure houses a variety of railroad memorabilia. An antique pullman, a brightly colored freight car and other vintage cars line the tracks.

## LAGUNA BEACH AREA LODGING

Boasting 70 rooms, a pool, spa and sundeck overlooking the sea, the **Inn at Laguna Beach** (211 North Coast Highway; 714-497-9722, 800-544-4479, fax 714-497-9972) offers great ocean views from its blufftop perch. Rooms are small, the construction uneven and the furnishings modern at this coastside property. Ultra-deluxe.

Even if you never stay there, you won't miss the **Hotel Laguna** (425 South Coast Highway; 714-494-1151, 800-524-2927, fax 714-497-2163). With its octagonal tower and Spanish motif, this huge, whitewashed building dominates downtown Laguna Beach. The oldest hotel in Laguna, it sits in the center of town, adjacent to Main Beach. In addition to 65 guest rooms there are a restaurant, lounge and a casual lobby terrace. The place shows signs of age and suffers some of the ills characteristic of large, old hotels. But for a place on the water *and* at the center of the action, it cannot be matched. Kids

---

### TUCKED IN FOR THE NIGHT

*A secluded canyon is the home of **Aliso Creek Inn and Golf Resort** (31106 South Coast Highway, Laguna Beach; 714-499-2271, 800-223-3309, fax 714-499-4601), an appealing, 83-acre resort complete with swimming pools, jacuzzi, Ben Brown's restaurant, lounge and nine-hole golf course. Particularly attractive for families, every unit includes a sitting area, patio and kitchen. Removed from the highway but within 400 yards of a beach, the resort is surrounded by steep hillsides populated by deer and raccoon. Tying this easy rusticity together is a small creek that tumbles through the resort. Studios and one-bedroom suites are deluxe to ultra-deluxe, two-bedroom complexes are ultra-deluxe. Kids* will enjoy the playground on the beach in front of the hotel. Deluxe to ultra-deluxe.

The premier resting place in Laguna Beach is a sprawling, 157-room establishment overhanging the sand. The **Surf & Sand Hotel** (1555 South Coast Highway; 714-497-4477, 800-524-8621, fax 714-494-2897) is a blocky, 1950s-era complex, an architectural mélange of five buildings and a shopping mall. The accent here is on the ocean: nearly every room has a sea view and private balcony, the pool sits just above the sand, and the beach, perfect for the kids, is a short step away. During weekends in the summer, the hotel staff will provide children's activities. A full-service hotel, the Surf & Sand has two restaurants and an art deco lounge. Guest rooms are understated but attractive with raw-silk furnishings, unfinished woods and sand-hued walls. Ultra-deluxe.

Accommodations with kitchen facilities are hard to come by in Laguna Beach. You'll find them in most of the units at **Capri Laguna** (1441 South Coast Highway; 714-494-6533, 800-225-4551, fax 714-497-6962), a multilevel, 46-unit motel on the beach. It provides contemporary, motel-style furnishings, plus a pool, sauna, workout room and sundeck with barbecue facilities ideal for families. Ultra-deluxe.

The **Ritz-Carlton Laguna Niguel** (1 Ritz-Carlton Drive, Dana Point; 714-240-2000, 800-287-2706, fax 714-240-0829), set on a cliff above the Pacific, is simply the finest resort hotel along the California coast. Built in the fashion of a Mediterranean villa, it dominates a broad sweep of coastline, a 393-room mansion replete with gourmet restaurants and dark-wood lounges. An Old World interior of arched windows and Italian marble is decorated with one of the finest hotel collections of 19th-century American and English art anywhere. The grounds are landscaped with willows, sycamores and a spectrum of flowering plants. Tile courtyards lead to two swimming pools, a pair of jacuzzis, four tennis courts and a fitness and massage center. A room for videos, video games and ping-pong provides entertainment for the kids, and there are also special supervised kids' programs during the summer holiday periods. The guest rooms are equal in luxury to the rest of the resort. Ultra-deluxe.

Most motels have a stream of traffic whizzing past outside, but the **Dana Marina Inn Motel** (34111 Coast Highway, Dana Point; 714-496-1300), situated on an island where the highway divides, manages to have traffic on both sides! The reason we're mentioning it is not because we're mean but because rooms in this 29-unit facility are inexpensive. The accommodations are roadside-motel style. Budget.

While San Juan Capistrano is lacking in accommodations, you'll find several places in neighboring San Clemente. **Algodon Motel** (135 Avenida Algodon; 714-492-3382) is a standard-type, 18-unit facility several blocks from the beach. Some units have kitchens. Not much to write home about, but it is clean and affordable. Budget to moderate.

Cheaper still is the **Hostelling International—San Clemente Beach** (233 Avenida Granada, San Clemente; 714-492-2848, 202-783-6161), an AYH facility in a stucco building on a residential street. The accommodations consist of bunk beds in dormitory rooms; one family room is also available in the summer. Visitors share a television room, kitchen and small patio. Open May through October. Budget.

## LAGUNA BEACH AREA DINING

Laguna Beach is never at a loss for oceanfront restaurants. But somehow the sea seems closer and more intimate at **Laguna Village Cafe** (577 South Coast Highway; 714-494-6344), probably because this informal eatery is partially outdoors, with about half of the tables placed at the very edge of the coastal bluff. The menu is simple: egg dishes in the morning, and a single menu with salads, sandwiches and smoothies during the rest of the day. There are also house specialties like calamari, abalone, scallops amandine, teriyaki chicken, Chinese-style chicken and skewered shrimp dumplings. Budget to moderate.

The **Penguin Malt Shop** (981 South Coast Highway; 714-494-1353) is from another era entirely—the 1930s to be exact. A tiny café featuring counter jukeboxes and swivel stools, it's a time capsule with a kitchen. Breakfast and lunch are all-American affairs from ham and eggs to hamburgers and milkshakes. It's affordable, so what have you got to lose? Step on it and order a chocolate malt with a side of fries. Budget.

**The White House** (340 South Coast Highway; 714-494-8088) seems nearly as permanent a Laguna Beach fixture as the ocean. Dating to early in the century, this simple, wooden structure serves as bar (with live music seven nights a week), restaurant and local landmark. Paneled in dark wood and trimmed with wallpaper, the White House is lined with historic photos of Laguna Beach. You can drop by from early morning until late evening to partake of a menu that includes pasta, steak, chicken and seafood dishes. Moderate to deluxe.

Choose one place to symbolize the easy elegance of Laguna and it inevitably will be **Las Brisas** (361 Cliff Drive; 714-497-5434). Something about this whitewashed Spanish building with arched windows captures the natural-living-but-class-conscious style of the Southland. Its cliffside locale on the water is part of this ambience. Then there is the dual kitchen arrangement that permits formal dining in a white-tablecloth room or bistro dining on an outdoor patio. The menu consists of continental Mexican seafood dishes and other specialties from south of the border, as well as chicken, steak and pasta. Out on the patio you can choose from sandwiches, salads and appetizers. Moderate to deluxe.

The most remarkable aspect of the **Cottage Restaurant** (308 North Coast Highway; 714-494-3023) is the cottage itself, an early-20th-century California bungalow. The place has been neatly decorated with turn-of-the-century antiques, oil paintings and stained glass. Meal time in this historic house is a traditional American affair. They serve classic egg-and-bacon breakfasts, while lunch consists of salads and sandwiches plus specials like top sirloin, fresh fish and steamed vegetables. For dinner there are chicken fettuccine, top sirloin, broiled lamb, fresh shrimp and swordfish as well as daily fish specials. Special entrées for the small fry include a junior breakfast featuring dollar-sized pancakes as well as dinner specialties like linguine and hamburgers. Budget to moderate.

The **Harbor Grill** (34499 Golden Lantern Street, Dana Point; 714-240-1416), located in spiffy Dana Point Harbor, lacks the view and polish of its splashy neighbors. But this understated restaurant serves excellent seafood dishes. The menu includes fresh swordfish and salmon with pesto sauce, but the real attraction is the list of daily specials. These might include sea bass with black bean sauce, gumbo and other fishy delights. Lunch, dinner and Sunday brunch are served in a light, bright dining room with contemporary artwork. There is also patio dining. For the kids, they serve grilled cheese sandwiches, burgers, fish and chips, or a half order of anything on the menu. Moderate to deluxe.

If you'd prefer to dine alfresco overlooking the harbor, there's **Proud Mary's** (34689 Golden Lantern Street, Dana Point; 714-493-5853), a hole-in-the-wall where you can order sandwiches, hot dogs, hamburgers and a few chicken and steak platters, then dine on picnic tables outside. They also have a full breakfast menu and a separate kids' menu. Budget.

Japanese food in these parts is spelled **Gen Kai** (34143 Pacific Coast Highway, Dana Point; 714-240-2004). In addition to a trimly appointed dining room, this chain restaurant features a sushi bar and comprehensive lunch and dinner menus. When we ate here the food was quite good. No lunch on weekends. Moderate.

One of San Juan Capistrano's many historic points, the 19th-century building **El Adobe de Capistrano** (31891 Camino Capistrano; 714-493-1163) has been converted into a restaurant. The interior is a warren of whitewashed rooms, supported by *vigas* and displaying the flourishes of Spanish California. The menu includes lunch, dinner and Sunday brunch. Naturally, the cuisine is Continental Mexican, and there's a special children's dinner. Budget to moderate.

## LAGUNA BEACH AREA BEACHES AND PARKS

A truly outstanding facility, **Crystal Cove State Park** (714-494-3539; admission) is a winding beach sometimes sectioned into a series of coves by high tides. The park stretches for over three miles along the coast and includes 2200 acres of the surrounding hill country. Grassy terraces grace the sea cliffs, and a 1200-acre offshore area is designated an underwater park, complete with a "trail." Join a tidepool walk or a backcountry hike (714-497-7647). Located along the Coast Highway between Laguna Beach and Corona del Mar.

Quite simply, **Doheny State Beach** (714-496-6171; admission) wrote the book on oceanside facilities. In addition to a broad swath

---

*MAIN BEACH*

*You'll have to venture north to Muscle Beach in Venice to find a scene equal to this one. It's near the very center of Laguna Beach, at Coast Highway and Broadway, with shopping streets radiating in several directions. A sinuous boardwalk winds along the waterfront, past basketball players, sunbathers, volleyball aficionados, little kids on swings and aging kids on rollerblades. Here and there an adventuresome soul has even dipped a toe in the wa-wa-water. In the midst of this humanity on holiday stands the lifeguard tower, an imposing, glass-encased structure that looks more like a conning tower and has become a Laguna Beach icon.*

of sandy beach, there is a five-acre lawn complete with private picnic areas, beach rentals and food concessions. The grassy area offers plenty of shade trees. Surfers work the north end of the beach, and divers explore an underwater park just offshore. The visitors center (open daily during the summer) has an indoor tidepool and five aquarium tanks. Call 714-496-6172 for the schedule during the rest of the year. Camping permitted (for reservations, call 800-444-7275). Dana Point Harbor, with complete marina facilities, borders the beach. Located off Dana Point Harbor Drive in Dana Point.

Walk down the deeply eroded cliffs guarding the coastline and you'll discover **San Clemente State Beach** (714-492-3156; admission). This narrow strip of sand curves north from San Diego County up to San Clemente City Beach. There are camping areas and picnic plots on top of the bluff. Kids camping here can participate in the Junior Ranger crafts and hiking program. Down below, a railroad track parallels the beach, and surfers paddle offshore. Year-round breaks at the north end of the beach make this a popular surfing area. Surf-fishing is best in spring. Swimmers should always beware of rip currents. Campfire nature talks are presented nightly during the summer and on most weekends during the rest of the year (information: 714-492-3156).

## The Sporting Life

### FISHING AND WHALE WATCHING

Among the Orange County outfits offering sportfishing charters are **Davey's Locker** (400 Main Street, Balboa; 714-673-1434) and **Dana Wharf Sportfishing** (34675 Golden Lantern Street, Dana Point; 714-496-5794). For those more interested in gazing at California's big grays, these companies also sponsor whale-watching cruises during the migratory season (late December through late March).

### SKINDIVING

The coastal waters abound in interesting kelp beds rich with sea life. To explore them contact **Aquatic Center** (4537 West Pacific Coast Highway, Newport Beach; 714-650-5440), **Laguna Sea Sports** (925 North Coast Highway, Laguna Beach; 714-494-6965) or **Beach Cities Scuba** (34283 Pacific Coast Highway, Dana Point; 714-496-

5891). **Aquatic Center** also operates a 24-hour surf and water condition line (714-650-5783).

## SURFING AND WINDSURFING

Orange County is surfer heaven. Grab a board from **Frog House** (6908 West Pacific Coast Highway, Newport Beach; 714-642-5690), **Hobie Sports** (24825 Del Prado, Dana Point; 714-496-2366) or **Stewart Sports** (2102 South El Camino Real, San Clemente; 714-492-1085) and head for the waves. For surf reports call 714-492-1011.

## GOLF

The climate and terrain make for excellent golfing. Anaheim and other inland sections of Orange County feature numerous golf links. Among them are **Dad Miller Golf Course** (430 North Gilbert Street; 714-774-8055), **Anaheim Hills Golf Course** (6501 Nohl Ranch Road; 714-998-3041), **Fullerton Golf Course** (2700 North Harbor Boulevard, Fullerton; 714-871-7411) or **Mile Square Golf Course** (10401 Warner Avenue, Fountain Valley; 714-968-4556).

On the coast you can tee up at **Newport Beach Golf Course** (3100 Irvine Avenue, Newport Beach; 714-852-8681), **Aliso Creek Golf Course** (31106 Coast Highway, Laguna Beach; 714-499-1919), **Monarch Beach Golf Links** (23841 Stonehill Drive, Dana Point; 714-240-8247), **San Clemente Municipal Golf Course** (150 East Avenida Magdalena; 714-361-8384) or **Shorecliffs Golf Course** (501 Avenida Vaquero, San Clemente; 714-492-1177).

## TENNIS

For tennis courts around the Anaheim and Buena Park area try **Anaheim Tennis Center** (975 South State College Boulevard, Anaheim; 714-991-9090) or **Ralph B. Clark Regional Park** (8800 Rosecrans Avenue, Buena Park; 714-670-8045).

Along the coast, try the **Marriott Tennis Club** (Marriott Hotel, 900 Newport Center Drive, Newport Beach; 714-729-3566), **Moulton Meadows Park** (Del Mar and Balboa avenues, Laguna Beach; 714-497-0716), **Laguna Niguel Regional Park** (28241 La Paz Road, Laguna Niguel; 714-831-2791), **Dana Hills Tennis Center** (24911 Calle de Tenis, Dana Point; 714-240-2104), **Bonito Canyon Park** (El Camino Real and Calle Valle, San Clemente; 714-361-8264), **San Luis Rey Park** (109 Avenida San Luis Rey, San Clemente; 714-361-8264) and **San Gorgonio Park** (2916 Via San Gorgonio, San Clemente; 714-361-8264).

## BOATING

With elaborate marina complexes at Huntington Beach, Newport Beach and Dana Point, this is a great area for boating. Sailboats and powerboats (including fishing skiffs) are rented at **Davey's Locker** (400 Main Street, Balboa; 714-673-1434), **Marina Sailing** (600 East Bay Avenue, Suite B6, Newport Beach; 714-673-7763), **Balboa Boat Rentals** (510 Edgewater Avenue, Balboa; 714-673-7200) and Embarcadero Marina (Embarcadero Place, public launch ramp, Dana Point; 714-496-6177).

## JOGGING

Mecca for Orange County runners is the Santa Ana Riverbed Trail, a smooth, asphalt ribbon stretching 20.6 miles from Anaheim to Huntington Beach State Park. There are par courses and excellent running trails at both Laguna Niguel Regional and Mile Square Regional parks. In Mission Viejo there's a beautiful 2.5-mile trail around Lake Mission Viejo. And then there are the miles and miles of beaches for which Orange County is renowned.

## BIKING

**Route 1** lets cyclists explore the Orange County coastline. The problem, of course, is the traffic. Along **Bolsa Chica State Beach**, however, a special pathway runs for six to seven miles along the length of the beach. Another way to avoid traffic is to mountain bike; Morro Canyon in Crystal Cove State Park is a favorite off-road riding area. Other interesting areas to explore are **Balboa Island** and the **Balboa Peninsula** in Newport Beach. Both offer quiet residential streets and are connected by a ferry that permits bicycles. A popular inland ride is along **Santiago Canyon Road**; leaving from Orange the route skirts Irvine Lake and Cleveland National Forest.

BIKE RENTALS   To rent bikes in Orange County try **Sandpiper Bicycle Repair** (231 Seal Beach Boulevard, Seal Beach; 562-594-6130), **Jack's Beach Concession** (2191 Pacific Coast Highway, Huntington Beach; 714-536-8328) and **Rainbow Bicycle Co.** (485 North Coast Highway, Laguna Beach; 714-494-5806).

# SEVEN

# San Diego Day Trips

The experts agree that San Diego is one of the best family vacation **167** cities in the United States. Who are we to argue? Famous for its zoo and wild animal park, beaches and missions, San Diego is one of California's most entertaining and relaxing destinations. You could spend a week exploring the museums of Balboa Park and still not see all that this cultural hub has to offer. And when it comes to family attractions you'll have a hard time beating delights like Sea World, Scripps Museum, Horton Plaza and Coronado.

The San Diego County Coast, with 76 sparkling miles stretching from the San Clemente area to the Mexican border, is the place to see the rare Torrey pines, ride one of the West Coast's two remaining classic roller coasters and visit California's first mission. With bays and beaches bathed in sunshine 75 percent of the time, less than ten inches of rainfall per year and average temperatures that mirror a proverbial day in June, San Diego offers the casual outdoor lifestyle that fulfills vacation dreams. There's a beach for every taste ranging from broad sweeps of white sand to slender scimitars beneath eroded sandstone bluffs.

Although waterfront resorts are a prime attraction, the San Diego region also offers many inland attractions. Old Town San Diego State Historic Park, Heritage Park, the Children's Museum of San Diego and the Aerospace Museum and Hall of Fame are just a few of the unique features of this alluring destination.

San Diego is also famous for its zoo, considered the world's best. It takes at least a day to get an overview of the lush habitat that is home to 800 species. Like the 2100-acre Wild Animal Park in northern San Diego County, the zoo is a center of wildlife conservation and offers a close look at the quiet war being waged to save the world's endangered species.

---

*Contrary to popular belief, koalas are marsupials, not bears.*

---

The city's downtown is a delight as well, thanks to attractions like Horton Plaza, an offbeat urban mall that doubles as a living museum showcasing more than a dozen architectural styles from the Renaissance to the Post Modern. The nearby Gaslamp Quarter historic district and the shops of Seaport Village also invite leisurely exploration.

Although they are within the boundaries of the city of San Diego, the seaside communities of Ocean Beach, Mission Beach and Pacific Beach have developed their own identities, moods and styles. "OB," as the first is fondly known, exults along with its two sister beach communities in the sunny, sporty, Southern California lifestyle fostered by nearby Mission Bay Park—home of Sea World. These neighboring communities are fronted by broad beaches and an almost continuous boardwalk that is jammed with joggers, skaters and cyclists.

The region's most upscale beach town, La Jolla, is scented with jasmine and hibiscus and looks like it was imported from Italy's Amalfi Coast. This university town makes an excellent base for exploring the best of San Diego's beaches, galleries, restaurants and family attractions.

Coronado, nestled on a peninsula jutting into San Diego Bay and connected to the mainland by a narrow sandbar known as the Silver Strand, is another community ideal for the sporting life.

All of these choices might make San Diego sound daunting. But in many ways this big city is like a small town, easy to navigate and surprisingly affordable. No matter where you go in this family-oriented region you'll likely only be minutes away from another great waterfront restaurant, a promising bike path or a marina that can rent you a ski or sailboat. Now, if you're ready, let's get started on the day trips that could easily turn into overnights.

## The San Diego Zoo

The San Diego Zoo has long been heralded as the best zoo in the world. But this glorious, 100-acre zoological park is not resting on its laurels. Having celebrated its 80th anniversary in 1996, it is now in the midst of a multimillion-dollar rebuilding and reorganization

*Yuck!!! Giraffes clean their ears and eyeballs with their long, black tongues.*

into ten bioclimactic zones. Several of these climate zones are already in place and have met with resounding success.

In addition to the lions, tigers and bears so common in zoos around the world, the animal population here includes many rare and endangered species that you'll be hard pressed to find elsewhere; you'll see giant pandas, Australian koalas, New Zealand kiwis and Fiji Island iguanas. You'll also witness the curious habits of feisty sun bears, acrobatic siamangs and playful meerkats.

The best thing about the zoo is that the animals seem relatively content to be here. You won't see any species cooped up in barred cages. Instead, the residents live in spacious, barless, moated enclosures carefully landscaped with plants from their native habitats.

**Arrival:** The zoo is just north of downtown San Diego on the east end of Balboa Park. Take the Park Boulevard exit off Route 163 and go north, following the signs to the zoo. The parking lot is located right off Park Boulevard. Parking is free and plentiful but be sure to make a note of where you left your car; each row is marked by a different animal. There is also a bus stop right in front of the zoo. Call San Diego Transit Information (619-233-3004) for route information.

**Ticket Options:** Visitors can choose between a one-day pass ($16 for adults, $7 for children age 3–11) or an annual membership ($57 for single adults or $70 for two adults in the same household, $15 for children age 3–15), which allows unlimited visits to both the San Diego Zoo and the San Diego Wild Animal Park.

**Sightseeing Strategies:** Covering a whopping 100 acres, the zoo seldom seems overcrowded. The most you have to worry about is having to crane your neck a little to see over the crowds that gather around the most popular enclosures. People don't linger in one spot for more than a few minutes, so you should always be able to work your way to the front for a good view.

Everyone is handed a map upon entering the zoo. You'll find it detailed and easy to follow. Signage within the zoo is so good that you might not even have to look at the map very often.

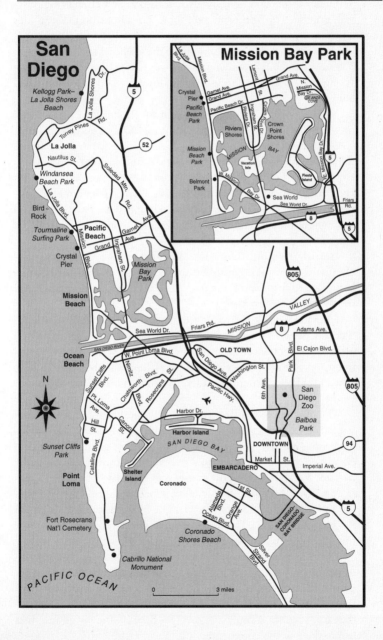

Some visitors find navigating zoo terrain to be a challenging physical exercise. This zoo is no exception, spread out over several hills and canyons, which means stairs, inclines and lots of walking. Several moving sidewalks carry visitors up the steepest inclines, but if you have a small child or an elderly relative, you may want to consider taking the 40-minute bus tour, which is described in greater detail below.

**Nuts & Bolts:** For general zoo information call 619-234-3153, or write San Diego Zoo Guest Relations, P.O. Box 551, San Diego, CA 92112. Wheelchair and stroller rentals are located just inside the main gate to the left. Here you'll also find an Information Center, Security, Lost & Found and a Camera and Film Shop. Lockers and First Aid are located by the Reptile House. Telephones, drinking fountains and restrooms with handicapped access are scattered throughout the zoo and clearly marked on the map. No animals are allowed.

**Getting Around:** This zoo is an enormous place, and it's possible that you may not get to see all the animals in one day. So it's a good idea to first consult the map and go directly to the animals and shows that you most want to see.

For a great bird's-eye view of the entire facility, climb aboard the **Skyfari Aerial Tram** ($1 each way). A station is located to the left of the main entrance. From your aerial cabin you'll see lush rainforests on one side, dry savanna on the other. Children love to look down over the enclosures and identify all the animals scurrying about below.

The 40-minute **Guided Bus Tour** is another alternative to seeing the entire zoo on foot, although it will cost you $4 extra. Double-decker buses cruise slowly through the canyons, giving passengers a chance to spot many animals. An extremely knowledgeable guide narrates the tour, giving the names and birthdays of celebrity animals, species anecdotes, conservation information and other interesting and often amusing bits of trivia. The information alone is worth the price of the tour. The seats on the top deck offer the best views, though you'll have to wait longer for them.

The **Kangaroo Bus** follows the same route as the Guided Bus route, but it has stops at eight locations throughout the zoo. After paying once ($8 for adults and $5 for kids) you may hop on and off the bus all day. This is ideal for families with small children because they can walk for a while and then get back on the bus to rest their feet and enjoy the commentary on the animals.

## TOURING THE ZOO

The **Children's Zoo** should be your first stop of the day. As in most zoos, this enclosure has the familiar petting paddock, filled with docile goats, sheep, deer and even pot-bellied pigs. But there's much more, like dozens of downy newborn chicks for touching; rabbits, guinea pigs and a miniature horse; and a nursery where newborn animals sometimes spend their first few months. Don't miss the pygmy marmosets housed in a glass enclosure at the entrance to Children's Zoo. The world's smallest monkeys, these tiny creatures weigh in at only four ounces when full grown.

Just inside the entrance to the left is **Tiger River**. A winding, downhill path takes you through a simulated Southeast Asian rain-forest with lush, live foliage. Hidden sprinklers provide cool, ambi-ent mist along the way. Reaching the bottom of the path, you'll be treated to glimpses of such rainforest natives as crocodiles and a 250-pound python. You will also see the playful "fishing cats," one of the only feline species that enjoys the water. But the stars of Tiger River are, of course, the magnificent Indochinese tigers, housed in a lush, green environment that slopes up the side of a hill. Visitors view these striped beasts from behind plexiglass at the bottom of the slope or from across an open moated area. You should be willing to linger here awhile, as these animals spend much of the day napping in the upper confines of their enclosure and are sometimes difficult to spot. But patience pays off when one of them suddenly rises to stretch its legs or get a drink of water.

---

### THEY ONLY COME OUT AT NIGHT

*If you've ever wondered about creatures of the night (and I'm not talking about human lounge lizards here), head on over to the San Diego Zoo during summer. From the end of June through August, the zoo features expanded hours that allow a peak into the lives of animals who might otherwise be getting shuteye. Indochinese tigers, snow leopards and lorises are just a few of the "night owls" you might want to see; the expanded hours also offer extra time to get a look at Bai Yun and Shi Shi, the zoo's visiting pandas. Of course, you can also visit with most of the regular zoo crew, with the exception of the great apes and siamangs who retire at dusk for a good night's sleep. Walk-through aviaries and birds-of-prey areas are also closed. Expanded hours are roughly 9 a.m. until 9 p.m., but check before you go.*

Because hippopotamuses spend the majority of their day submerged, when you stop by **Hippo Beach** that's likely how you'll find them: underwater and doing their infamous hippo ballet. As you watch the memorable moves of Funani and Jabba through the 105-foot-long observation window, you'll likely discover that they're just as curious about you as you are about them. The river hippos share this African marsh–like habitat with many fish and several species of birds including sacred ibis, African spoonbills and white-breasted cormorants. Adjacent to the hippos are rare forest-dwelling antelopes from central Africa called okapi.

Around the corner from Hippo Beach is the **Giant Panda Research Station,** home to temporary residents Bai Yun and Shi Shi. The visiting pandas, the only pair in the country, are on a 12-year loan from the People's Republic of China and can be seen intermittently, depending on availability (since the pandas are here for breeding research, caretakers have to be very sensitive to the animal's reproductive cycles). If you don't catch them up close, you may be able to see them in their exercise yards via "Panda Cam," and there's always some sort of video playing if the bears aren't available at all. Summer, when the bears are out for many hours at a time, is a particularly good season to see them. Because of the bears' popularity, the zoo has set up a hotline for information about viewing times: call 888-696-2632.

Overlooking the Giant Panda Research Station and Hippo Beach is **Gorilla Tropics**, a two-and-a-half acre simulated African rainforest that houses gorillas and thousands of African plants. Superstar

---

*ALL THE ZOO'S A STAGE*

*The zoo has two different shows to choose from, each taking place several times daily. Thankfully, you won't see costumed animals starring in silly, contrived skits. These shows aim to educate as well as entertain.*

*At Hunte Amphitheater in Cat Canyon, the **Wild Ones** focuses on residents of the rain forests. Many of the species featured are endangered, as their habitats are being systematically destroyed.*

*Wildlife native to California's offshore islands take to the Wegeforth Bowl pool for a splashy, informative **Wegeforth National Park Sea Lion Show** that focuses on the natural abilities of these animals to adapt to their environment and to one another.*

*Elephants have 40,000 muscles in their trunks alone.*

primates Memba and Alvila and family are truly a privileged bunch; their state-of-the-art home includes skylights, heated floors, custom-designed sleeping platforms and a 96-speaker compact disc stereo system that plays sounds recorded in actual African rainforests. The animals spend most of their time on a hillside clearing surrounded by bamboo, fig and banana trees, but frequent feedings afford visitors up-close views of the apes.

The **Scripp's Rain Forest Aviary**, built in 1923 but recently renovated, is also part of the Gorilla Tropics. Hundreds of exotic birds fly freely overhead through the thick canopy of African foliage. The roof of the mesh shell is painted sky-blue so it's nearly invisible from the inside.

A recent addition to Gorilla Tropics, **Pygmy Chimps at Bonobo Road**, is a replica of an African rainforest. Exhibits include the African crowned eagle and a variety of other birds. The stars are bonobos (also called pygmy chimpanzees) who entertain visitors with their antics.

**Sun Bear Forest**, judging from the crowds, is one of the most popular and entertaining zones within the zoo. Rambunctious lion-tailed macaques (rhymes with "attacks") swing from intertwined ropes and branches to the delight of crowds pressed up against the plexiglass wall of their enclosure. A sign informs visitors of these creatures' lofty heritage—some are descendants of a colony of macaques once owned by Prince Rainier of Monaco.

But the real celebrities are their neighbors, the sun bears. The world's smallest bear, this creature gets its name from the cream-colored starburst on its chest. Their long claws look threatening, but these clumsy, roly-poly bears seem anything but menacing. They appear to be the happiest creatures alive as they play in the waterfall and pools, and lumber about their spacious home, pestering their slumbering mates.

While you'll seldom see koalas doing much more than munching eucalyptus leaves, these creatures have always been among the most lovable residents of the zoo. Most of the time they stay curled up in a ball, doing what they do best—snoozing. This enclosure is also home to other intriguing creatures from Down Under, including several adorable wallabies and tree kangaroos.

The western end of the zoo, also known as **Horn and Hoof Mesa**, is reserved for giraffes, gazelles, buffalo and antelope. Continue south and you'll find more hoofstock such as deer, impala, and rare takin from China.

To visit **Polar Bear Plunge** is to be transported to the northern coast of Alaska in the summertime. At the center of this simulated Arctic tundra are the polar bears. As you watch them swimming gracefully underwater in their deep saltwater bay, you would never guess that they are fierce and persistent predators. Look closely at their fur. It's not the white or cream color that it appears; it's actually translucent and hollow, allowing sunlight to penetrate it. Other Arctic species that inhabit this wondrous exhibit are reindeer, Arctic foxes, snowy owls and yellow-throated martens.

In addition to these not-to-be-missed attractions, the zoo has hundreds of other intriguing animals to see should time permit. Up the hill from Sun Bear Forest you'll find **Elephant Mesa**, home to several rhinos and, of course, a herd of African and Asian elephants. Continue north and you'll pass bats, camels and tree kangaroos. The nearby **African Kopje Exhibit**, another of the zoo's climate zones, contains miniature antelope called klipspringers, dwarf mongooses, rock hyrax and a pair of majestic Verreaux's eagles. And don't miss the amusing meerkats just around the corner from the Kopje. These frisky critters are real crowd-pleasers, wrestling around in the dirt, standing on their hind legs and playing leapfrog.

Down the hill is **Dog and Cat Canyon** where you'll find several species of felines including the snow and Persian leopards, and a pair of stunning jaguars.

Alligators, tortoises and various rare frogs make their homes on **Reptile Mesa**. And don't forget to visit the slithering inhabitants of the **Reptile House** where dozens of varieties of snakes and lizards live in glass enclosures. Be sure to check out the rare Fiji island iguana and the two-headed corn snake named Thelma and Louise.

## SAN DIEGO ZOO DINING

The food at the zoo has improved greatly over the years. You'll find many favorite gourmet snacks such as frozen yogurt, Häagen-Dazs ice cream and Michelangelo calzones. The newest alternatives to the standard hot dogs, hamburgers and limp chicken sandwiches are found in the Treehouse, designed to recall a turn-of-the-century African manor house. On the upper level is the **Treehouse Café**, a buffet-style restaurant serving salads, sandwiches and hot dishes for

---

*The Wild Animal Park dispenses six tons of animal food daily at a cost of over $60,000 a month.*

---

budget prices. All the seating is on open-air decks. On the lower level is **Albert's**, which is named for the gorilla who once occupied the area where the Treehouse now stands. This sit-down eatery offers a variety of salads, sandwiches, fresh pastas and fish and meat entrées. There is a children's menu, and prices are moderate. For cuisine and ambience, the **Canyon Café**, at the bottom of Bear Canyon, tops our culinary list. This outdoor eatery is right next door to the Giant Panda Research Station. And in addition to the burgers, the menu includes some pretty decent fish tacos—a favorite dish of San Diegans.

You can also grab a bite at the handful of snack bars. **Safari Kitchen** near the Flamingo lagoon serves up burgers and chicken sandwiches, and **Safari Cones** across from the Reptile House has great gourmet hot dogs. Just inside the main entrance, the **Lagoon Terrace** and **Peacock and Raven** offer a more extensive menu served up cafeteria-style.

## San Diego Wild Animal Park

If you've always fantasized about going on an African safari, the San Diego Wild Animal Park—a 2200-acre sanctuary 30 miles north of San Diego—is the place for you. As your shaded monorail snakes slowly through the foothills, herds of antelope, rhinoceros, giraffes and zebras roam the vast plains below. Unlike most conventional zoos, the park's 3200 animals live together, creating one of the most realistic recreations of the wild you could think of anywhere.

Imagine a herd of giraffes, wildebeest or antelope charging pell-mell across the plains; a pair of young male gazelles locking horns, playfully sparring for territorial rights; mountain goats springing straight up a 100-foot rocky incline in mere seconds. These are just some of the things you can hope to see at this wonderful park.

**Arrival:** The park is at 15500 San Pasqual Valley Road in Escondido. From San Diego, take Route 15 to Via Rancho Parkway. From Los Angeles take Route 5 south to Route 78, then follow it east and pick up Route 15 south to Via Rancho Parkway. From Via Rancho Parkway a series of carefully placed signs leads you six more miles to the park. There is a fee for parking. (For information call 619-234-6541.)

**Ticket Options:** Choose between a one-day pass ($19.95 for adults, $12.95 for children age 3–11) or an annual membership ($57 for adults, $15 for children age 3–15), which allows unlimited visits to both the San Diego Wild Animal Park and the San Diego Zoo.

**Sightseeing Strategies:** Both humans and animals have plenty of space to roam, so the Wild Animal Park seldom seems congested. However, the 50-minute monorail safari, which is the highlight of the park, is what everyone heads for first. On slow days the wait usually runs about 20 minutes; when it's crowded you could be waiting twice as long. So it's best to take the monorail ride first. This will also give you an overview of the entire park and help you decide which animals you wish to return to later. The best strategy is to arrive at the park just as it opens and head immediately for the monorail station. When the ride is over, you can spend the rest of the day leisurely strolling through the park's many gardens, discovering pockets of wildlife around every corner.

One important thing to take into consideration: The San Diego Wild Animal Park is so far inland that temperatures reach the scorching point during late summer and early fall. Generally, the hotter the weather, the less active the animals. If possible, visit anytime from November through May when the weather is cooler.

**Nuts & Bolts:** For general park information call 619-234-6541, or write San Diego Wild Animal Park Guest Relations, 15500 San Pasqual Valley Road, Escondido, CA 92027. Lockers, strollers and wheelchair rentals are located just inside the main entrance. The Information Center (619-234-6541), situated north of the monorail

---

*UP CLOSE AND PERSONAL*

*How'd you like to get nose to nose with a rhino or eye to eye with an oryx? On a **Wild Animal Park Photo Caravan** anything is possible. Designed for photography buffs, these special tours take visitors into the animal habitats on a flatbed truck for close encounters with gazelles, giraffes, rhinos and more. Visitors have their choice of three tours, ranging from one-and-three-quarters to three-and-a-half hours. The journeys are $65 to $89 per person, but true nature buffs will tell you they're well worth it. The price includes park admission and a species-identification guide. Children must be at least 12 years old (ages 12 through 15 must be accompanied by an adult). Reservations required: 760-738-5022.*

*The "hump" on a rhino's back is really a ligament holding up the animal's heavy head. A rhino's head can weigh up to 1000 pounds.*

in the administration building, houses Lost & Found and a First Aid station. Major credit cards are accepted at the admission gate, in the gift shops and in some of the eateries. There is an ATM in the administration building. An information packet for visitors with disabilities is available at all ticket windows. Animals are not allowed, but kennels are available for guide dogs.

**Getting Around:** After entering the park, you'll find yourself in Nairobi Village. This is the main pedestrian area of the park and where you'll find all the shops, restaurants, restrooms and the homes of some of the park's smaller animals. The village, together with the Monorail Ride, the new Heart of Africa experience, the Kilimanjaro Safari Walk and the Animal Shows, are the Wild Animal Park's central attractions.

MONORAIL RIDE    The 50-minute, five-mile Wgasa Bush Line Monorail Ride is the core of the Wild Animal Park experience. The tour is a relaxing journey narrated by a knowledgeable guide who successfully mixes factual information with interesting anecdotes.

The shaded monorail travels through several sections of the park, each designed to simulate a different habitat. First you'll pass through the **Eastern Africa** and **Asian Plains** sections, home to elephants, giraffes, Sumatran tigers and zebras. Watch carefully for Indian rhinos; you may mistake them for large boulders.

Next you'll see the **Eurasian Watering Hole** where European bison and fallow deer live together. Look closely on the other side of the train or you might miss the many goats and sheep living in the **Mountain Habitat**. Camouflage is their best weapon against predators. That and speed: According to the guide they can scale this rocky mountain in under 20 seconds.

In **Southern Africa**, crowned cranes, rhinos, zebras and wildebeests peacefully coexist. To the other side of the train is a smaller habitat called the **Mongolian Steppe**. This area is reserved for a large herd of rare Przewalski's horses. The progenitor of domestic horses, there are only about 500 of these animals left in the world.

Shortly before the conclusion of the monorail journey, you'll pass a colony of **Western Lowland Gorillas**. Because the view from the monorail is largely obscured, you'll want to make sure you visit

---

*A giraffe's heart pumps three times as fast as a human heart in order to get blood up through that long neck.*

---

this enclosure later on foot. These somber beasts are undoubtedly the most popular residents of the park. About a dozen of the creatures loll about on a grassy hillside stretching, rolling on their backs and yawning, giving visitors a frightening display of teeth.

NAIROBI VILLAGE   After the monorail tour, you'll want to explore the park on foot. Walking trails wind all over the facility, through various habitats and nearly a dozen botanical gardens. After a visit to the gorillas, make your way along the **Bridge of Birds**, a wooden walkway that passes around an aviary.

Continuing through Nairobi Village, walk the path along **Mombasa Lagoon** and the **Congo Fishing Village** for a view of Chilean flamingos, Dalmatian pelicans and shoebill storks. A colony of adorable lemurs is right at home on **Lemur Isle**, in the center of the lagoon.

Children in particular enjoy the **Petting Kraal** where they can stroke and feed deer, antelope and gazelle. Next door, the **Animal Care Center** houses newborns that can be seen through large glass windows. Try to be on hand for the 11 a.m. or 4 p.m. feedings. Hundreds of insects, birds, amphibians, plants and reptiles inhabit the indoor rainforest of the **Hidden Jungle**. Visitors can observe these creatures in their natural environment, each performing a vital role in maintaining this 8800-square-foot ecosystem. A favorite among the visitors is the collection of butterflies from rainforests all over the world.

At Lorikeet Landing visitors can experience hand-feeding rainbow lorikeets. Lorikeet food is available for purchase. Nairobi Village is also dotted with enclosures containing gibbons, spider monkeys, meerkats and red river hogs. Don't miss the chance to see any of these playful mammals.

HEART OF AFRICA   With this attraction, the folks at the San Diego Wild Animal Park have taken their safari concept one giant step closer to the real thing. With lazy pathways winding through 30 acres of animal habitats, Heart of Africa is about the closest thing you'll get to the Serengeti without actually being there; exotic African wildlife seemingly roam as freely as the people. There are more than 200 animals here—cheetahs, rhinos, giraffes, and gazelles, to name a few—all ambling together (as they would in the wild) in authentically re-created homes flourishing with exotic African plants. The whole walk takes about an hour, and park staff are on hand at the area's research station where you'll have your best chance of actually interacting with some animals.

Designers of Heart of Africa have taken great pains to create the feeling of openness, installing camouflaged animal barriers that are largely imperceptible. Though the animals feel within reach, their accessibility is an illusion. Those cheetahs can't exactly come up and eat from your hand (although giraffes do occasionally make their way over to guests to be fed). But with invisible, low-lying boundaries such as trenches and brush-covered fences, it feels as if they can, and the effect is both real and startling.

KILIMANJARO SAFARI WALK    This mile-and-three-quarter trek through the eastern portion of the park passes lookout points that offer spectacular views of elephants, giraffes, lions, tigers and zebras. It also meanders through the park's many gardens, including a bed of herbs fragrant with culinary aromas. You can venture into **Tropical Asia** where hundreds of exotic birds live in the canopy overhead.

The Kilimanjaro Safari Walk ends at the park's far northeast corner. There you'll find a **Fuchsia Garden** as well as a **Bonsai Pavilion** and **Conifer Garden**. Double back and Nairobi Village is just a short hike away.

ANIMAL SHOWS    The Wild Animal Park offers several intriguing performances. The best is **Rare and Wild America**, which takes place twice daily at the Village Amphitheater. This wild and woolly revue stars a variety of animals native to North America. A pair of beavers named Ward and June demonstrate their swimming ability, a gray fox shimmies up a pole in seconds, and a raccoon obliges the audience with a wave of its dexterous paw.

The **Bird Show** at Benbough Amphitheater is almost as entertaining, with celebrity Amazon parrots that have appeared on the *David Letterman* show. These feathered creatures ham it up onstage singing "I Left My Heart in San Francisco" and mimic the sounds of sirens and human laughter. If you have small children along, be sure to catch this show; the tots delight in these crazy bird stunts.

The **Elephant Show** takes place on the outskirts of Nairobi Village along the Kilimanjaro Safari Walk. The Asian elephants are the stars of the show, which aims to educate the audience about the natural behavior of these behemoths.

**Hawk Talk** is an informal, gather-round question-and-answer session. A trainer brings out a variety of raptors and other predatory birds and fields questions about the creatures from onlookers. Hawk Talk can be heard twice daily on the bridge near the Water Wise Garden.

## SAN DIEGO WILD ANIMAL PARK DINING

Wild Animal Park fare is surprisingly good, a cut above the food served at most other theme parks. It's also apparent that a lot of thought went into creating a scenic atmosphere for each restaurant.

Our hands-down favorite lunch spot is the **Thorn Tree Terrace**. The one-third-pound gourmet hamburgers with onion rings are tasty, and the setting is sublime. Just across a moat from the shady patio tables, a group of playful spider monkeys puts on a lively floor show, swinging from their tails and pouncing on one another. Moderate.

The **Mombasa Cooker** is another scenic dining spot with a spacious patio overlooking the park's central lagoon. Best meals include the chicken sandwiches and pizza, pasta and stir-fry. Moderate.

There are half a dozen other snack bars and food stands throughout Nairobi Village. If you're in the mood for a hot dog, head for the **Congo Kitchen**, just north of the lagoon. If you have a hankering for something healthy, the **Kisangani Court**, just south of the lagoon, offers a fresh buffet of salads, fruits and vegetables. Moderate.

## San Diego

SEA WORLD AREA    One of the nation's largest and most diverse city-owned aquatic recreational areas, and home to Sea World, **Mission Bay Park** has something to suit just about everyone's interest. Here, visitors join with residents to enjoy swimming, sailing, windsurfing, waterskiing, fishing, jogging, cycling, golf and tennis. Or perhaps a relaxing day of kite flying and sunbathing. It is a mecca for San Diego's athletic set, a recreational paradise dotted with islands and lagoons and ringed by 27 miles of sandy beaches.

Key locations in this 4600-acre wonderland are as follows: **Dana Landing** and **Quivira Basin** make up the southwest portion of the park. Most boating activities begin here, home to port headquarters and a large marina. Adjacent is **Bonita Cove**, used for swimming, picnicking, softball and volleyball. Mission Boulevard shops, restaurants and recreational equipment rentals are within easy walking distance. **Ventura Cove** houses a large hotel complex, but its sandy beach is open to the public. Calm waters make it a popular swimming spot for small children.

**Vacation Isle** and **Ski Beach** are easily reached via the bridge on Ingraham Street, which bisects the island. The west side contains public swimming areas, boat rentals and a model-yacht basin. Ski Beach is on the east side and is the favorite spot in the bay for waterskiing. **Fiesta Island** is on the southwest side of the park. It's ringed with soft-sand swimming beaches and laced with jogging, cycling and skating paths. A favorite spot for fishing from the quieter coves and for kite flying.

Over on the **East Shore** you'll find landscaped picnic areas, playgrounds, a physical-fitness course, a sandy beach for swimming and the park information center. **De Anza Cove**, at the extreme northeast corner of the park, has a sandy beach for swimming plus a large private campground. **Crown Point Shores** provides a sandy beach, picnic area, nature-study area, physical-fitness course and waterski landing.

**Sail Bay** and **Riviera Shores** make up the northwest portion of Mission Bay and back up against the apartments and condominiums of Pacific Beach. Sail Bay's beaches aren't the best in the park and are usually submerged during high tides. Riviera Shores has a better beach with waterski areas.

**Santa Clara** and **El Carmel points** jut out into the westernmost side of the bay. Santa Clara Point is of interest to the visitor with its recreation center, tennis courts and softball field. A sandy beach fronts San Juan Cove between the two points.

---

## SEAPORT VILLAGE

*Near the south end of the Embarcadero sits the popular shopping and entertainment complex known as **Seaport Village** (Pacific Highway and Harbor Drive). Designed to replicate an early California seaport, it comprises 14 acres of bayfront parks and promenades, shops and galleries. On the south side, overlooking the water, is the 45-foot-high Mulkilto Lighthouse, official symbol of the village, a re-creation of a famous lighthouse in Washington state. Nearby is the Broadway Flying Horses Carousel, a hand-carved, turn-of-the-century model that originally whirled around Coney Island.*

---

*The Spreckels Organ in Balboa Park has 4416 pipes, making it one of the world's largest outdoor instruments.*

---

Just about every facility imaginable can be found somewhere in the park: catamaran and windsurfer rentals, playgrounds and parks, frisbee and golf. For further information contact the **Mission Bay Aquatic Center** (619-221-8900).

Not far from Mission Bay Park, the historic, 1925 "Giant Dipper" has come back to life after years of neglect at **Belmont Park** (3146 Mission Boulevard and West Mission Bay Drive; 619-488-0668). One of only two West Coast seaside coasters, this beauty is not all the park has to offer. There also are a carousel, video arcade, indoor swimming pool and a host of shops and eateries along the beach and boardwalk.

SAN DIEGO HARBOR   San Diego's beautiful harbor is a notable exception to the rule that big-city waterfronts lack appeal. Here, the city embraces its bay and presents its finest profile along the water.

The best way to see it all is on a harbor tour. A variety of vessels can be found near Harbor Drive at the foot of Broadway. **San Diego Harbor Excursion** (1050 North Harbor Drive; 619-234-4111; admission) provides leisurely trips around the 22-square-mile harbor, which is colorfully backdropped by commercial and naval vessels as well as the dramatic cityscape. A sunset dinner cruise is offered aboard the **Lord Hornblower** (1066 North Harbor Drive; 619-234-8687; admission).

All along the cityside of the harbor from the Coast Guard Station to Seaport Village is a lovely landscaped boardwalk called the **Embarcadero**. It offers parks where you can stroll and play, a floating maritime museum and a thriving assortment of waterfront diversions.

The **Maritime Museum of San Diego** (1492 North Harbor Drive; 619-234-9153; admission) is composed of three vintage ships. The most familiar is the 1863 *Star of India*, the nation's oldest iron-hulled merchant ship still afloat. Visitors go aboard for a hint of what life was like on the high seas more than a century ago. You can also visit the 1898 ferry *Berkeley*, which helped in the evacuation of San Francisco during the 1906 earthquake, and the 1904 steam yacht *Medea*.

The Marine Center presents colorful **military reviews** most Fridays. Marching ceremonies begin at exactly 10 a.m. at the Marine

Corps Recruiting Depot (619-524-1772). The center may be reached from downtown by going north on Pacific Highway to Barnett Avenue, then left to Gate 1.

One of the latest additions to the city skyline, the **San Diego Convention Center** (111 West Harbor Drive; 619-525-5000) looks like an erector set gone mad. An uncontained congeries of flying buttresses, giant tents and curved glass, it is fashioned in the from of a ship, seemingly poised to set sail across San Diego Harbor. This architectural exclamation mark is certainly worth a drive by or a quick tour.

DOWNTOWN SAN DIEGO    Billions of dollars invested in a stunning array of new buildings and in the restoration of many old ones have transformed downtown San Diego in recent years.

**Horton Plaza** (bounded by Broadway and G Street and 1st and 4th avenues) is totally unlike any other shopping mall. It has transcended its genre in a whimsical, multilevel, open-air, pastel-hued concoction of ramps, escalators, rambling paths, bridges, towers, piazzas, sculptures, fountains and live greenery. Mimes, minstrels and

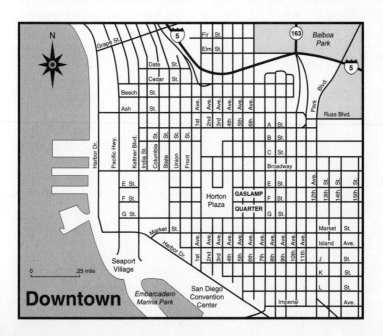

fortunetellers meander about the six-block complex performing for patrons.

Horton Plaza was inspired by European shopping streets and districts such as the Plaka of Athens, the Ramblas of Barcelona and Portobello Road in London. In all, 14 different styles, ranging from Renaissance to postmodern, are employed in the design.

If Horton Plaza doesn't have what you're looking for, try across the street at the **Paladion** (777 Front Street; 619-232-1627). The "bill of fare" at this small plaza includes clothes, jewelry and a wealth of other consumer goodies, most in the upper price range.

The **Gaslamp Quarter** is one of America's largest national historic districts, covering a 16-block strip along 4th, 5th and 6th avenues from Broadway to the waterfront. Architecturally, the Quarter reveals some of the finest Victorian-style commercial buildings constructed in San Diego during the 50 years between the Civil War and World War I. It was this area, along 5th Avenue, that became San Diego's first main street. The city's core began on the bay where Alonzo Horton first built a wharf in 1869.

During its redevelopment, the city added wide, brick sidewalks, period streetlamps, trees and benches. In all, more than 100 grand Victorian buildings have been restored to their original splendor.

BALBOA PARK    Home of the renowned San Diego Zoo, Balboa Park came about in 1868 when city fathers with a view to the future set aside 1400 acres for the public. The park's eventual development, and most of its lovely Spanish Baroque buildings, came as the result of two world's fairs—The Panama–California Exposition of 1915–16 and the California–Pacific International Exposition of 1935–36.

Today, Balboa Park ranks among the largest and finest of America's city parks. Wide avenues and walkways curve through luxurious subtropical foliage leading to nine major museums, three art galleries, four theaters, picnic groves, the zoo, a golf course and countless other recreation facilities. Its verdant grounds teem with cyclists, joggers, skaters, picnickers, weekend artists and museum mavens.

The main entrance is from 6th Avenue onto Laurel Street, which becomes El Prado as you cross Cabrillo Bridge. Begin your visit at the **Balboa Park Visitors Center** (619-239-0512), on the northeast corner of Plaza de Panama. They provide free pamphlets and maps on the park.

From here you can stroll about, taking in Balboa Park's main attractions. To the right, as you head east on the pedestrian-only section of El Prado, is the Casa de Balboa. It houses the **San Diego Model Railroad Museum** (619-696-0199; admission), which features the largest collection of small-gauge trains in the world. Closed Monday.

Sports fans will want to take in the **Hall of Champions Sports Museum** (619-234-2544; admission), in Casa de Balboa. It houses a "Hall of Fame" and has exhibits featuring world-class San Diego athletes from more than 40 sports.

Continuing east to the fountain, you'll see the **Reuben H. Fleet Space Theater and Science Center** (619-238-1233; admission) on your right. Among the park's finest attractions, it features one of the largest planetariums and most impressive multimedia theaters in the country. The hands-on Science Center features various exhibits and displays dealing with modern phenomena.

Located just across the courtyard is the **Natural History Museum** (619-232-3821; admission) with displays devoted mostly to the Southern California environment. There are also fossils (whales, dinosaurs, land mammals) galore.

Going back along El Prado, take a moment to admire your reflection in the Lily Pond. With the old, latticed **Botanical Building** in the background, the scene is a favorite among photographers. The fern collection inside is equally striking.

The grandest of all Balboa Park structures, built as the centerpiece for the 1915 Panama–California Exposition, is the 200-foot Spanish Renaissance California Tower. The **Museum of Man** (619-239-2001; admission), at the base of the tower, is a must for anthropology buffs and those interested in American Indian cultures.

Another museum not to be missed is the **San Diego Aerospace Museum** (619-234-8291; admission) several blocks south of the plaza. It contains over 65 aircraft including a replica of Charles Lindbergh's famous *Spirit of St. Louis*, the original of which was built in San Diego. Also on display is *Blackbird*, the world's fastest plane.

---

## HERITAGE PARK

*On the outskirts of Old Town lies **Heritage Park** (Juan and Harney streets), an area dedicated to the preservation of the city's Victorian past. Seven historic, 1880s-era houses and an old Jewish temple have been moved to the hillside site and beautifully restored.*

---

*Numerous movies, including* Some Like It Hot, *were filmed at the Hotel del Coronado.*

---

Balboa Park's museums charge an admission fee, but every Tuesday select museums can be visited free.

CORONADO   Once known as the "Nickel Snatcher," the Coronado Ferry for years crossed the waters of San Diego Harbor between the Embarcadero and Coronado. All for five cents each way. That fare is history, of course, but the 1940-vintage, double-deck *Silvergate* still plies the waters. The **San Diego Bay Ferry** (1050 North Harbor Drive; 619-234-4111; admission) leaves on the hour from the Bay Café on North Harbor Drive at the foot of Broadway and docks 15 minutes later at the Ferry Landing Marketplace on the Coronado side.

An isolated and exclusive community in San Diego Bay, Coronado is almost an island, connected to the mainland only by the graceful San Diego–Coronado Bay Bridge and by a long, narrow sandspit called the Silver Strand.

The town's main attraction is the **Hotel del Coronado** (1500 Orange Avenue; 619-435-6611), a red-roofed, Victorian-style, wooden wonder, a century-old National Historic Landmark. Explore the old palace and its manicured grounds, discovering the intricate corridors and cavernous public rooms. It was Elisha Babcock's dream when he purchased 4100 acres of barren, wind-blown peninsula in 1888 to build a hotel that would be the "talk of the Western world." Realizing Babcock's dream from the beginning, it attracted such famous guests as Thomas Edison, Robert Todd Lincoln, Henry Ford and a dozen U.S. presidents.

POINT LOMA   The Point Loma peninsula forms a high promontory that shelters San Diego Bay from the Pacific Ocean. It also provided Juan Rodríguez Cabrillo an excellent place from which to contemplate his 16th-century discovery of California. Naturally, **Cabrillo National Monument** (1800 Cabrillo Memorial Drive; 619-557-5450; admission), featuring a statue of the navigator, stands facing his landing site at Ballast Point. The sculpture itself, a gift from Cabrillo's native Portugal, isn't very impressive, but the view is outstanding. With the bay and city spread below, you can often see all the way from Mexico to the La Jolla mesa. The visitors center includes a small museum. The nearby **Old Point Loma Lighthouse** guided ships from 1855 to 1891.

On the ocean side of the peninsula is **Whale Watch Lookout Point** where, during winter months, you can observe the southward migration of California gray whales. Close by is a superb network of tidepools. Call 619-557-5450 for schedules and information.

OLD TOWN AND MISSION VALLEY    Back in 1769, Spanish explorer Gaspar de Portolá selected a hilltop site overlooking the bay for a mission that would begin the European settlement of California. A town soon spread out at the foot of the hill, complete with plaza, church, school and the tile-roofed adobe *casas* of California's first families.

Some of the buildings and relics of the early era survived and have been brought back to life at **Old Town San Diego State Historic Park** (4002 Wallace Street; 619-220-5423). Lined with adobe restorations and brightened with colorful shops, the six blocks of Old Town provide a lively and interesting opportunity for visitors to stroll, shop and sightsee.

The park sponsors a free walking tour at 2 p.m. daily, or you can easily do it on your own by picking up the *Old San Diego Gazette*. The paper, which comes out once a month and includes a map of the area, is free at local stores or the **Old Town San Diego Chamber of Commerce** (2461 San Diego Avenue #204; 619-291-4903). You can also hop aboard the **Old Town Trolley** (San Diego Avenue and Twiggs Street; 619-298-8687; admission) for a delightful, two-hour, narrated tour of Old Town and a variety of other highlights in San Diego and Coronado. The trolley makes nine stops, and you're allowed to get on and off all day long.

As it has for over a century, everything focuses on **Old Town Plaza**. Before 1872, this was the social and recreational center of the town; political meetings, barbecues, dances, shoot-outs and bullfights all happened here. Some of the community's early adobe houses, as well as a stagecoach station, stable and early newspaper office, can still be seen.

Shoppers seem to gravitate in large numbers toward the north side of the plaza to browse the unusual shops in **Bazaar del Mundo**. Built in circular fashion around a tropical courtyard, this complex also houses several restaurants.

The original mission and Spanish Presidio once stood high on a hill behind Old Town. This site of California's birthplace now houses **Junípero Serra Museum** (2727 Presidio Drive; 619-297-3258; admission), a handsome, Spanish Colonial structure containing an excellent collection of Mexican and Spanish artifacts from the state's pioneer days and relics from the Royal Presidio dig sites. Closed Monday.

Within five years after Father Serra dedicated the first of California's 21 missions, the site had become much too small for the growing numbers it served. So **Mission San Diego de Alcala** (10818 San Diego Mission Road; 619-281-8449; admission) was moved from Presidio Hill six miles east into Mission Valley. Surrounded now by shopping centers and suburban homes, the "Mother of Missions" retains its simple but striking white-adobe facade topped by a graceful campanile. There also are a museum containing mission records in Junípero Serra's handwriting and a lovely courtyard with gnarled pepper trees.

LA JOLLA   Another center of interest lies at the northern end of San Diego in the luxurious town of La Jolla. The best beaches are here, stretching from the ritzy La Jolla Shores to the scientific sands at Scripps Beach. The latter strand fronts Scripps Institute of Oceanography, the oldest institution in the nation devoted to oceanography and the home of the **Birch Aquarium at Scripps** (2300 Expedition Way; 619-534-3474; admission). Here you will find 33 marine-life tanks, breathtaking exhibits of coastal underwater habitats, a manmade tidepool, interactive displays for children and adults and displays illustrating recent advances in oceanographic research. The bronze whale sculpture that graces the entrance to the museum is the world's largest.

The **Children's Museum of San Diego** (200 West Island Avenue; 619-233-5437; admission) offers hands- and mind-on activities for the whole family. Kids may choose to play virtual reality basketball or visit Cora's Rainhouse, where they can do writing projects, watch videos or listen to storytellers. The art studio featuring recycled materials is a good place for young people to try their hand at finger painting and sand painting, mask making and quilting. In the Improv Theater your child will be a star. Every month there are new exhibits and programs. In addition, a gift shop offers toys, games and books the kids will enjoy during their travels. Closed Monday.

## SAN DIEGO LODGING

SEA WORLD AREA   Pacific Beach boasts the San Diego County motel with the most character of all. **Crystal Pier Hotel** (4500 Ocean Boulevard; 619-483-6983, 800-748-5894, fax 619-483-6811)

*billwilliee.com*

is a throwback to the 1930s, and this is only fitting because that's when this quaint-looking assemblage of 26 cottages on Crystal Pier was built. This blue-and-white woodframe complex, perched over the waves, features little cottages that are hardly more than huts. Each comes with a kitchen and a patio over the sea. A unique discovery that's ideally located for family beachcombing and sandcastle building. Ultra-deluxe.

One particularly pretty four-unit condominium, **Ventanas al Mar** (3631 Ocean Front Walk; phone/fax 619-459-7125, 800-869-7858), overlooks the ocean in Mission Beach. Its contemporary two- and three-bedroom units feature fireplaces, jacuzzi tubs, kitchens and washer-dryers. They sleep as many as eight people. In the summer, these rent by the week only. Families with small kids will appreciate fenced patios and the resort's proximity to the waterfront as well as a wide variety of restaurants and shops. Ultra-deluxe.

*3950*

*3% $2800*

*10.5% tx deposits ref.*

Most of the hotels within sprawling Mission Bay Park are upscale resorts in the deluxe to ultra-deluxe price range. But there's relief to be found at the **Western Shores Motel** (4345 Mission Bay Drive; 619-273-1121, fax 619-273-2944), located just across the street from

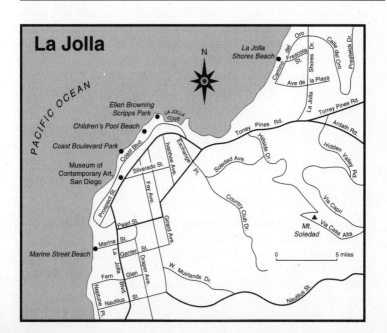

Mission Bay Golf Course. This quiet, 40-unit court simply can't be matched for value anywhere in the area. Budget.

Only one Mission Bay resort stands out as unique—the **San Diego Princess Resort** (1404 West Vacation Road; 619-274-4630, 800-344-2626, fax 619-581-5929). Over 40 acres of lush gardens, lagoons and white-sand beach surround the villas and cottages of this 462-room resort. Except for some fancy suites, room decor is motel-modern, with quality furnishings. But guests don't spend much time in their rooms anyway. At the Princess there's more than a mile of beach, catamaran rentals, bike rentals, six tennis courts, five pools, three restaurants, two lounges, and an 18-hole putting course. And if that's not enough to satisfy, this self-contained paradise also boasts a swim-up bar, a fitness center, a sauna, a jacuzzi and a sand volleyball court. If you're seeking a complete family resort, look no further. During Easter week and summer the Princess Day Camp program for children five to twelve features morning and afternoon recreation as well as evening movies. Friday and Saturday are teen nights offering movies, trivia and board games. Ultra-deluxe.

DOWNTOWN SAN DIEGO   The best value for your dollar among moderately priced downtown hotels is the 67-room **Comfort Inn** (719 Ash Street; 619-232-2525, 800-221-2222, fax 619-687-3024). A million-dollar renovation has left the rooms looking very slick. They feature wood furniture, designer color schemes and high-grade carpeting. Families will appreciate the convenience of microwaves and refrigerators in the larger rooms. The inn has a pool-sized jacuzzi and serves a continental breakfast. Guests are also welcome to use the pool at an adjacent motel. Conveniently located next to Balboa Park, a few blocks from the city center. Children 18 years old and under stay free. Moderate to deluxe.

---

### A HOSTEL FOR FAMILIES

*Ensconced in a plain-vanilla, two-story former church building, the **Hostelling International—Point Loma** (3790 Udall Street; 619-223-4778, fax 619-223-1883) is filled with 60 to 65 budget-minded guests almost every night in the summer. Comfortable bunk beds are grouped in 12 rooms housing from two to eight people in youth-hostel fashion. Family rooms are also available, and there is a common kitchen and dining area. Bring your own bedding.*

A recommended midtown hotel is **Best Western Bayside Inn** (555 West Ash Street; 619-233-7500, 800-528-1234, fax 619-239-8060). Small enough (122 rooms) to offer some degree of personalized service, this modern highrise promises nearly all the niceties you would pay extra for at more prestigious downtown hotels, including a harbor view. Furnishings and amenities are virtually at par with those found in the typical Hilton or Sheraton. There are a pool and spa, plus a restaurant and cocktail lounge. Deluxe.

No downtown hotel has a more colorful past than the **Horton Grand Hotel** (311 Island Avenue; 619-544-1886, 800-542-1886, fax 619-544-0058). This 132-room Victorian gem is actually two old hotels that were lavishly reconstructed and linked by an atrium-lobby and courtyard. The 1880s theme is faithfully executed, from the hotel's antique-furnished rooms (each with a fireplace) to its period-costumed staff. Suites with queen beds and pullout sofas will comfortably accommodate family groups. The hotel is within walking distance of two destinations that will appeal to families, the colorful Horton Plaza urban mall and Seaport Village. Ultra-deluxe.

CORONADO    Coronado has long been a playground of the rich and famous, and the city's hotel rates reflect its ritzy heritage. **El Cordova Hotel** (1351 Orange Avenue; 619-435-4131, 800-229-2032, fax 619-435-0632) is in the heart of Coronado. Originally built as a private mansion in 1902, El Cordova's moderate size (40 rooms) and lovely Spanish-hacienda architecture make it a relaxing getaway spot. A pool and patio restaurant are added features. Family suites are equipped with kitchenettes. Portable barbecue units are also available for cookouts. The kids will love the location, just half a block from Coronado Beach. Deluxe to ultra-deluxe.

Nothing can detract from the glamour of the **Hotel del Coronado** (1500 Orange Avenue; 619-522-8000, 800-468-3533, fax 619-522-8238). With its turrets, cupolas and gingerbread facade, this Victorian landmark is one of the great hotels of California. The last in a proud line of extravagant seaside resorts, the Hotel del Coronado has long been the lodging of choice for United States presidents and Hollywood stars. The 691-room "Del" has two pools, a long stretch of beach, tennis courts, a first-class health club and a gallery of shops. On one of the San Diego area's finest waterfronts, this resort is particularly appealing for children. A special Summer Play program offers day-long activities for children including games and beach sports. Teens can take a break from swimming at the video arcade. Ultra-deluxe.

---

*With a population of over one million, San Diego is the sixth-largest city in the United States.*

---

The **Coronado Victorian House** (1000 8th Street; 619-435-2200, 888-299-2822, fax 619-435-4760) is quite possibly the only hotel anywhere to include dance, exercise and gourmet cooking classes in a night's stay. Located in a historic landmark building near the beach and downtown Coronado, the decor of this seven-room bed and breakfast includes Persian rugs, stained-glass windows, and private baths with claw-foot tubs and jacuzzis. Those guests not interested in the extracurricular activities are invited to relax and enjoy such home-cooked specialties as baklava, stuffed grape leaves, homemade yogurt and potato casserole. Two-night minimum. Ultra-deluxe.

LA JOLLA  Like a Monopoly master, La Jolla possesses the lion's share of excellent accommodations in the San Diego area. Understandably, there are very few budget hotels in this fashionable village by the sea; only a few, in fact, offer affordably priced rooms. Among that scarce number, two stand out as the best values. **Sands of La Jolla** (5417 La Jolla Boulevard; 619-459-3336, 800-643-0530, fax 619-454-0922) is a small, 39-room motel on a busy thoroughfare. Rooms are not exactly designer showcases, but they are tastefully appointed and neatly maintained. Special two-room family suites feature kitchenettes with microwaves. The kids will enjoy splashing in the pool. Budget to deluxe.

Tucked away on the north fringe of the village is **Andrea Villa Inn** (2402 Torrey Pines Road; 619-459-3311, 800-411-2141, fax 619-459-1320), a classy-looking, 49-unit motel that packs more amenities than some resorts. Awaiting you are a pool, spa, and continental breakfast service. The rooms are spacious and professionally decorated with quality furniture. Kitchenettes are available. Andrea Villa is one of La Jolla's best hotel buys, located just six blocks from the beach and one block from a city park that's great for kids. Deluxe to ultra-deluxe.

La Jolla's only true beachfront hotel is **Sea Lodge on La Jolla Shores Beach** (8110 Camino del Oro; 619-459-8271, 800-237-5211, fax 619-456-9346). Designed and landscaped to resemble an old California hacienda, this 128-room retreat overlooks the Pacific on a mile-long beach. With its stuccoed arches, terra-cotta roofs, ceramic tilework, fountains and flowers, Sea Lodge offers a relaxing, south-of-the-border setting. Rooms are large and fittingly appointed with southwestern-style furnishings. All feature balconies and the usual amenities including pool and tennis courts. A children's wading pool, ping-pong and adjacent surf shops renting boogieboards make this laid-back resort popular with families. Babysitting service is available. Ultra-deluxe.

### SAN DIEGO DINING

SEA WORLD AREA   Critic's choice for the Pacific Beach area's best omelettes is **Broken Yoke Café** (1851 Garnet Avenue; 619-270-0045). Choose from nearly 30 of these eggy creations or invent your own. There are soups, sandwiches and salads, too. Pancakes, oatmeal, peanut-butter-and-jelly sandwiches and hamburgers are featured on the children's menu. Breakfast and lunch only. Budget.

DOWNTOWN SAN DIEGO   Attracting attention has never been a problem for the **Corvette Diner** (3946 5th Avenue; 619-542-1001). Cool 1950s music, a soda fountain (complete with resident jerks), rock-and-roll memorabilia, dancing waitresses and a classy Corvette have proven a magnetic formula. Simple "blue-plate" diner fare features meat loaf, chicken-fried steak and hefty hamburgers. A special kids' menu offers spaghetti, baby burgers, corn dogs, grilled cheese and peanut-butter-and-jelly sandwiches served with soft drink or milk and ice cream bar. Young people eager to catch up on their mid-20th-century musical history can place their requests with the resident DJ any evening. In addition, a magician performs on Tuesday and Wednesday, and on Friday and Saturday a guy does balloon tricks. Budget.

Everyone likes the warm, friendly atmosphere of a real family restaurant like **Hob Nob Hill** (2271 1st Avenue; 619-239-8176). Here's a place where the waitresses call the kids "hon" and remind them to finish their veggies. The owners have been serving breakfast, lunch and dinner since 1944, and a gang of grandmas couldn't do it better. Favorites are waffles, homemade breads, chicken and dumplings, potatoes with gravy, lamb shanks and corned beef cured in the restaurant's own vats. Silver-dollar pancakes, burgers, grilled cheese, turkey sandwiches and fish and chips are on the kid's menu. Wholesome, tasty food. Budget to moderate.

Visitors to Horton Plaza are bombarded with dining opportunities. But for those who can resist the temptation to chow down on pizza, French fries and enchiladas at nearby fast-food shops, there is

---

*San Diego County, measuring 4261 square miles, is as large as Connecticut.*

---

a special culinary reward. On the plaza's top level sits **Panda Inn** (506 Horton Plaza; 619-233-7800). Here the plush, contemporary design alludes only subtly to the Orient with a scattering of classic artwork. But the menu is all-Asian. Lunch and dinner menus together present more than 100 dishes. Dine on the glassed-in veranda for a great view of the harbor. Moderate.

For inexpensive Mexican food, families will want to head to **El Indio** (409 F Street; 619-239-8151). Dressed in a pink-and-white color scheme, this self-service café has chimichangas, shredded beef burritos and a host of other south-of-the-border dishes. Mini-bean or fruit burritos, mini-quesadillas and mini-chimichangas are perfect for smaller appetites. Closed Sunday. Budget.

Following a visit to Balboa Park or the zoo, there is nothing better than a plate of *poo ja* followed by a spicy serving of *gang ped*. Enjoy these and other wonderful Thai favorites at **Celedon** (3628 5th Avenue; 619-295-8800). Mild or spicy, Celedon's curried and stir-fried specialties are delicious. The stylish art deco surroundings, nicely appointed with original Thai brassworks and tapestries, add to the graceful flair of this excellent eatery. No lunch on Saturday. Closed Sunday. Moderate.

CORONADO    **Peohe's** (1201 1st Street; 619-437-4474) at the Ferry Landing Marketplace is primarily praised for its panoramic views of San Diego Bay and for its tropical decor. The aqua-accented dining room features green palms, and the children will get a kick out of dining next to rushing cascades of water flowing into ponds of live fish. The dinner menu is mostly fresh fish plus lobster, shrimp and scallops. There are also prime rib and lamb. We prefer the lunch, with a tasty soup/salad/sandwich combo at a moderate price. Featured on the children's menu are fish, chicken and hamburger plates. Moderate to deluxe.

POINT LOMA    The Point Loma neighborhood boasts San Diego's best soup-and-salad bar and our own favorite for healthy budget dining. **Souplantation** (3960 West Point Loma Boulevard; 619-222-7404) is also one of San Diego's best family dining deals. It features two bars loaded with the prettiest produce this side of the farmers market. Included are over 60 items to heap on your plate. Six tasty soups are made from scratch daily, and a variety of muffins is served hot from the oven. Fresh fruit rounds out this wholesome fare. It's a comfortable, wood-paneled environment. Children under 12 are half price, and kids under 3 eat free. Budget.

OLD TOWN AND MISSION VALLEY   Mexican food and atmosphere abound in Old Town, especially in the popular Bazaar del Mundo, a great spot for family dining. Two restaurants lure a steady stream of diners into festive, flowered courtyards. **Casa de Pico** (2754 Calhoun Street; 619-296-3267) is a favorite place to sit and munch nachos. Mexican entrées are served outside on the patio or in one of the hacienda-style dining rooms. Special kids' plates offer a choice of chicken flautas, burritos, tacos, quesadillas or beef taquitos with rice or beans. Budget to moderate.

Next door, in a magnificent hacienda built in 1829, **Casa de Bandini** (2754 Calhoun Street; 619-297-8211) has cuisine that's a bit more refined. Seafood is good here, especially the crab enchiladas. Mariachis often play at both restaurants. There's also a children's menu offering specialties like chicken enchiladas and beef tacos. Budget to moderate.

LA JOLLA   **Manhattan** (7766 Fay Avenue; 619-554-1444), which successfully replicates a New York City family-style Italian restaurant (despite the palms and pink stucco), features a singing maitre d'. The most popular dishes include zesty scampi *fra diavalo* over pasta, veal marsala and rack of lamb. There are wonderful Caesar salads and cannoli desserts every night. Moderate to deluxe.

**John's Waffle Shop** (7906 Girard Avenue; 619-454-7371) is a traditional La Jolla stopping place for old-fashioned, counter-style breakfasts or lunches. Locals start their day here with golden waffles, or eggs Benedict. The best lunches are the country-fried steak and grilled tuna melt on sourdough bread. Half portions are available for modest appetites. Kids will enjoy taking a seat at the counter, the heart of this community gathering place that's as much a part of La Jolla as the beach. Budget.

## SAN DIEGO BEACHES AND PARKS

SEA WORLD AREA   A major gathering place, the boardwalk at the south end of **Pacific Beach Park** is crowded with teenagers. But a few blocks north, just before Crystal Pier, the boardwalk becomes a quieter concrete promenade that follows scenic, sloping cliffs. The beach widens here, and the crowd becomes more family oriented. The surf is moderate and fine for swimming and bodysurfing. North of the pier, Ocean Boulevard becomes a pedestrian-only mall with a bike path, benches and picnic tables.

The wide, sandy beach at the southern end of Mission Bay Park, **Mission Beach Park** is a favorite haunt of high schoolers and college students. The most interesting spot is at the foot of Capistrano Court. A paved boardwalk runs along the beach and is busy with bicyclists, joggers and rollerbladers.

Where you toss down your towel at **Ocean Beach** will probably depend as much on your age as your interests. Surfers and sailors hang out around the pier; farther north, where the surf is milder and the beach wider, families can be found sunbathing and strolling. Take Ocean Beach Freeway (Route 8) west until it ends; turn left onto Sunset Cliffs Boulevard, then right on Voltaire Street.

A two-mile strip of fluffy white sand, **Silver Strand State Beach** (619-435-5184; admission) fronts a narrow isthmus separating the Pacific Ocean and San Diego Bay. It was named for the tiny silver seashells found in abundance along the shore. Swimming here is good on both bay and ocean side. The park is popular for surf-fishing and clamming. Camping for RVs and trailers only. Located on Silver Strand Boulevard between Imperial Beach and Coronado.

De Anza Cove, at the extreme northeast corner of the Mission Bay Park, has a sandy beach ideal for swimming plus the largest of San Diego's commercial campgrounds, **Campland On The Bay** (2211 Pacific Beach Drive; 619-581-4260), featuring hook-up sites for RVs, vans, tents and boats.

LA JOLLA   **Torrey Pines State Beach** (619-755-2063; admission) is a long, wide, sandy stretch adjacent to Los Peñasquitos Lagoon and Torrey Pines State Reserve. It's popular for sunning, swimming, surfing, surf-fishing and picnicking. Nearby trails lead through the rich reserves. Located just south of Carmel Valley Road in Del Mar.

With coastal bluffs above, narrow sand beach below and rich tidepools offshore, **Scripps Beach** is a great strand for beachcombers. Two underwater reserves are among the attractions. Located at the 8600 block of La Jolla Shores Drive.

The sand is wide and the swimming easy at **La Jolla Shores Beach**, so, naturally, it's covered with bodies whenever the sun appears. It's located off Camino del Oro and Costa Boulevard in La Jolla.

# The Sporting Life

## SPORTFISHING

The lure of sport and bottom fishing attracts thousands of enthusiasts to San Diego every year. Albacore and snapper are the close-in favorites, with marlin and tuna the prime objectives for longer charters. For deep-sea charters, see **Seaforth Sportfishing** (1717 Quivira Road, Mission Bay; 619-224-3383), **Islandia Sportfishing** (1551 West Mission Bay Drive, Mission Bay; 619-222-1164), **Point Loma Sportfishing** (1403 Scott Street, Point Loma; 619-223-1627) or **Fisherman's Landing** (2838 Garrison Street, Point Loma; 619-222-0391).

## WHALE WATCHING

For whale-watching tours contact **Islandia Sportfishing** (1551 West Mission Bay Drive; 619-222-1164) or **Point Loma Sportfishing** (1403 Scott Street, Point Loma; 619-223-1627).

## SKINDIVING

San Diego offers countless spots for diving. The rocky La Jolla coves boast the clearest water on the state's coast. Bird Rock, La Jolla Underwater Park and the underwater Scripp's Canyon are ideal havens for divers. In Point Loma try the colorful tidepools at Cabrillo Underwater Reserve.

For diving rentals, sales, instruction and dive tips contact **San Diego Diver's Supply** (4004 Sports Arena Boulevard, San Diego; 619-224-3439) and **Diving Locker** (1020 Grand Avenue, Pacific Beach; 619-272-1120).

## SURFING AND WINDSURFING

Surf's up in the San Diego area. Pacific, Mission and Ocean beaches, Tourmaline Surfing Park, and Windansea, La Jolla Shores, Swami and

---

### UP, UP AND AWAY

*Hot-air ballooning is a romantic pursuit that has soared in popularity in the Del Mar area. A growing number of ballooning companies offer spectacular dawn and sunset flights, most concluding with a traditional champagne toast. One of the companies in the Del Mar Valley is **A Skysurfer Balloon Company** (619-481-6800).*

*There's a glassed-in whale-watching observatory at Cabrillo National Monument on Point Loma.*

Moonlight beaches are well-known hangouts for surfers. Sailboarding is concentrated within Mission Bay. For surfboard and body board rentals try **Mitch's** (631 Pearl Street, La Jolla; 619-459-5933).

## BOATING

You can sail under the Coronado Bridge, skirt the gorgeous downtown skyline and even get a taste of open ocean in this Southern California sailing mecca. Several sailing companies operate out of Harbor Island West in San Diego, including **Harbor Sailboats** (2040 Harbor Island Drive, Suite 104; 619-291-9568) and **San Diego Sailing Club and School** (1880 Harbor Island Drive; 619-298-6623), which also has kayaks.

Other motorboat and sail rentals in the area can be found at **Seaforth Mission Bay Boat Rental** (1641 Quivira Road, Mission Bay; 619-223-1681) and **Coronado Boat Rentals** (1715 Strand Way, Coronado; 619-437-1514), where you can also rent kayaks and canoes.

Yacht charters are available through **Hornblower Dining Yachts** (1066 North Harbor Drive, San Diego; 619-238-1686).

## GOLF

For the golfing set there are **Torrey Pines Municipal Golf Course** (11480 North Torrey Pines Road, La Jolla; 619-570-1234), **Balboa Park Municipal Golf Course** (Golf Course Drive, Balboa Park; 619-235-1184), **Coronado Municipal Golf Course** (2000 Visalia Row, Coronado; 619-435-3121) and **Mission Bay Golf Resort** (2702 North Mission Bay Drive, Mission Bay; 619-490-3370).

## TENNIS

San Diego has many private and public courts open to traveling tennis buffs. Find some love (on the courts, that is!) at **Balboa Tennis Club** (2221 Morley Field Drive, San Diego; 619-295-9278), **Peninsula Tennis Club** (2525½ Bacon Street, Ocean Beach; 619-226-3407) and **La Jolla Recreation Center** (615 Prospect Street, La Jolla; 619-552-1658). In Coronado call the **Coronado Tennis Center** (1501 Glorietta Boulevard; 619-435-1616) for information on courts.

BIKING

Cycling has skyrocketed in popularity throughout San Diego County, especially in coastal areas. **Balboa Park** and **Mission Bay Park** both have excellent bike routes.

BIKE RENTALS    To rent a bicycle in San Diego, contact **Penny-farthings** (314 G Street; 619-233-7696); and **San Diego Bike** (127 East Island Avenue; 619-232-4700); and in Coronado call **Holland's Bicycles** (977 Orange Avenue at 10th Street; 619-435-3153).

WALKING TOURS

Several San Diego organizations and tour operators offer organized walks: **Gaslamp Quarter Historical Foundation** (410 Island Avenue; 619-233-4692) conducts walking tours of the restored downtown historic district. Walking tours of **Old Town State Historic Park** are offered daily through park headquarters (4002 Wallace Street; 619-220-5423). Join **Coronado Touring** (1110 Isabella Avenue, Coronado; 619-435-5993) for a leisurely, one-and-a-half-hour guided stroll through quaint Coronado.

# EIGHT

# Los Angeles Day Trips

From the beaches of the Pacific to the foothills of the San Gabriels, **203**
Los Angeles seems virtually inexhaustible. There is so much for families to do and see here that one day trip of the area simply won't see
m enough. The second-largest city in the country, it rests in a bowl
surrounded by five mountain ranges and an ocean and holds within
its ambit sandy beaches, hills and wind-ruffled deserts. The 74-mile
coastline extending north from Long Beach to Malibu is hard to pass
up. Along the way you'll have an opportunity to explore tidepools,
visit amusement parks and see the habitat of movie stars. Life here
reflects the culture of the beach, a freewheeling, pleasure-seeking philosophy that combines hedonism with healthfulness.

Inland Los Angeles County opens up even more possibilities. First
there is Six Flags California, one of today's greatest amusement parks.
Then there are the La Brea Tar Pits, dating back to the heyday of the
dinosaurs.

Many of the city's best family activities focus around Griffith Park,
home of the municipal zoo and planetarium. Of course, no visit to
the Los Angeles area is complete without a trip to Hollywood. The
NBC and Paramount Studios tours offer a chance to see both television production and motion picture sets. You could become part
of a studio audience and see the day-to-day activities of a multimedia complex.

All these features make the Los Angeles area worth a special trip.
An intriguing city with colorful murals, folk art, historic adobes and
offbeat shops, this is a great place for casual daytripping. If you can't
find it in Los Angeles, look again. It's probably just around the corner.

## Six Flags California

Spreading across 260 acres and featuring a private lake and a 4000-seat stadium, Six Flags California encompasses Six Flags Magic Mountain, a quintessential roller-coaster park, and Six Flags Hurricane Harbor, a family-oriented water park featuring water slides and a wave pool open in the summer. Though located adjacent to one another, Magic Mountain and Hurricane Harbor are separate parks with their own entrances and admission fees not to mention distinct personalities that draw different crowds. To know Magic Mountain is a thrill-ride heaven you only have to look at the mix of hand-holding teens in baggy shorts and high-tops who throng to the park each weekend. By 6 p.m. on a Saturday, anyone over 19 definitely is in the minority. Yet Magic Mountain maintains some family appeal with its less-intrepid rides, a beautifully restored 1912 carousel and a delightful collection of Warner Brothers/Looney Tunes characters. However, it's Hurricane Harbor that most appeals to families, especially those with young kids. The atmosphere is more easygoing, and most attractions are geared toward children.

Summer months are high season when the park reaches an effervescent energy level. The greatest number of shows will be up and operating then, and the crowds will also be colossal. The park is open daily during the summer. During the off-season, from mid-September to the end of May, the park is open weekends and holidays only. Hours vary, so call before setting out.

**Arrival:** The park is in Valencia in the Santa Clarita Valley, a half-hour drive north of Hollywood. Take the Magic Mountain Parkway exit off Route 5. It steers you directly into the park. You'll pay a $6 parking fee and be directed to a lot from which trams will deliver you to the main gate.

**Ticket Options:** Six Flags Magic Mountain only offers one-day passes. However, at certain times of the year they have a "Twicket," which allows the bearer a second day of admission for a nominal fee.

Available in the summer is a two-park combo ticket, which allows entrance to both Magic Mountain and Hurricane Harbor on a single day. The admission to Six Flags Magic Mountain is $35 for adults and $17 for children under 48 inches. Tickets to Six Flags Hurricane Harbor cost $18 for adults and $11 for children under 48 inches. Two-park combo tickets cost $50 for adults (no combo ticket for

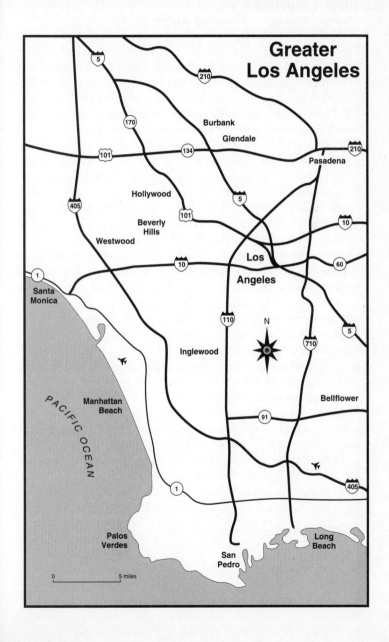

children). Season passes are $65. Children under 3 are free at both Magic Mountain and Hurricane Harbor.

**Sightseeing Strategies:** You'll be one of more than three million people to visit Magic Mountain this year, so it's wise to have a plan. Superman the Escape, Viper and Flashback develop lines within minutes of opening time, especially on summer weekends. If you have teens in your group (there are height restrictions on these rides), you'll want to be in line in your car when the parking-lot gates open, which is an hour before the park begins business.

If you can get through the parking gates within 15 minutes of the park's opening time, catch the tram or walk to the main gate. You won't be bored while standing in line because a Dixieland band performs while you wait. Then, if you can get through the entrance gates in the first ten minutes they're open and head for Superman the Escape, you'll be on the ride by 10:20. Dash over to Viper, where a small line will already have formed. You may have to wait 20 minutes or so, but it's nothing compared to the one-to-two-hour lines you can expect by the early afternoon. If you want to ride Flashback head there now since it draws crowds as well. From there, hit the rides of your choice wherever lines are shortest.

If you're with smaller children who can't make coaster height minimums, you can plan a more leisurely arrival. After coming through the main gate, go straight ahead to the red-brick Guest Relations building and pick up a park map. To help in planning your strategy, we have grouped rides and attractions in Magic Mountain by type rather than geographic location in the park.

Unlike Magic Mountain, there is no strategy for an enjoyable day at Hurricane Harbor. Lines and crowds are not as intense here as they are next door; just show up and have fun!

**Nuts & Bolts:** For general information regarding both parks call 805-255-4111 or 818-367-2271.

In Magic Mountain, lockers, strollers and wheelchair rentals are located in Six Flags Plaza near the entrance to Flashback. Free ken-

---

*FLASHBACK*

*The relentless Flashback coaster employs all the ingenuity of Swiss design to create a ride acclaimed as unique in the world. Each 20-person train carries four riders in each row who sit side by side and experience the feeling of falling face first from the height of an eight-story building. Nearly 130 tons of blue steel tubing were needed to build this $4 million thriller.*

nel services are located in the parking lot. At Guest Relations you'll find Lost and Found and Lost Children services. A nurse or paramedic is always on duty at First Aid, between the Gotham City Backlot entrance and Magic Moments Theatre. A convenient, free package service lets you make purchases in the park throughout the day, then pick them up before you leave at a shop called Flags near the front of the park. Most ATM cards are accepted at terminals in Six Flags Plaza.

In Hurricane Harbor, lockers are located in Buccaneer Village inside the entrance and to the left. You can rent strollers and wheelchairs at Magic Mountain and bring them into Hurricane Harbor. Guest Relations, also in Buccaneer Village, is where you'll find Lost and Found and Lost Children services. First Aid is located behind the lockers.

**Getting Around:** Working in a clockwise fashion, you enter the roughly circular-shape park at 6 o'clock. Moving to your left, the entrances to Viper and Revolution are within a few hundred feet of each other. Following the circle, Roaring Rapids, Ninja and Skytower are spaced inward from the park's perimeter. Psyclone is in the far corner, followed by Dive Devil, Batman Action Theatre and Freefall at high noon. Batman the Ride, Flashback and Colossus are along the opposite edge of the circle, with Superman the Escape in the middle of Samurai Summit.

For an overview, you can hop on the **Metro**, a comfortably modern monorail that stops at three different stations. It's also a good spot for a rest. To avoid a hill-climb, the **Orient Express**, a European-style funicular built in Zurich, takes you to Samurai Summit.

Working your way around Hurricane Harbor in a clockwise direction, you first come to Tiki Falls, the enclosed tube slides. Near the exit to Tiki Falls are the raft rentals to use in Forgotten Sea, a wave pool. Beyond that is Taboo Tower, three high-speed water slides. Lightning Falls and Lost Temple Rapids, two other water slides, are also located along the perimeter. In the center of Hurricane Harbor are Shipwreck Shores, River Cruise and Castaway Cove.

## SIX FLAGS MAGIC MOUNTAIN

The park has ten distinctively themed areas. **Cyclone Bay**, adjacent to the Psyclone wood roller coaster, has the flavor of a beachfront boardwalk and features food areas, specialty shops and live entertainment. **Samurai Summit** with its Oriental theme is home to Superman the Escape, Ninja, the Four Winds Restaurant and Skytower. The **Gotham City Backlot**, Batman's home, features Batman the

*Psyclone, a classic wood roller coaster, is a replica of New York's legendary Coney Island Cyclone built in 1927.*

Ride and a Batmobile replica. **Bugs Bunny World** and **Wile E. Coyote Critter Canyon** are planned especially for the small set. The **Six Flags Plaza**, located at the entrance, includes a Guest Relations center, shops and fountains where everyone seems to wait for lost friends.

ROLLER COASTERS AND THRILL RIDES    Southern California enjoys a longstanding love affair with coasters, and Magic Mountain caters to that addiction by introducing new terrifiers on a regular basis. These thrillers, from the classic wood varieties to those with cutting-edge technology, run the gamut of roller-coaster excitement.

Unless you've already booked passage on one of the space shuttle launches, **Superman the Escape** has got to be the next best thing. Six Flags has outdone itself with this one: strapped into one of two 15-passenger vehicles, you escape the Fortress of Solitude, a crystalline ice cavern atop the park's mountain ridge. Electromagnetic motors fire you through a special-effects tunnel and along an L-shaped dual track that spans 900 feet. Accelerating from 0 to 100 miles per hour in seven seconds, the vehicle blasts along the track, hits the curve at 100 mph, rockets straight up the 41-story tower, then free-falls back down. At one point during the ride, you'll experience a force of 4.5 Gs before you go to weightlessness for six and a half seconds. If you're just not up to this one, but would rather watch, the best viewing spot is from the plaza right in front of the Gotham City Gate.

On **Flashback**, the only diving roller coaster in the world, you're hauled upward through what appear to be stacks of track, then dropped from the top with a free-fall effect through six steeply banked, vertical 180-degree dives. Just when you think it's over, you enter a 540-degree upward spiral that seems to defy gravity.

**Psyclone** begins with an inky-black, 183-foot tunnel complete with maniacal laughter that prepares you for a 95-foot drop angled at 53 degrees. You'll hit 50 miles per hour as you race down ten steep hills and five banked turns. Psyclone got its name because of its reputation for messing with people's minds. Not surprising when you consider how much it looks like a Los Angeles freeway interchange.

In the opinion of many, **Viper** is the most frightening roller coaster in captivity. It turns you upside down seven times. Its snake-green cars seem to slither along the bright-red track, then "strike" with lightning speed. This mega-coaster, the largest looping roller coaster in the world, drops you 18 relentless stories as it spins through a classic corkscrew. Despite all, the ride is remarkably smooth, attesting to its high-tech perfection.

**Batman the Ride** takes you through hairpin turns, vertical loops, corkscrews and a zero-gravity spin. Experience all of this in a ski lift–style train that lacks a floor. Try to hit this ride early because lines can mean up to a two-hour wait.

**Dive Devil**, another new attraction, combines skydiving and hang gliding into one experience. Strapped into a harness, you're hoisted 150 feet in the air by cables attached to two towers. When one cable is released, you drop and soar in an arc at a speed of up to 60 mph. You can ride solo or with two pals, but you'll need to make a reservation. There's an extra cost to make this daredevil stunt ($15–$25), and divers must be at least 48 inches in height.

**Ninja**, set high above the park on Samurai Summit, is the West Coast's fastest suspended roller coaster. The out-of-control feeling here is intensified because trains hang from an overhead track and swing from side to side 180 degrees!

**Colossus**, the largest dual-track wood coaster ever built, is as notable for its architectural style as its ride. With almost two miles of track, this classic is the longest roller coaster in the park. Providing the rattly, clackety ride of a traditional coaster, it drops and flings you with abandon. If you like coaster thrills but aren't interested in being turned upside down, this is the ride for you.

One of the park's oldies but goodies, the **Revolution** is the first looping roller coaster ever built. Despite its age, this thriller hasn't lost a bit of its pizazz. At one point you're looped 360 degrees to

---

*GRAND CAROUSEL*

*This elegant dowager from another era was built in 1912 by the Philadelphia Toboggan Co. For 50 years it delighted guests at Savin Rock Amusement Park in West Haven, Connecticut, before being brought to Magic Mountain in 1971 and refurbished for the park's opening. Boasting 64 horses and two carriages, it glows with more than 1600 lights.*

---

*One shop close to Roaring Rapids claims that it does its biggest business in re-clothing folks soaked on this ride.*

---

find yourself staring down 90 feet at the Grand Carousel. For true coaster aficionados, this ride will have a touch of nostalgia.

The **Gold Rusher** opened with the park in 1971 and is still going strong. Here you board a runaway mine train that turns sharply, drops quickly and executes dual horizontal loops. It's tame compared to Viper and won't develop such long lines, so it's fun even for younger kids. Hit this one when crowds are at their peak.

These all have 42- to 54-inch height restrictions, so check before you stand in line.

FAMILY RIDES   How do you feel about jumping off a ten-story building? **Freefall** lets you do it in four-person cars that are cranked to the top of a tower, then pushed off the edge. You plunge at 55 miles per hour with your stomach in your throat, then end up on your back being air-braked to a halt. If the ride has a fault, it's that it's over before true terror has time to register.

You're guaranteed to get wet on **Tidal Wave** where 20-passenger boats plunge over a 50-foot waterfall, dunking those in the front seats and splashing onlookers.

You bounce through the waves and cross-currents of **Roaring Rapids** in huge, 12-passenger circular boats that serve as giant inner tubes careening off rocks and boulders. The sign at the entrance says, "You WILL get wet. You MAY get drenched." Count on the latter.

Another ride with a splashy finale, **Jet Stream** features jet boats that power up a hill, circle the back country and plummet into Jet Stream Lake via a 57-foot plunge, guaranteeing yet another shower.

On **Log Jammer**, riders float freely in four-person "logs" along a water flume. The final vertical drop looks worse than it is. You'll get damp, but nothing like on Roaring Rapids. Lines move quickly here so do this ride at peak hours.

In the Gotham City Backlot, **Gordon Gearworks** uses centrifugal force to hold you to the wall while you twirl into the air. Another Gotham ride, the **ACME Atom Smasher** is a fast-moving ride that sends you spinning.

**Buccaneer** swings back and forth, defying gravity in a "pirate ship." **Sandblasters** is an old-fashioned bumper-car ride.

For a park overview, **Skytower** lifts you gently 38 stories above the park to an enclosed circular viewing deck for a panorama of the entire Santa Clarita Valley. On windy days you can feel the tower sway.

All ages seem to take to the **Grand Carousel**. Its location, directly next to Revolution, clearly defines how amusement park rides have changed in the last half-century.

BUGS BUNNY WORLD    Warner Brothers/Looney Tunes characters welcome the guests to **Bugs Bunny World** at Magic Mountain, a six-acre funland for kids with seven pint-size rides and adventures here in their exclusive Southern California home. Bugs, Sylvester, Yosemite Sam, Pepe Le Pew and others are always ready to pose for photos.

At **Elmer Fudd's Orchard** kids climb into green "worms" that wind around a huge, red apple. Mini three-wheelers, complete with lights and throttles, putt around the **Tasmanian Devils** track. **Road Runner Racers** features scaled-down Grand Prix cars, or kids can steer dune buggies around the **Daffy Dunes** track. Even two-year-olds imitate their older siblings on the **Wile E. Coyote Coaster** as they ride the dips and turns shrieking and screaming with both hands in the air. Baron Von Fudd's World War I Fokker triplanes chase Sop with Camel biplanes. Kids can take the stick to control how high they go. **Tweety Bird Cages** swing little ones gently, and **Honey Bunny Bugs** circle around an oversized mushroom. At **Speedy Gonzalez Mouse Racers** kids can ride pink-eared rodents that chase one another around a piece of cheese.

WILE E. COYOTE CRITTER CANYON    From Bugs Bunny World, follow the paw prints to **Wile E. Coyote Critter Canyon**, a see-and-touch petting zoo housing more than 55 species of exotic and barnyard animals. Children here can pet woolly sheep and goats, watch a wallaby and admire the beauty of a regal golden eagle. Kids can see this eight-acre area from electrically powered miniature antique cars on the **Granny Gran Prix**, which takes them on a loop through the canyon.

SHOWS AND ENTERTAINMENT    At the Valencia Falls Pavilion Bugs Bunny is the president of the **Warner Bros. Kids Club**, a participatory game show suitable for the whole family. Learn about Hollywood stunts and special effects during the **Batman Forever Stunt Show**, held at the Batman Action Theater. The **Animals in Action Show** at the Animal Star Theatre features a menagerie of exotic animals. Celebrating **Looney Tunes Nights**, Bugs Bunny, Looney Tunes Characters and Comic Book Super-Heroes parade through the park finishing in Six Flags Plaza with a fireworks finale.

Not every show is available at all times of year, so check with the park for the latest schedule.

## SIX FLAGS HURRICANE HARBOR

If the soakings from Magic Mountain's Tidal Wave and Roaring Rapids rides aren't wet enough, it's probably time to head next door to Hurricane Harbor, Six Flags' extravagantly themed water park opened in 1995.

One of the nicest things about Hurricane Harbor is how kid-friendly it is. While Six Flags, with its emphasis on super-thrill rides and roller coasters, may not seem a particularly appropriate destination for small children, Hurricane Harbor is different; a fantasy entertainment environment of lost lagoons and pirate coves that was designed with children in mind (one attraction doesn't even allow adults). Of course with the addition of some new attractions, there's a nice balance in the thrill ride department too, and grown-ups will be plenty pleased with the selection of twisting water slides and daredevil drops.

The park is divided into several themed water areas. **Castaway Cove** is a large water play area for kids under 54 inches and includes waterfalls, water gadgets and swings. There are slides and some nice little pools to splash in, as well as a shady area on the outskirts lined with chaise longues. In **Shipwreck Shores**, a huge skull is mounted on the mast of Red Eye the Pirate's ship. This area is for all kids and adults. The skull dumps gallons of water on "intruders" every few minutes. On a raft, you can float along on **The River Cruise**, a 1300-foot-long lazy river that surrounds Castaway Cove and Shipwreck Shore, past the 45-foot volcano, **Geyser Peak**. A wave pool called **Forgotten Sea** is the park's largest "ocean," generating two-foot waves and measuring up to six feet deep. If you'd prefer to watch, you can take a seat on one of the surrounding lounge chairs. The park's newest themed area, **Lizard Lagoon**, is aimed at adult and teenage beach enthusiasts. The 3.2-acre recreation lagoon features water basketball, beach volleyball and comfortable lounge chairs set beneath swaying palm trees. Here's where you'll also find **Reptile Ridge**, a 35-foot-high structure housing five open and enclosed tubes ranging from a 255-foot-long gentle slide (Croc Creek), to a 70-foot-long straight drop (Gator Gorge).

Thrill riders, in fact, have a growing number of attractions to choose from, now that Hurricane Harbor has added to its stock of thrill slides. Most are enclosed- or open-tube slides that gently spiral or twist. One of the new themed areas, **Black Snake Summit**, features five new slides: **Twisted Fang** and **Coiled Cobra**, at 75 feet high each, the tallest fully enclosed speed slides in Southern California; the **Venom Drop**, an open tube offering a 75-foot near-vertical plunge; and the **Sidewinder** and **Boa Constrictor** slides, both 650-foot-long, fully enclosed tubes. The park's most novel addition may in fact be the **Bamboo Racer**, an attraction where six riders race along a 625-foot slide (head first, no less) on specially designed water "toboggans." Continuing old favorites include **Taboo Tower**, a crumbling temple with three routes of "escape": **Daredevil Plunge**, which has a 45-degree drop; the bumpy **Escape Chute**; and the **Secret Passage**, a 325-foot enclosed spiraling slide. The other water slides are **Lightning Falls** (twisting, open tubes), **Tiki Falls** (enclosed and semi-enclosed tubes) and **Lost Temple Rapids** (a four-person raft ride).

Hurricane Harbor features changing rooms with showers and lockers (extra charge) and raft rentals. A general admission admits you to all the attractions.

## SIX FLAGS CALIFORNIA DINING

SIX FLAGS MAGIC MOUNTAIN   Don't look for haute cuisine inside the park, but you will find plenty of variety among its 16 restaurants and stands. The **Laughing Dragon Pizza Co.** is probably the most attractive of the three moderately-priced sit-down restaurants, as much for its colorful and whimsical decor as for its location atop Samurai Summit, which affords great views of the park. As for the food, the name is a good indicator: individual California-style pizzas, salads and pastas. The **Mooseburger Lodge** resembles a High Sierra mountain lodge complete with a stuffed moose. The menu, which features the mooseburger, offers ribs and chicken dishes, as well as a buffet and salad bar. Bright, airy **Food Etc.** near Critter Canyon serves cafeteria-style barbecue, pasta, deli subs and salads. You can eat indoors or out on the patio.

The park's 12 budget-priced food stands all are adjacent to pleasant patios with outdoor seating. At **Dock Side Deli** in Cyclone Bay guests are entertained with live California pop music while they eat. **Cantina** has tostadas, tacos and enchiladas, and **Pizza Vector** specializes in pepperoni and sausage pizza. A good bet for dessert is **Plaza Cafe** where hand-dipped ice cream in super duper–sized cones will satisfy the biggest sweet-tooth. For an instant snack, popcorn and pretzel wagons roam the park.

SIX FLAGS HURRICANE HARBOR   Caribbean-style buildings house the food stands and souvenir shops in Hurricane Harbor. **Red Eye's Kitchen**, in Buccaneer Village, offers rotisserie chicken, burgers and hot dogs, salads and soft drinks. Fresh fruit and juices can be found at **Tradewind Treats** in Castaway Cove, while snacks like ices, churros and pretzels are at **Paradise Snacks** next to Forgotten Sea.

## SIX FLAGS CALIFORNIA AREA LODGING

There are dozens, perhaps hundreds, of hotels and motels in the San Fernando Valley within 20 to 30 minutes of Magic Mountain, ranging from super-budget to moderately elegant. Hotels here, all within five minutes of the park, have higher rates in summer.

The 152-room **Hilton Garden Inn** (27710 The Old Road, Valencia; 805-254-8800, 800-445-8667, fax 805-254-9399) is practically in Magic Mountain's lap. It's the most upscale of the close-to-the-park hotels, and is also the nearest (just a ten-minute walk from the gate). The two-story Spanish hacienda–style inn has oversized pastel-decor rooms with vaulted ceilings. Poolside lunch and beverage service give the place a resort-like feel as does the small workout center overlooking the pool and spa. It's one of the few hotels in the area that has a restaurant with room service. During the summer they provide games and activity programs for children. Deluxe to ultra-deluxe.

**Best Western Ranch House Inn** (27413 North Tourney Road, Valencia; 805-255-0555, 800-944-7446, fax 805-255-2216) is across the freeway from the park, about a 15-minute walk away. This two-story hostelry is made up of four different buildings. Room prices depend on which building you're in, with the least-expensive ones closest to the freeway. Rooms are homey and comfortable, if not particularly stylish. A spa, two pools plus a wading pool make it family-friendly. Children under 17 stay free. Moderate.

The **Hampton Inn** (25259 The Old Road, Santa Clarita; 805-253-2400, 800-426-7866, fax 805-253-1683) is three miles south of the park. Its rooms are fresh and pleasantly furnished in muted-tone Southwest style. Nightly cookie service in the lobby offers families a chance to defervesce after a busy day. There's no restaurant on premises, but the California breakfast buffet, included with rooms, is appealing and extensive. The palm-fringed pool and patio area add a Southern California touch. Deluxe.

The **Comfort Inn** (31558 Castaic Road, Castaic; 805-295-1100, 800-228-5150, fax 805-295-0379) offers reasonably priced, no-frills accommodations in a nondescript, two-story building. It's located five minutes north of the park, and although lacking in architectural grandeur it has an uncommonly helpful staff. Continental breakfast, included in the room rate, is more than adequate. Moderate.

## Long Beach

Anchoring the southern end of Los Angeles County is Long Beach, one of California's largest cities. Here you can visit the enclave of **Naples**, which was conceived early in the century. Modeled on Italy's fabled canal towns, it's a tiny community of three islands separated by canals and linked with walkways.

Adding to the sense of old Italia is the **Gondola Getaway** (5437 East Ocean Boulevard, Long Beach; 562-433-9595), a romantic, hour-long cruise through the canals of Naples. For a hefty price (less, however, than a ticket to Italy), you can climb aboard a gondola, dine on hors d'oeuvres and be serenaded with Italian music.

But the high point of any Long Beach tour is a visit to the **Queen Mary** (1126 Queen's Highway, Port of Long Beach; 562-435-3511; admission). Making her maiden voyage in 1936, the *Queen Mary* was the pride of Great Britain. Winston Churchill, the Duke and Duchess of Windsor, Greta Garbo and Fred Astaire all got to know her charms. Today this 1000-foot-long "city at sea" has been transformed into a floating museum and hotel. An art deco classic, the vessel was known as the "Ship of Beautiful Woods." An elaborate walking tour carries you down into the engine room (a world of pumps and propellers), out along the wooden decks and up to each level of this multistage behemoth. Dioramas throughout the ship realistically portray every aspect of sailing life during the great age of ocean liners. The *Queen Mary*, expertly refurbished and wonderfully laid out, is an important addition to the Long Beach seafront and the anchor attraction for Queen Mary Seaport, which also includes The Queen's Marketplace shopping and dining area.

*Queen Mary's* neighbor is the world's largest clear-span geodesic dome. The dome, now empty, once housed Howard Hughes' *Spruce Goose*, the largest plane ever built.

Since Marine World closed down years ago, the Los Angeles–Long Beach area has been without a major marine-themed attraction. The summer 1998 opening of the **Long Beach Aquarium of the Pacific** (100 Aquarium Way, Long Beach; 562-590-3100; admission) fills this void. The aquarium has three major permanent galleries designed to lead visitors on a "journey of discovery" through the waters of the Pacific Ocean. One exhibit features the huge Tropical Reef Tank, where microphone-equipped scuba divers swim along with schools of brilliant fish and sharks, answering questions for visitors. Kids will enjoy the touch tank full of marine creatures.

The Pacific Ocean may be Long Beach's biggest natural attraction, but many birds in the area prefer the **El Dorado Nature Center** (7550 East Spring Street; 562-570-1745; admission). Part of the 400-acre El Dorado East Regional Park, this wildlife sanctuary offers one- and two-mile hikes past two lakes and a stream. About 150 bird species as well as numerous land animals can be sighted. Though located in a heavily urbanized area, the facility encompasses several ecological zones. Closed Monday.

**Ports O' Call Village** (entrance at foot of 6th Street; 562-831-0287) in the nearby town of San Pedro is a shopping mall in the form of a 19th-century port town. In addition to shops and restaurants, it houses several outfits conducting harbor cruises. The boats sail around the San Pedro waterfront and venture out for glimpses of the surrounding shoreline; for information, contact **Spirit Cruises** (Ports O' Call Village, San Pedro; 562-548-8080).

For a view of how the waterfront used to look, stop by the **Los Angeles Maritime Museum** (Berth 84; 562-548-7618). This dockside showplace displays models of ships ranging from fully rigged brigs to 19th-century steam sloops to World War II battleships. There's even an 18-foot re-creation of the ill-starred *Titanic* and the ocean liner model used to film *The Poseidon Adventure*. Closed Monday.

Nearby at the **Cabrillo Marine Aquarium** (3720 Stephen M. White Drive; 562-548-7562) there is a modest collection of display cases with samples of shells, coral and shorebirds. Several dozen aquariums exhibit local fish and marine plants. Closed Monday.

Of greater interest is **Point Fermin Park** (807 Paseo del Mar; 562-548-7756), a 37-acre blufftop facility resting above spectacular tidepools and a marine preserve. The tidepools are accessible via steep trails from the park and from the Cabrillo Marine Aquarium, which sponsors exploratory tours. Also of note (though not open to the public), is the **Point Fermin Lighthouse**, a unique 19th-century clapboard house with a beacon set in a rooftop crow's nest. From

*Santa Monica has been a popular resort town since the 1870s.*

the park plateau, like lighthouse keepers of old, you'll have open vistas of the cliff-fringed coast and a perfect perch for sighting whales during their winter migration.

## *Santa Monica*

The capital of the Los Angeles beach scene is the resort city of Santa Monica, where white-sand beaches are framed by bald mountain peaks. The highlight of the beach promenade (and perhaps all Santa Monica) is the **Santa Monica Pier** (foot of Colorado Avenue; 562-458-8689). No doubt about it, the place is a scene. Acrobats work out on the playground below, surfers catch waves offshore, and street musicians strum guitars. And we haven't even mentioned the official attractions. There's a turn-of-the-century carousel with hand-painted horses that was featured in that cinematic classic, *The Sting*. There are video parlors, pinball machines, skee ball, bumper cars and a restaurant.

From here it's a short jaunt up to the **Santa Monica Visitors Center** information kiosk (1400 Ocean Avenue; 310-393-7593). Here are maps, brochures and helpful workers.

They can direct you to **Angels' Attic** (516 Colorado Avenue; 310-394-8331; admission), an 1895 Victorian that houses a unique museum of antique dollhouses. There's a Noah's ark worth of miniature animals plus a gallery of precious dolls. Closed Monday through Wednesday.

The **Museum of Flying** (2772 Donald Douglas Loop North; 310-392-8822; admission) is a miniature Smithsonian. Tracing the history of aviation in a single, brightly painted hangar, the museum houses everything from a 1924 Douglas World Cruiser (built in Santa Monica, it was the first plane to circle the globe) to a Douglas A-4 Skyhawk flown by the Blue Angels. Closed Monday and Tuesday.

**Santa Monica State Beach** (at the foot of Colorado Avenue; 310-458-8311) is part of the sandbox-gone-wild that stretches from Venice to Pacific Palisades—very white sand, blue water and broad beaches. Skaters, strollers and bicyclists pass along the promenade, sunbathers lie moribund in the sand, and volleyball players perform acrobatic shots.

Will Rogers once owned the two miles of neighboring beachfront property that's now **Will Rogers State Beach** (310-451-2906; admission). It's a wide, sandy strand looking up at the sharp cliffs that lend Pacific Palisades its name. Lifeguards are on duty. Located along Route 1 at Sunset Boulevard in Pacific Palisades.

At **Will Rogers State Historic Park** (1501 Will Rogers State Park Road, Pacific Palisades; 310-454-8212; admission), you can tour the ranch and home of America's greatest cowboy philosopher. The comedian whose humorous wisdom plucked a chord in the American psyche lived here from 1928 until his tragic death in 1935. The 31-room house is large but basic and unassuming, true to Rogers' Oklahoma roots. Western knickknacks adorn the tables, and one room is dominated by a full-sized stuffed calf that Rogers utilized for roping practice. Well worth visiting, the "house that jokes built" is a simple expression of a vital personality.

## Los Angeles

DOWNTOWN   The historic heart of the city is **El Pueblo de Los Angeles**, a 44-acre outdoor museum centered around Olvera Street. In 1781 a few dozen Spanish settlers established hardscrabble farms and built adobes here, breaking ground for what eventually became one of the world's largest metropolitan areas. The **visitors center** (622 North Main Street; 213-628-1274), providing maps, brochures and walking tours, sits in one of the pueblo's vintage buildings, a brick-faced Victorian built in 1887 called the Sepulveda House. Closed Monday.

Heart of hearts is the **Plaza** (North Main and Los Angeles streets), a tree-shaded courtyard adorned with statues and highlighted by a wrought-iron bandstand. A colorful gathering place, it's a frequent site for fiestas and open-air concerts.

Anchoring one corner of the plaza is **Firehouse No. 1** (134 Paseo de la Plaza), Los Angeles' original fire station. Today it's a miniature museum filled with horse-drawn fire wagons, old-time helmets and an ample inventory of memories. **Old Plaza Church** (535 North Main Street), first established as a chapel in 1784, also faces the square.

For the full flavor of Spanish California, wander down **Olvera Street**. Lined with *puestos* (stands) selling Mexican handicrafts, it provides a window on early Los Angeles. The brick-paved alleyway is also one of the West's first pedestrian shopping malls.

For information on Olvera Street and points of interest throughout the city, contact the information center at the **Greater Los Angeles Convention & Visitors Bureau** (685 South Figueroa Street; 213-689-8822). There you'll find maps, leaflets and a friendly staff to help point the way through this urban maze. Closed Sunday.

EXPOSITION PARK  A multiblock extravaganza bounded by Exposition Boulevard, Menlo Avenue, Martin Luther King Jr. Boulevard and Figueroa Street, Exposition Park is long on exposition and short on park. There *is* an enchanting **sunken garden** with a fountain, gazebos and almost 20,000 rose bushes representing nearly 200 varieties of roses. Otherwise the park blooms with museums and sports arenas.

The **California Museum of Science and Industry** (213-744-7400) is one of those hands-on, great-for-kids-of-all-ages complexes. Rambling between several buildings, it has halls devoted to health and economics and displays demonstrating everything from simple laws of science to the latest advances in high technology.

Over in the **California Museum's Aerospace Hall** there are exhibits explaining the principles of aerodynamics as well as planes, jets and space capsules suspended from the ceiling in mock flight. Climbing a catwalk-like series of staircases, you'll have a bird's-eye view of a 1920 glider, Air Force T-38, an F-20 Tiger Shark and Gemini II spacecraft.

The 75-foot screen in the **IMAX Theater** (213-744-2014; admission) takes viewers on film adventures of stunning, you-are-there

---

*A MUSEUM FOR KIDS*

*It's the noisiest museum in the world. The **Los Angeles Children's Museum** (310 North Main Street; 213-687-8800; admission), with countless hands-on and hands-all-over-everything exhibits, is probably the happiest as well. There are a bus and police motorcycle for kids to ride; make-up rooms for them to paint their faces; a dinosaur cave with holograms and sound effects; a water exhibit that lets kids get in touch with creatures inside aquariums; and a recording studio and video cameras to tape their own antics. During winter open weekends, and weekdays by appointment only. During summer open daily.*

realism. Several different films are screened daily. You might find yourself cruising with whales, sledding through Alaska or grazing with African wildlife.

The **Natural History Museum of Los Angeles County** (900 Exposition Boulevard; 213-263-3466; admission), reputedly the largest and most popular museum in California, is a world (and an afternoon) unto itself. Among the dozens of galleries are rock and gem displays; dioramas of bears, wolves and bison; set pieces from the American past, including a cut-away Conestoga wagon demonstrating life on the frontier; and, of course, the dinosaur skeletons required of every self-respecting natural history museum. If this is not enough, the museum contains bird specimens and a "discovery center" where kids can play scientist. Closed Monday.

Prettiest of all the buildings in this museum park is the **California African–American Museum** (600 State Drive; 213-744-7432) with its glass-roofed sculpture court and bright, airy galleries. Devoted to black culture and history, the center displays the work of artists from around the world. Closed Monday.

HOLLYWOOD    The best place to begin a visit to the film capital of the world is (where else?) the **Hollywood Visitor Information Center** (6541 Hollywood Boulevard; 213-236-2331). In addition to dispensing maps, brochures and a lot of good advice, they also happen to be located in the heart of the district on Hollywood Boulevard. Closed Sunday. From here it's a short stroll over to the **Hollywood Wax Museum** (6767 Hollywood Boulevard; 213-462-

---

## LA BREA TAR PITS

*Beauty gives way to the beast at the **George C. Page Museum of La Brea Discoveries** (5801 Wilshire Boulevard; 213-934-7243; admission). This paleontological showplace features displays of mammoths, mastodons and ground sloths. There are also extinct camels, ancient horses and ancestral condors. Together with over 200 varieties of other creatures they fell victim to the **La Brea Tar Pits**, which surround the museum. Dating to the Pleistocene Era, these oozing oil pools trapped birds, mammals, insects and reptiles, creating fossil deposits that are still being discovered by scientists. American Indians once used the tar to caulk boats and roofs. Today you can wander past the pits, which bubble menacingly with methane gas and lie covered in globs of black tar. Closed Monday.*

8860; admission) where you can "see your favorite stars in living wax." Here they are—Marilyn Monroe and Elvis Presley, Clint Eastwood and Sylvester Stallone—complete with that classic grin or sneer frozen forevermore.

**Mann's Chinese Theater** (6925 Hollywood Boulevard; 213-464-8111) is a 1927 movie palace fashioned in "Oriental Baroque" style with pagoda roof, Asian masks and beautiful bas-reliefs. Though the architecture is splendid, the theater is actually known for its sidewalk. Embedded in the cement forecourt are the handprints and footprints of Hollywood's greatest stars. Jean Harlow, Rock Hudson, Cary Grant and Jimmy Stewart have left their signatures in this grandest of all autograph collections. Not every celebrity simply signed and stepped, however: there are also cement images of Jimmy Durante's nose and the webbed feet of Donald Duck.

Throughout this area—extending for three-and-a-half miles along Hollywood Boulevard from Gower Street to La Brea Boulevard and on Vine Street between Sunset Boulevard and Yucca Street—is the **Walk of Fame**, a star-studded terrazzo commemorating notables from the film, television, radio, theater and music industries. The names of nearly 2100 legends appear on brass-rimmed stars embedded in the sidewalk. Pride of Hollywood, it represents the only walkway in Los Angeles to be washed several times weekly.

The Hollywood street scene centers along Sunset Boulevard, a flashy avenue studded with nightclubs and fresh-cuisine restaurants. During the 1930s and 1940s, the section between Crescent Heights Boulevard and Doheny Drive formed the fabled **Sunset Strip**. Center of Los Angeles night action, it was an avenue of dreams, housing nightclubs like Ciro's and the Trocadero. As picture magazines of the times illustrated, starlets bedecked with diamonds emerged from limousines with their leading men. During the 1950s, Ed "Kookie" Byrnes immortalized the street on the television show 77 *Sunset Strip*.

Another vestige of tinseltown's history stands across the street from the Hollywood Bowl. Back in 1913, a young director named Cecil B. De Mille found a farm town called Hollywood with an empty barn he could convert into a studio. The barn, a kind of wood-frame keepsake, moved around with De Mille over the years, seeing use as an office, a set and even a gymnasium for stars like Gary Cooper and Kirk Douglas. Eventually moved to its present site, the historic building became the **Hollywood Studio Museum** (2100

---

*Maps of the stars' homes are sold on street corners and in shops through-
out Hollywood.*

---

North Highland Avenue; 213-874-4005; admission), a showplace
dedicated to the era of silent films and containing a replica of De
Mille's original office. The museum is currently closed for repairs
and is slated to reopen in late 1998.

Of course, the ultimate Hollywood experience is a visit to a studio. The **NBC Studio Tour** (3000 West Alameda Avenue, Burbank;
818-840-3537; admission) provides a brief view of the television
industry. Though only 75 minutes long, it takes in a special-effects
center and visits a mini-studio where visitors participate in a mock
game show. The wardrobe area, set-construction shop and make-up
room are also on the itinerary. Closed weekends during winter;
closed Sunday during summer. Here and at **CBS Ticket Information** (7800 Beverly Boulevard, Los Angeles; 213-852-2458) and
**ABC Tickets** (4151 Prospect Avenue, Hollywood; 562-557-7777),
free tickets to television shows are available. Or contact **Audiences
Unlimited** (100 Universal City Plaza, Building 153, Universal City;
818-506-0067), which provides tickets for several different networks.

The **Warner Brothers VIP Tour** (4000 Warner Boulevard, Burbank; 818-954-1744; admission), by contrast, takes you behind the
scenes to see the day-to-day activities of a multimedia complex. Reservations suggested. Closed weekends. **Paramount Studios** (5555
Melrose Avenue; 213-956-5575; admission) operates weekday tours
in a behind-the-scenes fashion with a historical overview. You must
be over the age of ten.

To learn more about the architectural history of Los Angeles,
visit the **Hollyhock House** (4808 Hollywood Boulevard; 213-485-
4581; admission). A masterwork by Frank Lloyd Wright, it is a
sprawling 6200-square-foot home that represents his California Ro-
manza style. Constructed of poured concrete and stucco, the house
incorporates a geometric motif based on the hollyhock. Guided tours
of the house are available. Closed Monday and Tuesday.

PASADENA   One of the Southland's most spectacular complexes and certainly the premier attraction in the Pasadena area is
the **Huntington Library, Art Collections and Botanical Gardens** (1151 Oxford Road, San Marino; 626-405-2141; admission).
Closed Monday.

The focal point of the 207-acre aesthetic preserve, the **Hunting-ton Gallery** was originally philanthropist Henry E. Huntington's home. Today the mansion is dedicated to 18th- and 19th-century English and French art and houses one of the finest collections of its kind in the country. Another gallery contains Renaissance paintings and French sculpture from the 18th century; the **Virginia Steele Scott Gallery of American Art**, housed in an enchanting build-ing, traces American painting from 1730 to 1930. Moving from oil to ink, and from mansion to mansion, the **Huntington Library** contains one of the world's finest collections of rare British and American manuscripts and first editions.

This describes only the *buildings* on the property! There are also the grounds, a heavenly labyrinth of **gardens** ranging from a ver-dant jungle setting to the austerely elegant Desert Garden. Rolling lawns are adorned with Italian statuary and bordered by plots of roses and camellias. The Shakespearean garden is filled with plants mentioned by the playwright, and the Japanese garden features an arched bridge, koi pond and 19th-century teahouse.

The **Arboretum of Los Angeles County** (301 North Baldwin Avenue; 626-821-3222; admission) in neighboring Arcadia may be the most photographed location in the world. Everything from Tar-zan movies to weekly television shows have been filmed in this 127-acre garden. With plants from every corner of the globe, it has por-trayed Hawaii, Burma, Africa, Samoa and Devil's Island.

The history of the surrounding region, captured in several his-toric structures still standing on the grounds, long precedes the mov-ies. There are *wickiups* similar to those of the original Gabrieleño Indians who used the local spring-fed pond as a watering hole. Representing the Spanish era is the **Hugo Reid Adobe**, an 1839 structure built with over 3000 mud bricks. Crudely furnished in 19th-century Spanish fashion, the adobe dates to the days when the area was part of a huge Spanish land grant. E. J. "Lucky" Baldwin,

---

*KIDSPACE MUSEUM*

*The little ones can play with hands-on exhibits at **Kidspace Museum** (390 South El Molino Avenue, Pasadena; 626-449-9144; admission). This innovative facility has a television studio, critter caverns climbing structure and everything else a futuristic child might desire.*

the silver-mining magnate who helped introduce horse racing to Southern California, bought the ranch in 1875 and built a **Queen Anne Cottage**. His castle-in-the-sky dream house is a gingerbread Victorian that was often featured on the "Fantasy Island" television show. Also part of this never-ending complex is the **Santa Anita Depot**. Built in 1890, it's a classic brick train station filled with equipment and memorabilia from the great age of railroads. Open Tuesday, Wednesday and Sunday only.

SAN GABRIEL MOUNTAINS   Set in the foothills, **Eaton Canyon** (626-398-5420) is a 184-acre park laced with hiking trails that traverse an arroyo and four different plant communities. Trails meander through the park and lead deep into the adjacent Angeles National Forest. In 1993 about half of Eaton Canyon, including the interpretive center, burned in a fire, but a temporary trailer is staffed to greet visitors, and a fire ecology trail shows the amazing regeneration of foothill flora.

Another of the region's botanic preserves, **Descanso Gardens** (1418 Descanso Drive, La Cañada; 818-952-4400; admission), stretches across 165 acres at the foot of the San Gabriel Mountains. This former estate has the largest camellia garden in the world, numbering 100,000 plants, as well as a rose garden where strains of species are cultivated. You'll also find a Japanese garden and teahouse (tea is served weekends only) and a section devoted to native California plants.

To explore the **San Gabriel Mountains** fully, follow the Angeles Crest Highway (Route 2) in its sinuous course upward from La Cañada. With their sharp-faced cliffs and granite outcroppings, the San Gabriels from a natural barrier between the Los Angeles Basin and the Mojave Desert. A side road from Route 2 leads to 5710-foot Mount Wilson, from which you can gaze across the entire expanse of Los Angeles to the Pacific Ocean. **Mount Wilson Observatory**, the area's most famous landmark, supports a 100-inch reflecting telescope. For more information call 626-793-3100. Open weekends only.

GRIFFITH PARK   Every great city boasts a great park. Consider New York's Central Park, Golden Gate Park in San Francisco and in Los Angeles, Griffith Park (entrances near Western Canyon Road, Vermont Avenue, Riverside Drive and Route 5). Set astride the Hollywood Hills between the Westside and the San Fernando Valley, this 4000-acre facility offers a flatlands area complete with golf

*James Dean filmed a famous scene from* Rebel Without a Cause *at the Griffith Observatory.*

courses, playgrounds and picnic areas, plus a vast hillside section featuring meadows, forests and miles of mountain roads.

Along Crystal Springs Drive, traversing the eastern edge of the park, you'll pass the **Griffith Park & Southern Railroad** (213-664-6788), a miniature train ride; nearby is a track offering **pony rides** (213-664-3266). The **ranger station** (213-665-5188) will provide maps and information while directing you across the street to the **merry-go-round**, a beautiful, 1926 vintage carousel, which is open weekends only.

Featuring real-life versions of these whirling animals, the **L. A. Zoo** (5333 Zoo Drive; 213-666-4650; admission) is among the highlights of the park. More than 1200 animals inhabit this 113-acre facility, many in environments simulating their natural habitats. The African exhibit houses elephants, rhinos, giraffes and monkeys; Eurasia is represented by tigers and black leopards; there are also jaguars and spectacle bears and, from Australia, kangaroos, koalas and cassowaries. The adjacent **Nursery** is where newborn mammals are bottle-fed. You can see the baby animals in an exhibition area.

**Travel Town** (5200 West Zoo Drive; 213-662-5874; admission) is a transportation museum featuring a train yard full of cabooses, steam engines and passenger cars from the railroad's glory days. The exhibit also includes a fleet of 1920-era fire trucks and old milk wagons. For the kids there are narrow-gauge train rides here and at **Live Steamers** next door.

For Hollywood's version of American history, there's the **Autry Museum of Western Heritage** (4700 Western Heritage Way; 213-667-2000; admission). The focus here is more on Westerns than the West, but it's great fun for kids nonetheless. There are displays of saloons and stagecoaches, silver saddles and ivory-handled six-shooters, plus photos and film-clips of all your favorite stars. Closed Monday.

Standing above the urban fray at the southern end of the park is the **Griffith Observatory and Planetarium** (Observatory Drive; 213-664-1191; admission), a copper-domed beauty that perfectly represents the public-monument architecture of the 1930s. With its bas-reliefs and interior murals, this eerie site also resembles a kind of interplanetary temple. In fact it has been the setting for numerous science fiction films such as *When Worlds Collide* (1951). Apart from a movie setting, the Observatory features a Planetarium Theatre and a space-age Laserium (admission) complete with high-tech light shows. The Hall of Science offers museum displays on astronomy and meteorology. Closed Monday.

## LOS ANGELES LODGING

SANTA MONICA   Ocean Avenue, which runs the length of Santa Monica paralleling the ocean one block above the beach, boasts the most hotels and the best location in town. Among its varied facilities are several generic motels. One such establishment, the **Pacific Sands Motel** (1515 Ocean Avenue; 562-395-6133), is a 52-unit facility which features a small swimming pool. The location is quite convenient to the beach. Moderate.

A better bargain by far is the **Bayside Hotel** (2001 Ocean Avenue; 562-396-6000, 800-525-4447, fax 562-451-1111). Laid out in motel fashion, this two-story complex offers plusher carpets and plumper furniture than motels hereabouts. More important, it's just 50 yards from the beach across a palm-studded park. Some rooms have ocean views; no pool. Deluxe.

Of course the ultimate bargain in town is found at the **Hostelling International—Santa Monica** (1436 2nd Street; 562-393-9913, 800-909-4776 ext. 05, fax 562-393-1769). This four-story, dorm-like structure boasts 30,000 square feet, room for 228 beds. There are several common rooms, a central courtyard, library and kitchen. In addition to facilities for independent travelers, the hostel has set aside six private rooms for couples and families. Budget.

**Loews Santa Monica Beach Hotel** (1700 Ocean Avenue; 562-458-6700, 800-235-6397, fax 562-458-6761), which opened in 1989, was the first Los Angeles luxury hotel with direct beach access. The peach, blue and seafoam-green "contemporary Victorian" features a mock turn-of-the-century design. Its spectacular five-story glass atrium lobby and most of the 343 rooms provide views of the famed Santa Monica Pier. Rooms are furnished in rattan and wicker and offer special amenities. One-bedroom suites are ideal for families. Babysitting service is available. Non-beachies love the shallow ocean-view indoor/outdoor pool. Ultra-deluxe.

DOWNTOWN   In the reasonable price range it's hard to top the **Figueroa Hotel** (939 South Figueroa Street; 213-627-8971, 800-421-9092, fax 213-689-0305). A 1927 Spanish-style building, it offers a beautiful lobby with tile floor and hand-painted ceiling. The palm-fringed courtyard contains a swimming pool, jacuzzi and lounge. The rooms are very large, adequately furnished and decorated with wall-hangings. Tile baths add a touch of class to this very appealing establishment. Coffee shop and restaurants on the premises. Moderate to deluxe.

What can you say about a place that became a landmark as soon as it was built? To call the **Westin Bonaventure** (404 South Figueroa Street; 213-624-1000, 800-228-3000, fax 213-612-4800) ultra-modern would belittle the structure. "Post Future" is a more appropriate tag. Its dark-glass silos rise 35 stories from the street like a way station on the road to the 21st century. Within are two levels of shops, 20 restaurants, a revolving cocktail lounge, at least 1300 rooms, and many suites. The atrium lobby furthers the Buck Rogers theme with reflecting pools, glass-shaft elevators and lattice skylights. Considering all this, the guest rooms seem almost an afterthought; because of the building's configuration they are small and pie-shaped but offer good views of the surrounding financial district. The hotel is a short drive from the Los Angeles Children's Museum, the Natural History Museum and the Museum of Science and Industry. Ultra-deluxe.

HOLLYWOOD    The **Hollywood Celebrity Hotel** (1775 North Orchid Avenue; 213-850-6464, 800-222-7090, fax 213-850-7667) occupies a 1930s art deco building just above Hollywood Boulevard. The 40 rooms are nicely refurbished, furnished in neo-deco style and decorated in a Hollywood motif. The rooms are spacious and include a continental breakfast. Children 12 and under are free. Moderate.

One of Hollywood's best bargains is found at the **Magic Hotel** (7025 Franklin Avenue; 213-851-0800, 800-741-4915, fax 213-851-4926), a 40-unit establishment next to the famed Magic Castle, a private club for magicians. Suites with kitchens are furnished in oak and decorated (presto!) with magic posters. They are big and well maintained. Pool and sundeck. Moderate to deluxe.

It's as much a part of Hollywood as the Academy Awards. In fact, the very first Oscars were presented at the **Clarion Hollywood Roosevelt Hotel** (7000 Hollywood Boulevard; 213-466-7000, 800-950-7667, fax 213-462-8056). Built in 1927, the Spanish Revival building offers 320 rooms, plus a restaurant, lounges and a palm-studded courtyard with pool and sauna. This classic caravansary has many features of the finest hostelries. The lobby is a recessed-ceiling affair with colonnades and hand-painted beams. Guest rooms are small but commodiously furnished with plump armchairs and hardwood pieces. Family suites are available. Across the street from Mann's Chinese Theater, this historic hotel is convenient to the heart of Hollywood. Deluxe.

PASADENA   Motel row in Pasadena lies along Colorado Boulevard, route of the famous Rose Parade. **Pasadena Central Travelodge** (2131 East Colorado Boulevard; 626-796-3121, 800-578-7878, fax 626-793-4713), an 80-unit stucco complex, is typical of the accommodations. It offers standard rooms with cinderblock walls, stall showers, wall-to-wall carpeting and other basic amenities. The kids will enjoy frolicking in the swimming pool and jacuzzi. Budget.

Over $100 million was poured into the revered **Ritz-Carlton Huntington Hotel** (1401 South Oak Knoll Avenue; 626-568-3900, 800-784-3748, fax 626-568-1842), returning the 1907 grande dame to her turn-of-the-century glory. Situated on 20 manicured acres, this 383-room hotel combines modern amenities with the style and charm of another era. The Olympic-size swimming pool (reputed to be the first in California) has been restored, as have the hotel's Japanese and Horseshoe gardens. If you are seeking Old World ele-

---

## PARAMOUNT RANCH

*An enchanting version of the Wild West awaits at **Paramount Ranch** (in Santa Monica Mountains National Recreation Area; 818-597-9192), a 335-acre park which once served as the film location for Westerns. Paramount owned the spread for two decades beginning in the 1920s, using it as a set for many movies, including* Adventures of Marco Polo *(1937), the Samuel Goldwyn extravaganza that included a fortress, elephants and 2000 horses. During the heyday of television Westerns in the 1950s, the property was a location for* The Cisco Kid, Bat Masterson *and* Have Gun, Will Travel.

*Today you can hike around the ranch, past the rolling meadows, willow-lined streams, grassy hillsides and rocky heights that made it such an ideal set. "Western Town" still stands, a collection of falsefront buildings that change their signs depending on what's being filmed. If you're lucky, a film crew will be shooting a commercial or even producing the last of that dying breed of movie, the Western.*

gance, this is the address. Special note for families: The fitness center sets up croquet, volleyball, badminton and other games for kids.
Bike rentals are also available. Ultra-deluxe.

## LOS ANGELES DINING

LONG BEACH    What more elegant a setting than aboard the
**Queen Mary** (1126 Queen's Highway; 562-435-3511), where you
will find everything from snack kiosks to coffee shops to first-class
dining rooms. The menu at the **Promenade Café** focuses on steak,
chicken, seafood and vegetarian dishes. They also have salads, sandwiches and hamburgers. The coffee shop is a lovely art deco room
featuring wicker furnishings and period lamps. Kids will enjoy the
harbor view and a special menu featuring hamburgers, fish and chips,
nachos and grilled ham and cheese. Moderate to deluxe.

For a true taste of regal life aboard the old ship, cast anchor at **Sir
Winston's** (562-435-3511). The Continental cuisine in this dining
emporium includes lamb chops macadamia, breast of capon, beef
phyllo, roast duckling with raspberry sauce, sautéed scallops and
broiled swordfish with caviar. Open only for dinner, Sir Winston's is
a wood-paneled dining room with copper-rimmed mirrors, white
tablecloths and upholstered armchairs. The walls are adorned with
photos of the great prime minister, and every window opens onto
a view of Long Beach. Ultra-deluxe.

SANTA MONICA    One of the best places in Southern California
for stuffing yourself with junk food while soaking up sun and having
a whale of a good time is the **Santa Monica Pier** (foot of Colorado Avenue). There are taco stands, fish and chips shops, hot dog
vendors, oyster bars, snack shops, pizzerias and all those good things
guaranteed to leave you clutching your stomach. Budget.

There's a sense of the Mediterranean at the sidewalk cafés lining
Santa Monica's Ocean Avenue: palm trees along the boulevard, ocean
views in the distance and (usually) a warm breeze blowing. Any of
these bistros will do (since it's atmosphere we're seeking), so try **Ivy
at the Shore** (1541 Ocean Avenue; 562-393-3113). It features a full
bar, serves espresso and, if you want to get serious about it, has a full
lunch and dinner menu with pizza, pastas and Cajun dishes. Deluxe.

Every type of cuisine imaginable is found on the bottom level of
**Santa Monica Place** (Broadway between 2nd and 4th streets). This
multitiered shopping mall has an entire floor of take-out food stands.
It's like the United Nations of dining. Budget.

Along the Third Street Promenade is **Benita's Frites** (1437 3rd Street; 562-458-2889), a Belgian French-fry stand. This diminutive entry in Santa Monica's rough-and-tumble restaurant race does not just serve plain old fries, however. They feature 20 different dips, including spicy barbecue, peanut sauce and garlic mayonnaise, as well as full lunch and dinner fare. Budget.

Benita's is only one of many excellent eateries along Santa Monica's vaunted Third Street Promenade. This three-block-long walkway, filled with movie theaters and located in the downtown district, boasts some of the best coffeehouses and restaurants in the area.

**Sabor** (3221 Pico Boulevard; 562-829-3781) offers a wonderfully eclectic melange of Creole and Latin cuisine. Set in a Mission-style building with whitewashed walls and Latin sculpture, this restaurant serves up such exotic fare as Salvadoran *pupusa* and Brazilian *coxinha* (buttermilk puff pastry filled with chicken, goat cheese and fresh herb mousse). No lunch on Saturday and Sunday. Moderate to deluxe.

**El Cholo** (1025 Wilshire Boulevard; 562-899-1106) is long on atmosphere. Laid out in courtyard style, the dining room is surrounded by a wrought-iron balcony and illuminated through a skylight. Potted ferns and palms decorate the place, and the floor is inlaid with brick. The menu is similarly inspired. Rather than simply serving the standard Mexican dishes, El Cholo offers specialties like green corn tamales, crabmeat enchiladas and shrimp fajitas. A children's menu includes a grilled-cheese sandwich, hamburger, taco or cheese enchilada with rice and beans. Moderate.

DOWNTOWN   Olvera Street, where the Spanish originally located the pueblo of Los Angeles, is still a prime place for Mexican food. Tiny **taco stands** line this brick-paved alley. Little more than open-air kitchens, they dispense fresh Mexican dishes. You'll also find bakeries and candy stands, where old Mexican ladies sell churros (Mexican donuts) and candied squash. Budget.

**La Golondrina** (West 17 Olvera Street; 213-628-4349) provides something more formal. Set in the historic Pelanconi House, an 1850-era home built of fired brick, it features an open-air patio and a dining room with stone fireplace and *viga* ceiling. The bill of fare includes a standard selection of tacos, tostadas and enchiladas as well as specialties such as fajitas, crab-meat enchiladas and grilled jumbo shrimp. Children will enjoy specialties like cheese burritos and taquitos. Moderate to deluxe.

Across from Union Station, midway between Olvera Street and Chinatown, stands one of the city's most famous cafeterias. **Philippe The Original** (1001 North Alameda Street; 213-628-3781) has been around since 1908, serving pork, beef, turkey and lamb sandwiches in a French-dip style. With sawdust on the floors and memories tacked to the walls, this antique eatery still serves ten-cent cups of coffee. Open for breakfast, lunch and dinner. Budget.

HOLLYWOOD    Hollywood's oldest restaurant, **Musso & Frank's Grill** (6667 Hollywood Boulevard; 213-467-7788) is a 1919 original with dark paneling, murals and red leather booths. A bar and open grill create a clubby atmosphere that reflects the eatery's long tradition. Among the American-style dishes offered are cracked crab, fresh clams, roast lamb, plus assorted steaks and chops. Closed Sunday and Monday. Deluxe to ultra-deluxe.

**Hampton's Hollywood Cafe** (1342 North Highland Avenue; 213-469-1090) may be the world's only hamburger joint with valet parking. This well-known noshing spot has transformed the art of hamburgers to a science, preparing over 340 different combinations. You can order them with sour-plum jam, peanut butter or creamed horseradish. If you disagree with the when-in-Rome philosophy, there are broiled shrimp, chicken, pasta and vegetarian platters. Budget to moderate.

The celebrity photos covering every inch of **Formosa Cafe** (7156 Santa Monica Boulevard; 213-850-9050) tell a tale of Hollywood that reaches back to the 1940s. This crowded café, originally fashioned from a streetcar, has seen more stars than heaven. Over the years they've poured in from the surrounding studios, leaving autographs and memories. Today you'll find a Chinese restaurant, a kind of museum with meals. No lunch on weekends. Moderate.

---

### FARMERS MARKET

*Back in 1934 local farmers created a cooperative market where they could congregate and sell their goods. Today **Farmers Market** (6333 West 3rd Street; 213-933-9211) is an open-air labyrinth of stalls, shops and vendor stands. There are tables overflowing with vegetables, fruits, meats, cheeses and baked goods, a total of over 120 outlets. Stop by for groceries, gifts and finger foods or simply to catch Los Angeles at its relaxed and informal best.*

Hollywood's prettiest restaurant is a re-created Japanese palace called **Yamashiro** (1999 North Sycamore Avenue; 213-466-5125). Set in the hills overlooking Los Angeles, the mansion was built earlier in the century, modeled after an estate in the high mountains of Japan, and trimmed with ornamental gardens. Dine here and you are surrounded by hand-carved columns, *shoji* screens and Asian statuary. The courtyard garden contains a waterfall, koi pond and miniature trees. For dinner the kimono-clad servers offer a complete Japanese menu as well as Western-style entrées. Dinner only. Deluxe to ultra-deluxe.

**Barney's Beanery** (8447 Santa Monica Boulevard; 213-654-2287) is the only place around where you can shoot pool while eating chili, pizza, ribs, burritos and hamburgers. Or where you can choose from nearly 300 varieties of beer. A dive with character, Barney's has rainbow-colored booths, license plates on the ceiling and a road-sign decor. Native funk. Budget to moderate.

PASADENA   One of the San Gabriel Valley's best food bargains is **Restaurant Mérida** (20 East Colorado Boulevard; 626-792-7371). Serving Yucatán-style dishes, this brick-walled eatery with a patio courtyard offers *birria de chivo* (goat in spicy sauce), *oriental de pavo* (turkey, onions and garlic in rich broth) and *cochinita pibil* (pork wrapped in banana leaves). For those accustomed to dining closer to Mexico City there are enchiladas, burritos and tostadas. With three meals daily and a menu numbering over 100 items, it's an exceptional place. Budget to moderate.

For another great buy, try **Burger Continental** (535 South Lake Avenue; 626-792-6634), a congested and crazy café where you order at the counter, then dine indoors or on a patio. Portions are bountiful and the prices ridiculously low. In addition to hamburgers they serve steaks, seafood, sandwiches and an enticing array of Middle Eastern dishes. The best bargain is the "Armenian feast," a combination of kebab dishes and Mideastern appetizers capable of feeding a large family or small army. Breakfast, lunch and dinner are served. Budget to moderate.

## The Sporting Life

### FISHING

Fish the waters around Los Angeles and you can try your hand at landing a barracuda, white croaker, halibut, calico bass or maybe even a relative of Jaws. For sportfishing outfits call **L.A. Harbor Sportfishing** (Berth 79, San Pedro; 562-547-9916 or 562-832-2274) and **Long Beach Sportfishing** (555 Pico Avenue, Long Beach; 562-432-8993).

## SKINDIVING

To explore Los Angeles' submerged depths, contact **Pacific Sporting Goods** (11 39th Place; Long Beach, 562-434-1604), **Pacific Wilderness Ocean Sports** (1719 South Pacific Avenue, San Pedro; 562-833-2422), **Blue Cheer Ocean Water Sport**s (1110 Wilshire Boulevard, Santa Monica; 562-828-1217) or **Scuba Haus** (2501 Wilshire Boulevard, Santa Monica; 562-828-2916) to rent gear and/or take a dive trip.

## WHALE WATCHING

During the annual migration the following outfits offer whale-watching trips: **Mickey's Belmont Inc.** (Belmont Pier, Long Beach; 562-434-6781), **Long Beach Sportfishing** (555 Pico Avenue, Long Beach; 562-432-8993), **Spirit Cruises** (Berth 77, San Pedro; 562-831-1073), **Los Angeles Harbor Cruise** (Berth 78, San Pedro; 562-831-0996), and **L.A. Harbor Sportfishing** (Berth 79, San Pedro; 562-547-9916).

## WINDSURFING, SURFING AND SEA KAYAKING

"Surfing is the only life," so grab a board from **Fun Bunns** (1116 Manhattan Avenue, Manhattan Beach; 562-372-8500), **Jeffers** (39 14th Street, Hermosa Beach; 562-372-9492) or **Zuma Jay Surfboards** (22775 Pacific Coast Highway, Malibu; 562-456-8044).

---

*RAGING WATERS*

*With 50 acres of aquatic attractions, **Raging Waters** (111 Raging Waters Drive, San Dimas; 909-592-6453; admission) is a great place to get all wet on a blazing Southern California day. Located 40 minutes east of downtown Los Angeles, this aquatic hot spot offers 25 thrill rides including a water slide journey that descends seven stories. Also here are tube and sled rides, the six-person raft journey down Thunder Rapids, wave pools and a slide that shoots down a dark hole. Two activity areas for smaller children feature waterfalls, dinosaur-shaped slide rides and swimming areas. Nine restaurants, activity islands, a surf shop and video arcades make this a complete kid's playland. Closed October to April.*

*Santa Monica Bay stretches 30 miles from Redondo Beach to Point Dume.*

## SKATING

Los Angeles may well be the roller-skating capital of California. To rent roller skates, rollerblades or maybe even a skateboard call **Spokes 'n Stuff** (1715 Oceanfront Walk, 562-395-4748; and near the Santa Monica Pier, 562-395-4748).

## HANG GLIDING

What better way to let yourself go than by coasting or floating on high? The adventurous can try hang gliding at **Windsports Soaring Center** (16145 Victory Boulevard, Van Nuys; 818-988-0111). Closed Sunday and Monday.

## HORSEBACK RIDING

With its curving hills and flowering meadows, Griffith Park is a favorite spot among urban equestrians. Several places on the edge of the park provide facilities. Try **Sunset Ranch** (3400 North Beachwood Drive, Hollywood; 213-464-9612), **Circle K Stables** (914 Mariposa Street, Burbank; 818-843-9890), **Griffith Park Horse Rentals** (480 Riverside Drive, Burbank; 818-840-8401) or **Bar S Stables** (1850 Riverside Drive, Glendale; 818-242-8443).

## GOLF

For the golfers in the crowd, try **El Dorado Park Municipal Golf Course** (2400 North Studebaker Road, Long Beach; 562-430-5411), **Skylink Golf Course** (4800 East Wardlow Road, Long Beach; 562-421-3388) and **Recreation Park** (5001 Deukmejian Drive, Long Beach; 562-494-5000). Farther inland are the **Rancho Park Golf Course** (10460 West Pico Boulevard, West Los Angeles; 562-838-7373), **Brookside Golf Course** (1133 North Rosemont Avenue, Pasadena; 818-796-0177) and **Wilson Harding Golf Course** (Griffith Park; 213-663-2555).

## TENNIS

There are public tennis courts at the **Billie Jean King Tennis Center** (1040 Park Avenue, Long Beach; 562-438-8509), **Lincoln Park** (1133 7th Street, Santa Monica; 562-394-6011) and **Ocean View Park** (Barnard Way south of Ocean Park Boulevard, Santa

Monica; 562-394-6011). The city's largest facility, **Griffith Park** (4730 Crystal Springs Drive, Los Angeles; 213-662-7772) has many tennis courts. For information on other local parks, contact the nearest Los Angeles City and County Parks and Recreation Department office.

Tennis clubs dot the county; one such club, the **Racquet Center** (10933 Ventura Boulevard, Studio City, 818-760-2303; and 920 Lohman Lane, South Pasadena, 213-258-4178), is open to the public. For further information about clubs, contact the **Southern California Tennis Association** (P.O. Box 240015, Los Angeles, CA 90024; 562-208-3838).

BIKING

Though Los Angeles might seem like one giant freeway, there are scores of shoreline bike trails and routes for scenic excursions. Foremost is the **South Bay Bike Trail**, with over 22 miles of coastal vistas. The trail, an easy ride, is extremely popular and runs from RAT Beach in Torrance to Will Rogers State Beach in Pacific Palisades. The path intersects the Ballona Creek Bikeway in Marina Del Rey, which extends seven miles east and passes the Venice Boardwalk, as well as piers and marinas along the way.

**Naples**, a Venice-like neighborhood in Long Beach, provides a charming area for freeform bike rides.

The **Santa Monica Loop** is an easy ride starting at Ocean Avenue and going up San Vicente Boulevard, past Palisades Park and the Santa Monica Pier. Most of the trail is on bike lanes and paths. It's a ten-mile round trip.

Over 14 miles of bike routes wind through Griffith Park. Two notable excursions skirt many of the park attractions: **Crystal Springs Loop**, which follows Crystal Springs Drive and Zoo Drive along the park's eastern edge, passes the merry-go-round and Travel Town; **Mineral Wells Loop**, an arduous uphill climb, passes Harding Golf Course, then coasts downhill to Zoo Drive, taking in Travel Town and the zoo.

For a look at the good life, check out the route from **San Gabriel Mission to the Huntington Library**, which winds from San Gabriel through the exclusive town of San Marino.

A strenuous but worthwhile excursion is a bike ride along **Mulholland Drive**. Not recommended during commute hours, this route traverses the spine of the Santa Monica Mountains and offers fabulous views of the city and ocean.

For maps, brochures and additional information on bike routes in Los Angeles contact the **Department of Transportation** (205 South Broadway; 213-485-4277).

BIKE RENTALS    To rent bikes in coastal Los Angeles try **Spokes 'n Stuff** (4175 Admiralty Way at Jamaica Bay Inn Hotel, Marina del Rey, 562-306-3332; and near the Santa Monica Pier, 562-395-4748) and **Sea Mist Skate Rentals** (1619 Ocean Front Walk, Santa Monica; 562-395-7076).

# Index

**238** A Walk in Walt's Footsteps, 36

ABC Tickets, 222

ACME Atom Smasher, 210

Adventureland, 40–43; dining, 69–70; shopping, 75

Aerospace Hall, 219

African Kopje Exhibit, 176

Air travel, 10

Alice in Wonderland, 56

Amtrak, 10

Anaheim area: camping, 68; dining, 71–74; lodging, 63–67; nightlife, 76; sightseeing, 144, 146, 148

Angels' Attic, 217

Animal shows (San Diego Wild Animal Park), 181–82

Animals in Action Show, 211

Arboretum of Los Angeles County, 223

Astro Orbitor, 61

AT&T at the Movies, 119

ATMs. *See* Banking and ATMs

Audiences Unlimited, 222

Autopias, 58, 63

Autry Museum of Western Heritage, 225

Baby services, 20; (Disneyland) 36; (Knott's Berry Farm) 83; (Sea World) 132; (Universal Studios) 113

Babysitters, 20

Back Lot Tram Tour, 113–16

Back to the Future—The Ride, 120

Backdraft, 117

Balboa Island, 150

Balboa Island Ferry, 152

Balboa Park, 186–88

Balboa Pavilion, 150, 151

Balboa Peninsula, 150, 151

Balboa Pier, 152

Ballooning, 199

Bamboo Racer, 213

Banking and ATMs, 17; (Disneyland) 37; (Knott's Berry Farm) 83; (San Diego Wild Animal Park) 179; (Sea World) 133; (Six Flags California) 207; (Universal Studios) 113

Batman Forever Stunt Show, 211

Batman the Ride, 209

Bayside Skyride, 141

Bazaar del Mundo, 189

Beagle Ballroom, 96

Beary Tales Playhouse, 97

Beethoven's Animal Actors Stage, 122–23

Beetlejuice's Rockin' Graveyard Revue, 123

Behind-the-Scenes tour (Sea World), 134

Belmont Park, 184

Big Thunder Mountain Railroad, 47–48

Bigfoot Rapids, 88

Biking, 166, 201, 235–36

Birch Aquarium at Scripps, 190

Black Snake Summit, 213

Blacksmith Shop, 105

The Boardwalk, 89–93; dining, 102

Boat tours, 216

Boating and sailing, 166, 200

Bolsa Chica Ecological Reserve, 148

Bolsa Chica State Beach, 149–50

Boomerang, 90–91

Botanical Building, 187

Breastfeeding nooks, 21

Buccaneer, 210

Buena Park area: dining, 103–104; lodging, 100–102; nightlife,

105–106; sightseeing, 144, 146, 148

Bugs Bunny World, 208, 211

Bus travel, 10

Butterfield Stagecoach, 85

Cabrillo Marine Aquarium, 216

Cabrillo National Monument, 188

Calendar of events, 6–8

Calico Mine Train, 85–86

California African-American Museum, 220

California MarketPlace, 103; dining, 102–103; shopping, 105

California Museum of Science and Industry, 219

Cameras, 18; (Knott's Berry Farm) 83; (San Diego Zoo) 172; (Sea World) 132

Camp Bus, 97

Camp Snoopy, 95–99; dining, 102; shopping, 105

Camp Snoopy Theatre, 98–99

Camping, 19, 67–68. *See also* Beaches and parks *in area and town entries*

Campland On The Bay, 198

Capistrano Depot, 159

Car rentals, 10–11

Car repair, 10

Car travel, 9

Carousels, 57, 94, 209, 211, 225

Casey Jr. Circus Train, 57–58

Cash advances. *See* Banking and ATMs

Castaic: lodging, 215

Castaway Cove, 212

Catalina Island, 152

CBS Ticket Information, 222

Character meals (Disneyland), 71

Children's Camp, 100

Children's Museum (La Habra), 144

Children's Museum of San Diego, 190

Children's Zoo, 173

City Hall, 38

Climate, 5–6

Clydesdale Hamlet, 139

Colossus, 209

Corona del Mar State Beach, 156

Corona del Mar Tidepool Reserve, 156

Coronado: dining, 196; lodging, 193–94; sightseeing, 188

Country Bear Playhouse, 46–47

Credit cards, 17

Critter Country, 45–47; dining, 70; shopping, 75

Crystal Cove State Park, 163

Cyclone Bay, 207

Cyprus: dining, 104

Daffy Dunes, 211

Dana Point: beaches and parks, 163–64; dining, 162–63; lodging, 160–61; sightseeing, 157–58

Daredevil Plunge, 213

Daytrips: Los Angeles area, 203–36; Orange County area, 143–66; San Diego area, 167–201

Denver & Rio Grande Railroad, 86

Descanso Gardens, 224

Dining, 19–20. *See also* Dining *in town and theme park entries; see also Dining Index*

Disabled travelers, 21–22. *See also* Wheelchairs

Discounts, 15

Discovery Center, 89

Discovery Museum of Orange County, 146

Disney dollars, 15

Disney Gallery, 45

Disneyland, 31–76; camping, 67–68; dining, 68–74; discounts, 15–16; hours, 12; introduction, 31–32; lodging, 63–67; map, 33; nightlife, 76; nuts and bolts of visiting, 36–37; shopping, 74–76; sightseeing strategies, 34–36; tickets, 13, 14, 34; transportation in, 11, 37; transportation to, 32, 34; visitor information, 11, 36. *See also park areas and attractions*

Disneyland and beyond map, 3

Disneyland Monorail, 12, 62, 63

Disneyland Railroad, 39–40

Dive Devil, 209

Dog and Cat Canyon, 176

Doheny State Beach, 163–64

Doll City USA, 146

Dolphin Interaction Program, 135–36

Dolphin Stadium, 135

Downtown Los Angeles. *See* Los Angeles downtown

Downtown San Diego. *See* San Diego downtown

Dragon Swing, 94

Dumbo the Flying Elephant, 55–56

E.T. Adventure, 117

Eaton Canyon, 224

Edison's Inventor's Workshop, 98

El Dorado Nature Center, 216

El Pueblo de Los Angeles, 218

Elephant Mesa, 176

Elmer Fudd's Orchard, 211

Enchanted Tiki Room, 43

Escape Chute, 213

Exposition Park, 219–20

Fantasmic!, 49–50

Fantasyland, 53–58; dining, 71; shopping, 76

Fantasyland Autopia, 58

Farmers Market (Los Angeles), 231

Ferris Wheel, 96

Festival of the Arts, 157

Fiesta Village, 93–95; dining, 102

Firehouse No. 1, 218

First aid: (Disneyland) 37; (Knott's Berry Farm) 83; (San Diego Wild Animal Park) 179; (San Diego Zoo) 172; (Sea World) 132; (Six Flags California) 207; (Universal Studios) 113

Fishing, 164, 199, 232–33

Flashback, 206, 208

Flying Ace Balloon Race, 99

Forbidden Reef, 137

Foreign travelers, 22–24

Forgotten Sea, 212

Freefall, 210

Freshwater Aquarium, 137

Frontierland, 47–50; dining, 70–71; shopping, 76

Frontierland Shootin' Exposition, 50

Fun Zone, 152

Gadget's Go Coaster, 52–53

Garden Grove: camping, 68; dining, 74

Gaslamp Quarter (San Diego), 186

George C. Page Museum of La Brea Discoveries, 220

Geyser Peak, 212

Ghost Town, 84–87; shopping, 104–105

Giant Panda Research Station, 174

Glassblower, 138

Gold Rusher, 210

Golden Horseshoe Stage, 50

Golf, 165, 200, 234

Gondola Getaway, 215

Gordon Gearworks, 210

Gorilla Tropics, 174–75

Gotham City Backlot, 207–208

Grand Carousel, 209, 211

Grand Sierra Scenic Railroad, 97–98

Grand Slammer, 95

Granny Gran Prix, 211

"Great Moments With Mr. Lincoln," 39

Greater Los Angeles area, 203–36; introduction, 203; map, 205; sports, 232–36. *See also towns in the Los Angeles area*

Greater San Diego area, 167–201; introduction, 167–68; maps, 171, 185, 191; sports, 199–201; weather, 167. *See also towns in the San Diego area*

Griffith Observatory and Planetarium, 225–26
Griffith Park, 224–26
Griffith Park & Southern Railroad, 225

Hall of Champions Sports Museum, 187
HammerHead, 90
Hang gliding, 234
Haunted Mansion, 44–45
Haunted Shack, 86–87
HeadAche, 90
HeadSpin, 90
Heart of Africa, 180–81
Height restrictions on rides, 8. *See also specific rides*
Heisler Park, 157
Heritage Park, 187
Hippo Beach, 174
Hobby City, 144
Hollyhock House, 222
Hollywood: dining, 231–32; lodging, 227–28; sightseeing, 220–22; visitor information, 220
Hollywood Studio Museum, 221–22
Hollywood Walk of Fame, 221
Hollywood Wax Museum, 220–21
Honey Bunny Bugs, 211
Honey, I Shrunk the Audience, 61–62
Horn and Hoof Mesa, 176
Horseback riding, 234
Horton Plaza, 185–86
Hostels, 161, 192, 226
Hotel del Coronado, 188
Hotels, 18–19. *See also* Lodging *in town and theme park entries; see also Lodging Index*
Hours, 12. *See also* Hours *in theme park entries*
Huff and Puff, 97
Hugo Reid Adobe, 223–24
Huntington Beach (town), 148–50; beaches and parks, 149–50; dining, 149; sightseeing, 148

Huntington City Beach, 150
Huntington Library, Art Collections and Botanical Gardens, 222–23
Huntington Pier, 148
Huntington State Beach, 150
Hurricane Harbor, 212–13. *See also* Six Flags California

IMAX Theater, 219–20
Incredible Waterworks Show, 92
Independence Hall, 82
Indian Trails, 99–100
Indiana Jones Adventure, 41
International Surfing Museum Huntington Beach, 148
International travelers, 22–24
Irvine: sightseeing, 146, 148
Itineraries, sample, 25–29
It's a Small World, 55

Jaguar, 93–94
Jet Stream, 210
Jogging, 166
John Wayne International Airport, 10
Jungle Cruise, 42–43
Junípero Serra Museum, 189–90
Jurassic Park—The Ride, 116–17

Kangaroo Bus, 172
Kayaking, 233
Kennels, 17; (Disneyland) 36; (Knott's Berry Farm) 83; (San Diego Wild Animal Park) 179; (Six Flags California) 206–207; (Universal Studios), 113
Kidspace Museum, 223
Kilimanjaro Safari Walk, 181
King Arthur Carrousel, 57
Kingdom of the Dinosaurs, 89–90
Knott's Berry Farm, 77–106; dining, 102–104; introduction, 77–78, 80; lodging, 100–102; map, 81; nightlife, 105–106; nuts and bolts of visiting, 83; shopping, 104–105; sightseeing strategies, 80, 82–83; tickets, 13, 15, 80; transportation

in, 83–84; transportation to, 80; visitor information, 83. *See also park areas and attractions*

La Brea Tar Pits, 220
La Habra: sightseeing, 144
La Jolla: beaches and parks, 198; dining, 197; lodging, 194–95; map, 191; sightseeing, 190
La Jolla Shores Beach, 198
Laguna Beach area, 156–64; beaches and parks, 163–64; dining, 161–63; lodging, 159–61; sightseeing, 156–59; visitor information, 157
Lightning Falls, 213
Little Corona del Mar State Beach, 156
Live Steamers, 225
Lizard Lagoon, 212
Lockers, 17; (Disneyland) 36; (Knott's Berry Farm) 83; (San Diego Wild Animal Park) 178; (San Diego Zoo) 172; (Sea World) 132; (Six Flags California) 206, 207; (Universal Studios) 113
Lodging, 18–19. *See also* Lodging *in town and theme park entries; see also Lodging Index*
Log Jammer, 210
Log Peeler, 96
Long Beach: dining, 229; sightseeing, 215–17
Long Beach Aquarium of the Pacific, 216
Looney Tunes Nights, 211
Los Angeles area, 218–32; dining, 229–32; lodging, 226–29; sightseeing, 218–26; visitor information, 219. *See also* Greater Los Angeles area
Los Angeles Children's Museum, 219
Los Angeles downtown: dining, 230–31; lodging, 226–27; sightseeing, 218–19; visitor information, 219

Los Angeles Maritime Museum, 216
Los Angeles Zoo, 225
Lost and found: (Disneyland) 37; (Knott's Berry Farm) 83; (San Diego Wild Animal Park) 179; (San Diego Zoo) 172; (Sea World) 132; (Six Flags California) 207; (Universal Studios) 113
Lost children: (Disneyland) 36; (Knott's Berry Farm) 83; (Sea World) 132; (Six Flags California) 207; (Universal Studios), 113
Lower Lot, 116–19; dining, 124; shopping, 127
Lucy: A Tribute, 118

Mad Tea Party, 57
Magic Kingdom Club, 15
Magic Mountain, 207–12. *See also* Six Flags California
Main Beach, 163
Main Street Cinema, 38–39
Main Street U.S.A., 37–40; dining, 69; shopping, 74–75
Mann's Chinese Theater, 221
Marine Aquarium, 137
Maritime Museum of San Diego, 184
*Mark Twain* Steamboat, 48
Matterhorn Bobsleds, 54–55
Matterhorn Mountain, 54
Medieval Times, 105–106
Merry-Go-Round, 94. *See also* Carousels
Metro, 207
Mexican Hat Dance, 94
Mickey's House, 51–52
Mickey's Toontown, 50–53
Mike Fink Keelboats, 49
Minnie's House, 52
Mission Bay Aquatic Center, 184
Mission Bay Park: lodging, 191–92; map, 171; sightseeing, 182–84
Mission Beach (town): lodging, 191
Mission Beach Park, 198
Mission San Diego de Alcala, 190

Mission San Juan Capistrano, 158
Mission Valley. *See* Old Town and Mission Valley
Mr. Toad's Wild Ride, 56
Monorails: (Disneyland), 12, 62, 63; (San Diego Wild Animal Park), 179–80; (Six Flags California) 207
Montezooma's Revenge, 93
Mount Wilson Observatory, 224
Movieland Wax Museum, 144, 146
Museum of Flying, 217
Museum of La Brea Discoveries, 220
Museum of Man, 187
Mystery Lodge, 87–88

Nairobi Village, 180
Naples: sightseeing, 215
Natural History Museum (San Diego), 187
Natural History Museum of Los Angeles County, 220
Nature Center, 87
NBC Studio Tour, 222
New Orleans Square, 43–45; dining, 70; shopping, 75
Newland House Museum, 148
Newport Beach (town), 150–56; beaches and parks, 156; dining, 154–55; lodging, 153–54; map, 151; sightseeing, 150–53; visitor information, 150
Newport Dory Fishing Fleet, 152
Newport Dunes RV Resort, 156
Newport Pier, 152
Ninja, 209
North Hollywood: lodging, 124
Nu-Wave Theater, 91–92
Nursing nooks, 21

Ocean Beach, 198
Old Plaza Church, 218
Old Point Loma Lighthouse, 188
Old Town and Mission Valley: dining, 197; sightseeing, 189–90; visitor information, 189

Old Town San Diego State Historic Park, 189
Old Town Trolley, 189
Older travelers, 22; discounts, 16
Olvera Street (Los Angeles), 218–19; dining, 230
O'Neill Museum, 158–59
Operating hours, 12. *See also* Hours *in theme park entries*
Orange County area, 143–66; introduction, 143–44; map, 147; sports, 164–66. *See also towns in the Orange County area*
Orange County Marine Institute, 158
Orange County Museum of Art, 150
Orient Express, 207

Pacific Beach (town): lodging, 190–91
Pacific Beach Park, 197–98
Pacific Pavilion, 90
Package pickup: (Disneyland) 37; (Sea World) 133; (Six Flags California) 207
Packing, 8–9
Pageant of the Masters, 157
Paladion, 186
Parachute Sky Jump, 91
Parades (Disneyland), 52
Paramount Ranch, 228
Paramount Studios, 222
Parking. *See* Transportation in/to *in theme park entries*
Pasadena: dining, 232; lodging, 228–29; sightseeing, 222–24
Penguin Encounter, 138
Penny Arcade, 38
Peter Pan's Flight, 55
Pets, 17; (Disneyland) 36; (Knott's Berry Farm) 83; (San Diego Wild Animal Park) 179; (Six Flags California) 206–207; (Universal Studios) 113
Petting Zoo, 99
Photography. *See* Cameras

Pinocchio's Daring Journey, 57

Pirates of the Caribbean, 44

Plaza del Sol, 139

Point Fermin Park and Lighthouse, 216–17

Point Loma: dining, 196–97; lodging, 192; sightseeing, 188–89

Polar Bear Plunge, 176

Ports O' Call Village, 216

Price ranges: dining, 20; lodging, 19

Psyclone, 208

Pygmy Chimps at Bonobo Road, 175

Queen Anne Cottage, 224

*Queen Mary* (ship), 215

Raging Waters, 233

Rainfall, 5

Ralph B. Clark Regional Park, 146

Red Baron, 99

Reptile Mesa and House, 176

Reptile Ridge, 212

Restaurants, 19. *See also* Dining *in town and theme park entries; see also* Dining Index

Reuben H. Fleet Space Theater and Science Center, 187

Revolution, 209–10

River Cruise, 212

Road Runner Racers, 211

Roaring Rapids, 210

Rocky Point Preserve, 138

Rocky Road Trucking Company, 96

Roger Rabbit's Car Toon Spin, 53

Roller skating, 234

Sailing and boating, 166, 200

Sailing Ship *Columbia*, 48–49

Sample itineraries, 25–29

Samurai Summit, 207

San Clemente: lodging, 161

San Clemente State Beach, 164

San Diego, 182–98; beaches and parks, 197–98; dining, 195–97; lodging, 190–95; maps, 171, 185; sightseeing, 182–90. *See also* Greater San Diego area

San Diego Aerospace Museum, 187

San Diego Bay Ferry, 188

San Diego Convention Center, 185

San Diego downtown: dining, 195–96; lodging, 192–93; map, 185; sightseeing 185–86

San Diego Embarcadero, 184

San Diego Harbor area: sightseeing, 184–85

San Diego Model Railroad Museum, 187

San Diego Wild Animal Park, 177–82; dining, 182; nuts and bolts of visiting, 178–79; sightseeing strategies, 178; tickets, 14, 178; transportation in, 179; transportation to, 177; visitor information, 178; weather, 178

San Diego Zoo, 168, 170, 172–77; dining, 176–77; hours, 173; nuts and bolts of visiting, 172; sightseeing strategies, 170, 172; tickets, 13–14, 170; tours, 172; transportation in, 172; transportation to, 170; visitor information, 172

San Dimas: sights, 233

San Gabriel Mountains: sightseeing, 224

San Juan Capistrano: beaches and parks, 164; dining, 163; sightseeing, 158–59

San Marino: sightseeing, 222–23

San Pedro: sightseeing, 216

Sandblasters, 210

Santa Ana: sightseeing, 146

Santa Anita Depot, 224

Santa Clarita: lodging, 214

Santa Monica: dining, 229–30; lodging, 226; sightseeing, 217–18; visitor information, 217

Santa Monica Pier, 217

Santa Monica State Beach, 217

Sawdust Festival, 157

Scripps Beach, 198

Scripp's Rain Forest Aviary, 175
Sea kayaking, 233
Sea Lion and Otter Stadium, 136
Sea World, 129–42; dining, 141;
    introduction, 129–30; map, 131;
    nightlife, 141–42; nuts and bolts
    of visiting, 132–33; shopping,
    141; sightseeing strategies, 132;
    tickets, 13, 14, 130; transporta-
    tion in, 133; transportation to,
    130; visitor information, 132.
    *See also park areas and attractions*
Seal Beach (town): dining, 149
Seal Beach, 149
Seaport Village, 183
Secret Passage, 213
Senior travelers, 22; discounts, 16
Shamu Stadium, 133–34
Shamu's Happy Harbor, 138–39
Shark Encounter, 139
Shipwreck Shores, 212
Silver Strand State Beach, 198
Six Flags California, 204, 206–17;
    dining, 213–14; hours, 204;
    Hurricane Harbor, 212–13; lodg-
    ing, 214–15; Magic Mountain,
    207–12; nuts and bolts of visiting,
    206–207; sightseeing strategies,
    206; tickets, 14, 15, 204, 206;
    transportation in, 207; transporta-
    tion to, 204; visitor information,
    206
Six Flags Plaza, 208
Skating, 234
Skindiving, 164–65, 199, 233
Skyfari Aerial Tram, 172
Skytower (Sea World), 140–41
Skytower (Six Flags California),
    210–11
Sleeping Beauty Castle, 54
Sling Shot, 94
Smog, 5
Snoopy's Bounce, 96
Snow White's Scary Adventures, 56
Southern California: calendar of
    events, 6–8; map, 3; transporta-

tion to, 9–11; weather, 5–6. *See
    also towns and areas*
Space Mountain, 60–61
Speedy Gonzalez Mouse Racers, 211
Splash Mountain, 46
Sportfishing, 199. *See also* Fishing
Sports, 164–66, 199–201, 232–36
Star system used in book, 17–18
Star Tours, 59–60
Storage lockers. *See* Lockers
Storybook Land Canal Boats, 58
Streets of the World, 119
Strollers for children, 20;
    (Disneyland) 36; (Knott's Berry
    Farm) 83; (San Diego Wild Ani-
    mal Park) 178; (San Diego Zoo)
    172; (Sea World) 132; (Six Flags
    California) 206, 207; (Universal
    Studios) 113
Studio City: dining, 125–26
Studio tours, 222
Submarine Voyage, 62
Sun Bear Forest, 175
Sunset Strip (Hollywood), 221
Superman the Escape, 208
Supreme Scream, 93
Surfing, 165, 199–200, 233
Swiss Family Treehouse, 41–42

Taboo Tower, 213
Tampico Tumbler, 95
Tasmanian Devils, 211
Teddi Barra's Swingin' Arcade, 47
Television ticket information, 222
Temple Rapids, 213
Tennis, 165–66, 200, 234–35
Ticket options/prices, 13–15. *See
    also* Tickets *in theme park entries*
Tidal Wave, 210
Tiger River, 173
Tiki Falls, 213
Timber Mountain Log Ride, 85
Timberline Twister, 97
Tom Sawyer Island River Rafts, 48
Tomorrowland, 58–63; dining, 71;
    shopping, 76

Tomorrowland Autopia, 63
Toontown, 50–53
Torrey Pines State Beach, 198
Totally Nickelodeon, 120–21
Tourist seasons, 4–5
Train travel, 10
Travel Town, 225
TV Audience ticket booth, 112
TV ticket information, 222
Tweety Bird Cages, 211

Universal City: dining, 125, 126; lodging, 123–24; sightseeing, 125
Universal City Walk, 125
Universal Studios Hollywood, 107–27; dining, 124–26; introduction, 107–108; lodging, 123–24; map, 111; nuts and bolts of visiting, 112–13; shopping, 126–27; sightseeing strategies, 110, 112; tickets, 13, 110; transportation in, 113; transportation to, 108, 110; visitor information, 112. *See also park areas and attractions*
Upper Lot, 119–23; dining, 124–25; shopping, 127
Upper Newport Bay Ecological Reserve, 153

Vacation packages, 16–17
Valencia: lodging, 214
Viper, 209
Virginia Steele Scott Gallery of American Art, 223
Visitor information, 11–12. *See also towns and theme parks*

Walk of Fame, 221
Walking tours (San Diego), 201
Walt Disney Story "Great Moments With Mr. Lincoln," 39

Warner Brothers Kids Club, 211
Warner Brothers VIP Tour, 222
Water Ski Lagoon, 134
WaterWorld—A Live Sea War Spectacular, 121–22
Weather, 5–6
Wegeforth National Park Sea Lion Show, 174
West Jetty View Park, 152–53
Whale Watch Lookout Point, 189
Whale watching, 164, 199, 233
Wheelchairs, 21; (Disneyland) 36; (Knott's Berry Farm) 83; (San Diego Wild Animal Park) 178; (San Diego Zoo) 172; (Sea World) 132; (Six Flags California) 206, 207; (Universal Studios) 113
Wild Animal Park Photo Caravan, 178
Wild Arctic, 140
Wild Ones, 174
Wild Rivers, 146, 148
Wild Water Wilderness, 87–88; dining, 102
Wild West Stunt Show, 86
Wild, Wild, Wild West Stunt Show, 122
Wile E. Coyote Coaster, 211
Wile E. Coyote Critter Canyon, 208, 211
Will Rogers State Beach, 218
Will Rogers State Historic Park, 218
Windjammer, 92
Window to the Sea, 135
Windsurfing, 165, 199–200, 233
Wings of the World, 136–37
World of Cinemagic, 117–18
World of the Sea Aquarium, 137

XK-1, 92–93

Algodon Motel, 161
Aliso Creek Inn and Golf Resort, 159
Alpine Motel, 66
Anaheim Desert Palm Inn and Suites, 66
Anaheim Fairfield Inn by Marriott, 67
Anaheim Hilton and Towers, 65–66
Anaheim KOA, 68
Anaheim Marriott, 65
Anaheim Vacation Park, 68
Andrea Villa Inn, 194

Balboa Inn, 153
Bayside Hotel, 226
Best Western Bayside Inn, 193
Best Western Buena Park Inn, 101–102
Best Western Park Place Inn, 67
Best Western Raffles Inn, 67
Best Western Ranch House Inn, 214
Beverly Garland's Holiday Inn, 124
Buena Park Courtyard by Marriott, 100–101
Buena Park Hotel, 100

Candy Cane Inn, 66
Capri Laguna, 160
Castle Inn and Suites, 66
CC Camperland, 68
Clarion Hollywood Roosevelt Hotel, 227–28
Colony Inn, 102
Comfort Inn (Castaic), 215
Comfort Inn (San Diego), 192
Coronado Victorian House, 194
Crystal Pier Hotel, 190–91

Dana Marina Inn Motel, 160–61
Disneyland Hotel, 64–65
Disneyland Pacific Hotel, 65

El Cordova Hotel, 193
Embassy Suites, 100

Fairfield Inn, 101
Figueroa Hotel, 226–27

Hampton Inn, 214
Hanford Hotel, 101
Hilton Garden Inn, 214
Holiday Inn, 101
Hollywood Celebrity Hotel, 227
Horton Grand Hotel, 193
Hostelling International—Point Loma, 192
Hostelling International—San Clemente Beach, 161
Hostelling International—Santa Monica, 226
Hotel del Coronado, 193
Hotel Laguna, 159–60
Hyatt Newporter Resort, 153–54

Inn at Laguna Beach, 159
Innsuites Hotel, 101

Loews Santa Monica Beach Hotel, 226

Magic Hotel, 227

Pacific Sands Motel, 226
Pasadena Central Travelodge, 228

Ramada Conestoga, 67
Ritz-Carlton Huntington Hotel, 228–29
Ritz-Carlton Laguna Niguel, 160

Sail Inn Motel, 153
San Diego Princess Resort, 192

Sands of La Jolla, 194
Sea Lodge on La Jolla Shores Beach,
    194–95
Sheraton Universal, 123
Surf & Sand Hotel, 160

Travelers Inn, 101
Travelers World, 68

Universal City Hilton, 123–24

Ventanas al Mar, 191

Western Shores Motel, 191–92
Westin Bonaventure, 227

LODGING SERVICES
Walt Disney Travel Company, 64

Acapulco Mexican Restaurant, 74
AirHeadz, 102
Aladdin's Oasis, 69–70
Albert's, 177
Allie's American Grill, 72
Amelia's, 155

B. B. King's Blues Club, 126
Balboa Pavilion, 154
Barney's Beanery, 232
Belisle's Restaurant, 74
Bengal Barbecue, 70
Benita's Frites, 230
Big Thunder Barbecue, 70
Blue Bayou, 70
Blue Ribbon Bakery, 69
Broken Yoke Café, 195
Burger Continental, 232

Café Orleans, 70
The Cannery Restaurant and Cruises, 154
Cantina, 213
Canyon Café, 177
Carnation Ice Cream Parlor and Restaurant, 69
Carnation Plaza Gardens, 69
Casa de Bandini, 197
Casa de Pico, 197
Casa Mexicana, 70
Celedon, 196
Character Meals, 71
Chicken Dinner Restaurant, 102–103
Churro Cart, 70
Claim Jumper, 104
Congo Kitchen, 182
Corvette Diner, 195
Cottage Restaurant, 162
Crab Cooker, 154
Crepe de Paris, 125

Doc Brown's Fancy Fried Chicken, **249**
125
Dock Side Deli, 213

El Adobe de Capistrano, 163
El Cholo, 230
El Indio, 196

Fashion Island, 155
Flaky Jake's, 73
Food Etc., 213
Formosa Cafe, 231
French Market Restaurant, 70
Fresh Fruit Cart, 71
Fung Lum Restaurant, 124

Gen Kai, 163
Glide 'er Inn, 149
Golden Horseshoe, 71
Good Neighbor Restaurant, 126
Goofy's Kitchen, 71–72
Grizzly Creek Lodge, 102

Hampton's Hollywood Cafe, 231
Hansa House, 73
Harbor Grill, 162
Harbor House Café, 149
Harborside Cafe, 141
Harbour Galley, 70
Hard Rock Cafe Hollywood, 126
Herdez Cantina, 102
Hob Nob Hill, 195
Hollywood Cantina, 125
Hospitality Center Deli, 141
Hungry Bear Restaurant, 70

Ice Cream Train, 71
Ivy at the Shore, 229

John's Waffle Shop, 197
JW's Steakhouse, 72

Kisangani Court, 182
Knott's Family Steak House, 103

La Golondrina, 230
Lagoon Terrace, 177
Laguna Village Cafe, 161
Las Brisas, 162
Laughing Dragon Pizza Co., 213
Louise's Trattoria, 149
Lunching Pad, 71

Mama Stella's Kitchen, 141
Manhattan, 197
Marvel Mania Hollywood, 124
Mel's Diner, 125
Miceli's Restaurant, 126
Ming Delight Restaurant, 73
Mint Julep Bar, 70
Mr. Stox, 72
Mombasa Cooker, 182
Mooseburger Lodge, 213
Musso & Frank's Grill, 231

Newport Landing, 154

Olive Garden, 104

Panda Inn, 196
Papa Geppetto's, 72–73
Paradise Snacks, 214
Peacock and Raven, 177
Penguin Malt Shop, 161
Peohe's, 196
Philippe The Original, 231
Pizza Vector, 213
Plaza Cafe, 213
Plaza Inn, 69
PoFolks, 103–104
Promenade Café, 229
Proud Mary's, 162–63

Queen Mary, 229

Ranch House Grill, 141
Red Eye's Kitchen, 214
Restaurant Mérida, 232
Ristorante Italia, 125
River Belle Terrace, 70
River Princess, 125
Royal Street Veranda, 70
Ruby's Diner, 155

Sabor, 230
Safari Cones, 177
Safari Kitchen, 177
Santa Monica Pier, 229
Santa Monica Place, 229
Sir Winston's, 229
Souplantation, 196–97
Spaghetti Station Restaurant, 74
Stage Door Café, 71
Studio Commissary, 124

Teru Sushi, 126
Thai BBQ Restaurant, 126
Thorn Tree Terrace, 182
Tiffy's Family Restaurant & Ice
    Cream Parlor, 73
Tomorrowland Terrace, 71
Tradewind Treats, 214
Treehouse Café, 176–77

Village Haus Restaurant, 71

White House, 161–62
Wilderness Broiler, 102
Wilma's Patio, 155

Yamabuki, 72
Yamashiro, 232

## HIDDEN GUIDES

Adventure travel or a relaxing vacation?—"Hidden" guidebooks are the only travel books in the business to provide detailed information on both. Aimed at environmentally aware travelers, our motto is "Adventure Travel Plus." These books combine details on unique hotels, restaurants and sightseeing with information on camping, sports and hiking for the outdoor enthusiast.

## THE NEW KEY GUIDES

Based on the concept of ecotourism, The New Key Guides are dedicated to the preservation of Central America's rare and endangered species, architecture and archaeology. Filled with helpful tips, they give travelers everything they need to know about these exotic destinations.

## ULTIMATE FAMILY GUIDES

These innovative guides present the best and most unique features of a family destination. Quality is the keynote. In addition to thoroughly covering each destination, they feature short articles and one-line "teasers" that are both fun and informative.

# Order Form

## HIDDEN GUIDEBOOKS

____ Hidden Arizona, $13.95

____ Hidden Bahamas, $12.95

____ Hidden Baja, $14.95

____ Hidden Boston and Cape Cod, $11.95

____ Hidden Carolinas, $16.95

____ Hidden Coast of California, $16.95

____ Hidden Colorado, $13.95

____ Hidden Florida, $16.95

____ Hidden Florida Keys & Everglades, $11.95

____ Hidden Hawaii, $16.95

____ Hidden Idaho, $13.95

____ Hidden Maui, $12.95

____ Hidden Montana, $13.95

____ Hidden New England, $17.95

____ Hidden New Mexico, $13.95

____ Hidden Oahu, $12.95

____ Hidden Oregon, $13.95

____ Hidden Pacific Northwest, $17.95

____ Hidden Rockies, $16.95

____ Hidden San Francisco and Northern California, $17.95

____ Hidden Southern California, $17.95

____ Hidden Southwest, $17.95

____ Hidden Tahiti, $16.95

____ Hidden Tennessee, $15.95

____ Hidden Wyoming, $13.95

## THE NEW KEY GUIDEBOOKS

____ The New Key to Belize, $14.95

____ The New Key to Cancún and the Yucatán, $14.95

____ The New Key to Costa Rica, $16.95

____ The New Key to Ecuador and the Galápagos, $16.95

____ The New Key to Guatemala, $14.95

## ULTIMATE FAMILY GUIDEBOOKS

____ Disneyland and Beyond, $12.95

____ Disney World and Beyond, $13.95

Mark the book(s) you're ordering and enter the total cost here ⇨ [          ]

California residents add 8% sales tax here ⇨ [          ]

**Shipping**, check box for preferred method and enter cost here ⇨ [          ]

❑ BOOK RATE  **FREE! FREE! FREE!**

❑ PRIORITY MAIL  $3.00 first book, $1.00/each additional book

❑ UPS 2-DAY AIR  $7.00 first book, $1.00/each additional book

[          ]

**Billing**, enter total amount due and check payment method ⇨

❑ CHECK  ❑ MONEY ORDER

❑ VISA/MASTERCARD _____ EXP. DATE _____

NAME _____ PHONE _____

ADDRESS _____

_____

CITY _____ STATE _____ ZIP _____

MONEY-BACK GUARANTEE ON DIRECT ORDERS PLACED THROUGH ULYSSES PRESS

## About the Authors

Judy Wade is a contributing editor for *Walking* and *Valley Magazine*. She also writes for *Cosmopolitan*, *Cruise Travel*, *TravelAmerica*, the Los Angeles Times Syndicate and other national publications. A member of the Society of American Travel Writers, she packs and unpacks in Phoenix, Arizona.

Sharon K. Gillenwater, a former editor at *San Diego Magazine*, is a freelance writer living in San Diego. She has written for various publications, including *Los Angeles Magazine*, Fodor's Travel Guides, Access Press and *Travel Life*. She also writes features and travel stories for Copley News Service.

Stacy Ritz is the author of *Disney World and Beyond: Orlando Family Attractions* and *Hidden Carolinas*. She also co-authored *Hidden Florida* and *Hidden New England*. Formerly a staff writer for the *Tampa Tribune*, she has written for the *Washington Post*, the *Fort Lauderdale Sun-Sentinel*, *Parents* and *Bride's*.

## About the Illustrator

Glenn Kim is a freelance illustrator residing in San Francisco. His work appears in numerous Ulysses Press titles, including *Hidden Tahiti*, *Hidden Southwest* and *The New Key to Belize*. He has also done illustrations for the National Forest Service, magazines, book covers, greeting cards and advertising agencies.